BUTLER'S
LIVES OF THE SAINTS

NEW
FULL EDITION

MAY

BUTLER'S
LIVES OF THE SAINTS

NEW FULL EDITION

Patron

H. E. CARDINAL BASIL HUME, O.S.B.
Archbishop of Westminster

EDITORIAL BOARD

General Consultant Editor
DAVID HUGH FARMER

General Consultant, U.S.A.
ERIC HOLLAS, O.S.B.

Specialist Consultants
PHILIP CARAMAN, S.J.
JOHN HARWOOD
KATHLEEN JONES
DANIEL REES, O.S.B.
RICHARD SHARPE, MA, PhD
AYLWARD SHORTER, W.F.
ALBERIC STACPOOLE, O.S.B., MA, FRHS
HENRY WANSBROUGH, O.S.B., MA, STL
BENEDICTA WARD, SLG, MA, DPhil

Managing Editor
PAUL BURNS

BUTLER'S LIVES OF THE SAINTS

NEW
FULL EDITION

MAY

Revised by
DAVID HUGH FARMER

BURNS & OATES

THE LITURGICAL PRESS
Collegeville, Minnesota

First published 1996 in Great Britain by
BURNS & OATES
Wellwood, North Farm Road,
Tunbridge Wells, Kent TN2 3DR

First published 1996 in North America by
THE LITURGICAL PRESS
St John's Abbey, Collegeville,
Minnesota 56321

Reprinted, with revisions, 1998

ISBN 0 86012 254 9   Burns & Oates
ISBN 0-8146-2381-6   The Liturgical Press

The emblems appearing at the foot of some pages are taken from W. Ellwood Post,
Saints, Signs and Symbols: A Concise Dictionary. © Copyright 1962, 1974, by
Morehouse Publishing, with the permission of the publishers.

The woodcuts on pages 91 and 111 are by Robert Gibbings, originally published
in Helen Waddell, *Beasts and Saints* (Constable, 1934; n.e. Darton, Longman &
Todd, 1995). Reproduced by permission.

Library of Congress Catalog Card Number: 95-81671

Typeset by Search Press Limited
Printed in the United States of America

CONTENTS

Preface   *page*   *xi*

Abbreviations and Short Forms   *xv*

Maps   *xvii*

(Entries in capital letters indicate that the feast or saint is commemorated throughout the Roman Catholic Church with the rank of Solemnity, Feast, Memorial, or
Optional Memorial, according to the 1969 revised Calendar of the Latin [Roman]
Rite of the Catholic Church, published in the Roman Missal of 1970, or that the
saint is of particular importance for the English-speaking world. These entries are
placed first on their dates. All others are in chronological order. The paragraph at
the end of each day headed "*R.M.*" lists those saints and blessed who appear in the
new Roman Martyrology but are not given an entry in this volume.)

1. ST JOSEPH THE WORKER   1

    St Amator of Auxerre, bishop, 2; St Brioc, 2; St Sigismund of
    Burgundy, 3; St Marculf, abbot, 4; St Asaph, bishop, 4; St Theodard
    of Narbonne, bishop, 4; St Mafalda of Portugal, 5; St Peregrine
    Laziosi, 5; St Richard Pampuri, 6

2. ST ATHANASIUS, bishop and doctor   8

    St Waldebert, abbot, 11; St Wiborada, martyr, 11; Bd Conrad of
    Seldenbüren, 12; Bd Nicholas Hermansson, 12; St Antoninus of
    Florence, 13; Bd Joseph Mary Rubio Peralta, 15

3. SS PHILIP and JAMES, apostles   17

    SS Timothy and Maura, martyrs, 19; St Juvenal of Narni, 19; St
    Conleth of Kildare, 20; St Ansfrid of Utrecht, bishop, 20; Bd Mary
    Paradis, 20

4. BB MARTYRS OF ENGLAND AND WALES   22

    St Florian, martyr, 25; Bd Gregory of Verucchio, 26; Bd Michael
    Giedroyc, 26; Bd Ladislas of Warsaw, 26; Bd John Martin Moye,
    founder, 27

5. St Maximus of Jerusalem, bishop   29

    St Hilary of Arles, bishop, 29; St Maurontius, abbot, 30; St Gothard
    of Hildesheim, bishop, 30; St Angelo, martyr, 31; Bd Nuntius
    Sulprizio, 31

Contents

6. St Evodius of Antioch, bishop 33

    SS Marian and James, martyrs, 33; St Edbert of Lindisfarne, 34; Bd Bartholomew of Montepulciano, 34; BB Edward Jones and Antony Middleton, martyrs, 35; Bd Francis of Quebec, 35; Bd Mary-Catherine of Cairo, 36

7. ST JOHN OF BEVERLEY, bishop 37

    St Flavia Domitilla, martyr, 38; St Domitian of Maastricht, bishop, 38; St Serenicus, 39; Bd Giselle of Bavaria, abbess, 39; Bd Rose Venerini, 39

8. St Victor the Moor, martyr 41

    St Acacius, martyr, 41; St Gibrian, 41; St Desideratus of Bourges, bishop, 42; St Boniface IV, pope, 42; St Benedict II, pope, 43; St Indract of Glastonbury, 43; St Wiro of Utrecht, bishop, 44; Bd Mary Catherine de Longpré, 44; Bd Frances Nisch, 45

9. St Pachomius, abbot 47

    St Gerontius, bishop and martyr, 48; Bd Thomas Pickering, martyr, 49; Bd Mary-Teresa Gerhardinger, 50

10. SS Gordian and Epimachus, martyrs 51

    SS Alphius and Companions, martyrs, 51; St Comgall of Bangor, abbot, 52; St Catald, 54; St Solangia, 54; Bd Beatrice d'Este, 55; Bd Nicholas Albergati, 55; St John of Avila, 56

11. St Mamertus of Vienne, bishop 58

    St Gengulf, 59; St Majolus of Cluny, abbot, 59; St Walter of L'Esterp, 60; St Francis di Girolamo, 61; St Ignatius of Laconi, 62

12. SS Nereus and Achilleus, martyrs 64

    St Pancras, martyr, 65; St Epiphanius of Salamis, bishop, 65; St Modoaldus, bishop, 66; St Rictrudis, abbess, 67; St Germanus of Constantinople, patriarch, 67; St Dominic of the Causeway, 68; Bd Imelda Lambertini, 69; Bd Jane of Portugal, 69

13. St Servatius, bishop 71

    SS Mel and Sulian, 71; SS Argentea and Wulfram of Córdoba, martyrs, 72; Bd Gerard Meccati, 72; Bd Gemma of Solmona, 73; Bd Madeleine Albrici, 73; St Andrew Fournet, founder, 74

14. ST MATTHIAS, apostle   76

St Boniface of Tarsus, martyr, 76; St Carthach, bishop and abbot, 77; St Erembert, 78; St Hallvard of Oslo, martyr, 78; Bd Giles of Portugal, 79; St Michael Garicoïts, founder, 80; St Mary Mazzarello, 80; St Leopold Mandic, 81

15. SS Torquatus and Companions, martyrs   83

St Rheticius, bishop, 83; St Rupert of Bingen, 83; St Vitesindus of Córdoba, martyr, 83; St Isaiah of Rostov, abbot and bishop, 84; St Isidore the Farmer, 84; Bd Andrew Abellon, 85

16. St Alexander of Caesarea, bishop and martyr   86

St Possidius, bishop, 86; St Brendan of Clonfert, abbot, 87; St Carantoc, bishop, 88; Forty-Four Martyrs of Palestine, 89; St Simon Stock, 89; St Andrew Bobola, martyr, 90

17. St Paschal Baylon   92

Bd Peter Lieou, martyr, 93; Bd Antonia Mesina, martyr, 93

18. St John 1, pope and martyr   95

St Potamon, bishop and martyr, 96; SS Theodotus and Companions, martyrs, 96; St Eric of Sweden, king and martyr, 97; Bd William of Toulouse, 98; St Felix of Cantalice, 98; Bd Blandina Merten, 99

19. ST DUNSTAN OF CANTERBURY, abbot and bishop   100

St Urban I, pope, 102; SS Calocerus and Parthenius, martyrs, 102; St Peter Celestine, pope, 102; St Ivo of Brittany, 104; Bd Peter Wright, martyr, 105; St Crispin of Viterbo, 105

20. ST BERNARDINO OF SIENA   107

St Thalalaeus, martyr, 108; St Austregisilus, bishop, 109; St Ethelbert of East Anglia, 109; Bd Columba of Rieti, 110

21. ST GODRIC OF FINCHALE   112

St Paternus of Vannes, 114; St Theobald of Vienne, bishop, 114; Bd Charles de Mazenod, bishop and founder, 114

22. St Quiteria, martyr   116

St Julia, martyr, 116; St John of Parma, abbot, 117; St Humility of Florence, 117; St Hemming of Abo, bishop, 118; St Rita of Cascia, 118; Bd John Forest, martyr, 119

23. SS Montanus, Lucius, and Companions, martyrs   121

St Desiderius of Vienne, bishop and martyr, 122; St Leontius of
Rostov, bishop and martyr, 122; St Euphrosyne of Polotsk, 123; St
William of Rochester, 123; St John Baptist Rossi, 123

24. SS Donatian and Rogatian, martyrs   125

St Vincent of Lérins, 125; St Simeon Stylites the Younger, 126; St
David of Scotland, 127; Bd John of Prado, martyr, 128; Bd Louis
Moreau, bishop, 129

25. ST BEDE THE VENERABLE, doctor   130

ST GREGORY VII, pope, 133; St Denis of Milan, bishop, 135; St
Zenobius of Florence, bishop, 135; St Aldhelm, abbot and bishop,
136; St Gennadius, abbot and bishop, 138; St Mary Magdalen de'
Pazzi, 139; St Madeleine Sophie Barat, foundress, 141

26. ST PHILIP NERI, founder   144

St Eleutherius, pope, 147; Bd Andrew Franchi, 148; St Mary Ann
of Quito, 148; Bd Peter Sanz and Companions, martyrs, 149

27. ST AUGUSTINE OF CANTERBURY, abbot and bishop   150

St Julius the Veteran, martyr, 154; St Eutropius, bishop, 154; St
Melangell, 155; BB Edmund Duke and Companions, martyrs, 155

28. St Justus of Urgel   157

St Germanus of Paris, 157; St William of Gellone, 158; St Gizur of
Iceland, 159; Bd Lanfranc of Canterbury, bishop, 160; St Ignatius
of Rostov, abbot, 161; Bd Margaret Pole, 161; Bd Mary Bartholomaea
Bagnesi, 162; BB Thomas Ford and Companions, martyrs, 162

29. St Maximinus of Trier, bishop   164

SS Sisinnius and Companions, martyrs, 164; St Bona of Pisa, 164;
BB William Arnaud and Companions, martyrs, 165; St Andrew of
Constantinople, martyr, 166; Bd Richard Thirkeld, martyr, 166;
Bd Joseph Gerard, 166; Bd Ursula Ledochowska, foundress, 167

30. SS Basil and Emmelia   168

St Isaac of Constantinople, 168; St Exuperantius, bishop, 168; St
Dympna, martyr, 169; St Walstan of Bawburgh, 169; St Hubert of
Liège, 170; St Ferdinand of Castile, 171; St Joan of Arc, 171; BB
William Scott and Richard Newport, martyrs, 173; BB Luke Kirby
and Companions, martyrs, 174

31. THE VISITATION OF THE BLESSED VIRGIN MARY   176

St Petronilla, martyr, 177; SS Cantius, Cantianus, and Cantianella, martyrs, 177; Bd James Salomoni, 177; BB Robert Thorpe and Thomas Watkinson, martyrs, 178; Bd Felix of Nicosia, 178

Glossary   *179*
Alphabetical List of Entries   *184*

PREFACE

The saints reveal the life of Christ: in venerating them, we venerate him. The saints of May are of special interest. They represent each century from the first to the twentieth. This wide assembly, in place as well as time, inevitably causes problems to the reader of this volume. Some background knowledge of the history of their times is desirable, even necessary, for full understanding. In the course of history the Church developed both doctrine and religious outlook in relation to events and ideas in the society around it. Sometimes saints' actions may seem misguided or erroneous. While none of them was perfect in every respect, it is good not to judge or criticize them too hastily, but rather to try to understand them and their actions in the context of their own lifetimes, not ours. This volume is no substitute for such a study, rather an encouragement toward it.

The Calendar of May begins with St Joseph the Worker (1) and ends with the Blessed Virgin in her visit of charity to her cousin Elizabeth (31). The intervening days introduce us to saints of every period. The apostles Philip and James (3), as well as Matthias (14) remind us of saints close to Christ's mission, which they and subsequent saints continued. This would be with healings, exorcisms and speaking in tongues: above all, in their preaching, Christ would work with them, confirming the word with the signs that followed (see Mark 16:15-20).

After the apostolic age the work of Christ in his saints by no means ceased. It was especially evident in the witness of the early martyrs. Among these are the comparatively unfamiliar names of SS Montanus and Companions from third-century Carthage (23), SS Marian and James (6) and St Julius the Veteran (27) from present-day Bulgaria. Their authentic words, accurately recorded, speak movingly to us across the centuries.

When the Peace of the Church came under Constantine in the early fourth century, a new hazard threatened the Church. This was the heresy of Arianism, often supported by emperors, but refuted and eventually overcome, principally by St Athanasius (2). For his fidelity to the council of Nicaea in spite of repeated persecution and for his spiritual teaching inspired by the Incarnation, he surely deserves to be reckoned among the greatest saints. This was also the time of Christian monasticism's development as in some way an alternative to martyrdom. Pachomius (9) was of crucial importance in the formulation of community monasticism, also supported and esteemed by Athanasius. He influenced St Benedict (11 July) as well as the saintly abbots of Cluny such as Majolus (11).

In the time of the barbarian invasions and the fall of the Roman Empire the Church faced new challenges. Where the old diocesan structure, both civil and religious, survived (as in Italy and southern France) the problems seemed less. But the rise of half-converted Merovingian kings with records of violence was a new and unwelcome obstacle. St Sigismund of Burgundy (1) did at least repent of his misdeeds, but courageous bishops like St Germanus of Paris (28) and others reproved rulers at their peril. In England, however, St Augustine of Canterbury (27), whose achievements have been both overestimated and underestimated, made a new beginning, establishing his see in Canterbury rather than London. This was in relation to the changed political circumstances of the time. His pioneering work was consolidated in different ways by the scholarly Bede (25), England's only Doctor of the Church, and by the later St Dunstan, monastic founder and archbishop (19). Meanwhile Ireland had formed impressive monastic saints like St Brendan of Clonfert (16) and St Comgall of Bagnor (10).

Other medieval saints who find a place in this book are two popes, the energetic St Gregory VII (25) and the diffident St Peter Celestine (19), who uniquely resigned this highest office. Also here are two outstanding friars, St Antoninus of Florence (2), the Dominican, and St Bernardino of Siena (2), the Franciscan. Each combined deep study of the mystery of Christ with dynamic preaching and almsgiving. Antoninus was a bishop, but Bernardino refused three sees.

The Reformation period was critical for the Church, but numbers of saints illumined it. Two came from Florence: the outstanding apostle, St Philip Neri (26) and the unique mystic, St Mary Magdalen de' Pazzi (25). From Spain came St John of Avila (10), canonized as recently as 1970, yet known for centuries as an eminent spiritual writer. From England came a succession of martyrs (1535–1678), many of whom are commemorated on 4 May. Although from the human point of view they may not attract as many as do the more famous Forty Martyrs of 25 October, their fine example inspired and continues to inspire their fellow-Catholics in England and elsewhere.

Saints of the seventeenth and eighteenth centuries are harder to find in the calendar for May, but three Jesuit saints should be noted: St Francis di Girolamo of Naples (11), the martyred St Andrew Bobola (16), and Bd Joseph Peralta from Spain (2). Meanwhile Franciscan laybrothers such as St Pascal Baylon (17) and St Ignatius Laconi (11) provide salutary reminders that sanctity can be attained in humble and humdrum surroundings.

To the nineteenth century belongs a patron of youth, Bd Nuntius Sulprizio (5), whose example in a short life of severe suffering was solemnly approved by two recent popes. Here also are found famous founders like Bd Charles de Mazenod (21), whose Oblates of Mary Immaculate contributed strongly to the growth of the Church in Canada, the United States, and elsewhere. St Madeleine Sophie Barat (25) and St Mary Mazarello (14) provide contrasting examples of saintly foundresses, whose Congregations also have long since spread into the New World.

The majority of canonized saints at present come, almost inevitably, from Europe, but in fifty or a hundred years' time the picture may be very different.

Canonizations achieved by Pope John Paul II so far are marginally fewer than those of Pope Pius XII, but geographically are more widely based. The same is even more true of beatifications. Here at least the numbers have far exceeded those of earlier popes this century. Most of the candidates are either from non-European countries or else are European candidates whose causes have been started long ago, but have met some sort of obstacle in the process. Some of these recent beatifications and canonizations are represented in this volume. Others, mentioned in the Roman Martyrology, belong to groups of martyrs whose communal feasts occur elsewhere in the Calendar.

Within Europe itself, it has long ago been noted that for various historical reasons the bulk of the European saints come from Italy, France and Spain. In this volume, as it happens, a more balanced representation occurs with the presence of Scandinavian saints such as SS Eric, king of Sweden (18), and Bd Nicholas Hermansson, bishop of Linkoping, and St Hemming, Swedish apostle of southern Finland (21). Also present are St Hallvard of Norway, patron of Oslo (14), and St Gizur of Iceland (28), closely linked with the early history of the Church there. Polish saints are present in the Jesuit martyr St Andrew Bobola (16), Bd Ladislas of Warsaw (4) and the much more recent Bd Ursula Ledochowska (29). The troubled land of Croatia is represented by the recently canonized St Leopold Mandic (14), small in stature, but great in unwearying commitment.

It will come as no surprise that German saints also figure in May, even if they are not the best known ones, who occur in other months of the calendar. St Gothard (5) and St Rupert (15) are here, together with two recently beatified nuns, Blandina Merten (10) and Mary-Teresa Gerhardinger (9). The Low Countries are represented by four bishops: St Hubert of Liège (30), St Ansfrid and St Wiro of Utrecht (3 and 8), with St Domitian of Maastricht (7).

Among the countries of the New World, Canada is the most strongly characterized, if not with a canonized saint in May, at least with several notable *beati*, beginning with Bd Francis Montmorency-Laval, first bishop of Quebec (6), and some recently honoured nuns as well.

Another geographical area which figures here is the Near East. Forty-four martyrs of Palestine are commemorated on 16 May, while both Constantinople and Russia are represented, one by St Germanus the Patriarch (12) and the two martyrs Andrew (29) and Isaac (30), and the other by the two saints of Rostov, Leontius (23) and Ignatius (28), as well as the mysterious Euphrosyne of Polotsk (23). All these belong to the period before the tragic separation of the Eastern Churches from Rome, whether this is dated to 1054 (the "official" date, but one not universally recognized as such) or to 1204, the date of the sack of Constantinople by Crusaders, which made the separation even more bitter and general. In this work Eastern saints before the break with Rome are included; after it only those whose cults have been authorized by the Holy See. Among many ecumenical ventures in recent years, the most important of all, both historically and numerically, must surely be the attempts toward the reunion of the Churches of

Eastern and Western Christendom, and in particular the reunion of Constantinople and Moscow with Rome.

* * * * *

"Happy is the saint who finds a biographer worthy of him." Thus spoke an eminent Bollandist of our time. This remark has its importance for readers of this volume. Inevitably much of what we know of saints comes from their biographers, lesser men (like Boswell) than the heroes they depict. Nonetheless the best of them provide character-studies as well as records of achievements: SS Godric of Finchale, Philip Neri and Antoninus were all fortunate in this respect; they can all be known as real people. Too often, however, record of very recent saints is inspired by too close adherence to a narrow tradition of hagiography. The final wish of this editor is for these modern saints to be provided with worthy biographers.

In conclusion I must thank Dom Henry Wansbrough O.S.B. and Fr Philip Caraman S.J. for their specialist help, and Paul Burns, the Managing Editor, for his general help and for retrieving the products of a faulty word-processor. Above all, my thanks are due to my wife Ann, who has contributed much by her constant and patient support.

---

1 June 1996, Feast of St Justin, martyr

Abbreviations and Short Forms

A.A.S.	*Acta Apostolicae Sedis*. Rome, 1909- .
AA.SS.	*Acta Sanctorum*. 64 vols., Antwerp, 1643- . (* after a page reference refers to supplementary pages in a volume.)
A.C.M.	H. Musurillo. *The Acts of the Christian Martyrs*. Oxford, 1972.
Anal. Boll.	*Analecta Bollandiana* (1882-).
A.S.C.	*Anglo-Saxon Chronicle* in *E.H.D.*, vol. 1
Bede, *H.E.*	*Historia Ecclesiastica* (ed. B. Colgrave and R.A.B. Mynors). Oxford, 1969.
B.H.L.	*Bibliotheca Hagiographica Latina Antiquae et Mediae Aetatis*. 1898-1901; supplement, 1911.
Bibl. SS.	*Bibliotheca Sanctorum*. 13 vols. and supplement. Rome, 1960-87.
C.M.H.	H. Delehaye. *Commentarius Perpetuus in Martyrologium Hieronymianum* (*AA.SS.*, 65). 1931.
C.S.E.L.	*Corpus Scriptorum Ecclesiasticorm Latinorum*. Vienna, 1886.
D.H.G.E.	*Dictionnaire d'Histoire et de Géographie Ecclésiastique* (ed. A. Baudrillart). 1912- .
D.T.C.	*Dictionnaire de Théologie Catholique*. Paris, 1903-50.
E.H.D.	D. C. Douglas *et al.* (eds.). *English Historical Documents*. London, 1953- .
E.H.R.	*English Historical Review* (1886-).
E.M.C.A.	Edward G. Tasker. *Encyclopedia of Medieval Church Art*. Ed. John Beaumont, London, 1993.
Eusebius, *H.E.*	Eusebius. *The History of the Church* (ed. G.A. Williamson). London, 1965.
G.C.S.	*Die griechischen christlichen Schriftseller der ersten drei Jahrhunderte*. Leipzig & Berlin, 1897.
H.S.S.C.	F. Chiovaro (ed.), *Histoire des Saints et de la Sainteté Chrétienne*. 12 vols., Paris, 1972- .
J.E.H.	*Journal of Ecclesiastical History* (1950-).
M.G.H.	*Monumenta Germaniae Historica*.
M.M.P.	R. Challoner. *Memoirs of Missionary Priests* (ed J. H. Pollen). London, 1924.
M.O.	D. Knowles. *The Monastic Order in England*. 2d edition. Cambridge, 1969.

N.C.E.	*New Catholic Encyclopedia*, 14 vols. New York, 1967- .
N.L.A.	*The Kalendre of the Newe Legende of Englande* (ed. M. Gorlach). Heidelberg, 1994.
O.D.C.C.	*Oxford Dictionary of the Christian Church.* 2d edition (ed. F.L. Cross and E. A. Livingstone). London, New York and Toronto, 1974.
O.D.P.	J. N. D. Kelly, *Oxford Dictionary of Popes.* Oxford, 1985.
O.D.S.	D. H. Farmer, *The Oxford Dictionary of Saints*, 3d edition. Oxford and New York, 1993.
P.G.	J. P. Migne (ed.). *Patrologiae Cursus Completus. Series Graeca.* 162 vols., Paris, 1857-66.
P.L.	J. P. Migne (ed.). *Patrologiae Cursus Completus. Series Latina.* 221 vols., Paris, 1844-64.
Propylaeum	*Propylaeum ad Acta Sanctorum Decembris.* Brussels, 1940.
Rev. Ben.	*Revue Benedictine* (1885-).
R.H.E.	*Revue d'Histoire Ecclésiastique* (1900-).
R.S.	Rolls Series (1858-).
s.d.	*sub die*, under the day
s.v.	*sub verbo*, under the word
T.R.H.S.	*Transactions of the Royal Historical Society* (1871-).
V.S.H.	C. Plummer (ed.). *Vitae Sanctorum Hiberniae.* 2 vols., 1910; 2d ed., 1968.

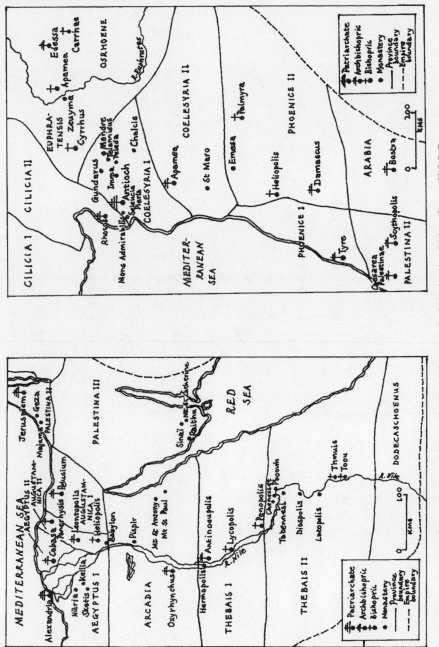

Episcopal Sees and Monasteries in Egypt and Syria in the Fourth Century. *See St Pachomius, 9 May. Source: H.S.S.C.*

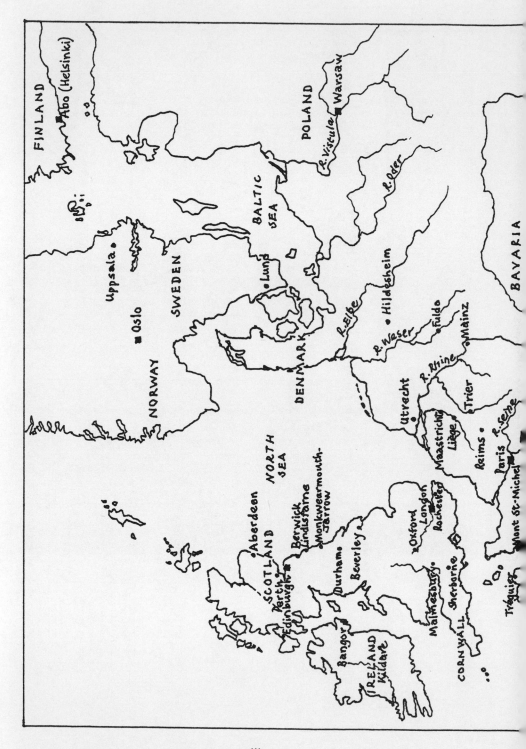

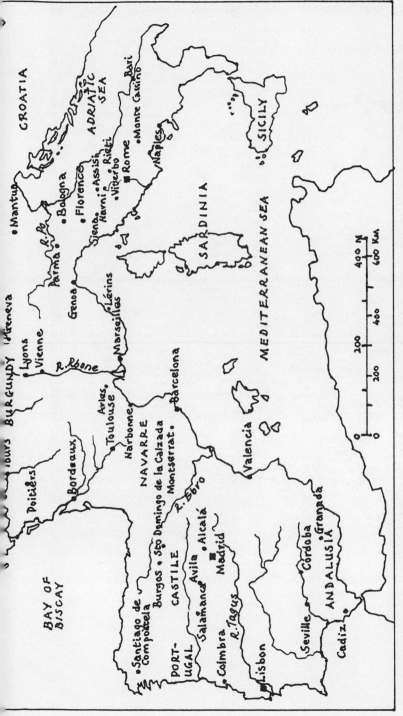

Western Europe. Places of significance mentioned in the text of this volume. (Several periods are covered; names have been modernized, and political boundaries, which have changed over the centuries, omitted.)

England and Wales: Principal monasteries following the Rule of St Benedict in the Middle Ages. *See*: St John of Beverley, 7 May; St Indract of Glastonbury, 8 May; St Dunstan of Canterbury, 19 May; St Bede the Venerable, 25 May; St Aldhelm, 25 May; St Augustine of Canterbury, 27 May; Bd Lanfranc of Canterbury, 28 May. *Source*: D. H. Farmer (ed.), *Benedict's Disciples* (1980, 1995).

England and Wales: Towns where Martyrs were executed in the Reign of Elizabeth I. The figures show the number put to death in each place. *See*: BB Martyrs of England and Wales, 4 May. *Source*: P. Hughes, *The Reformation in England* (1950, 1963).

1

ST JOSEPH THE WORKER (First Century)

Today is the "Memory of St Joseph the craftsman, who as as a carpenter at Nazareth provided for the needs of Jesus and Mary by his labour, and initiated the Son of God into human work. Therefore on the day when the feast of labour is celebrated in many countries, Christian workers venerate him as their exemplar and protector." In these words the Roman Martyrology describes the nature of this feast. Its history, however, is somewhat complex.

The principal feast of St Joseph has always been 19 March. The martyrologies of Reichenau and of the Irishman Oengus (both of the ninth century) were the first to record him. Other martyrologies soon did the same, but his feast was firmly established only in the early fifteenth century. Gerson, chancellor of Paris University, was its prominent advocate, not least as a means of reuniting the Church after the divisions of the conciliar movement. Late medieval saints such as Bernardino of Siena (below, 20 May), Vincent Ferrer (5 Apr.), and Bridget of Sweden (23 July) all helped to propagate devotion to St Joseph, especially in face of some medieval mystery plays which treated him with disrespect and derision. Like Gerson, these saints saw Joseph both as a patron of Christian families and as a model for workmen.

Thus the idea behind today's feast is ancient, although its implementation is modern. After the Council of Trent (1545-63) extended the feast of Joseph to the whole Catholic world, helped by both St Teresa of Avila (d. 1582; 15 Oct.) and the Carmelite friars, who successfully petitioned for a feast of Joseph's Patronage, this was extended to the Universal Church in 1847 by Pius IX with the new name of the Solemnity. In 1913 its day was altered from the third Sunday to the third Wednesday after Easter. In 1956, however, this feast was replaced by that of St Joseph the Worker: Pius XI deliberately attempted to give a Christian meaning to Labour Day on 1 May.

The Gospels, especially Matthew 2 and Luke 1-2 (see also Matt. 13:55 and Luke 4:22), provide the firm basis for the veneration of St Joseph and for meditation on his role in the story of our redemption. He was chosen by God to be the legal father of Jesus and the husband of Mary. In the time of her pregnancy and Christ's infancy he was the protector of them both. His care extended to finding a birthplace for Jesus and a safe refuge during the flight into Egypt. Afterward Jesus was known as the son of Joseph the Carpenter. This trade in those days included that of builder, as most houses were made of wood. Joseph and the young Jesus earned their living by working at such crafts. By the time that Jesus began his public life at the age of about thirty, Joseph disappears from the Gospels, and it is usually thought that he had died by this time. His age must be a matter for speculation, but it seems reasonable to suppose that he was about thirty-five to forty when Jesus was born. It is possible that references to Christ's "brothers and sisters" refer to the fruit of an earlier marriage by Joseph and that he was a widower when he married the Blessed Virgin. However that may be, Matthew's infancy narrative is written largely from the point of view of Joseph, while Luke's represents that of Mary. Both agree that Joseph was descended from King David. Apocryphal writings like the Gospel of James and the History of Joseph the Carpenter (Greek, fifth-sixth century) add legendary details, as did some later private revelations, but the Gospels of Matthew and Luke provide us with the indispensable authentic information about him.

In the course of time Joseph's name was added to the Litany of Saints (1350) and to the Canon of the Roman Mass (1962). He is invoked as the special patron of fathers of families, of procurators, of carpenters and other manual workers. Paintings of him with Jesus and Mary are innumerable. Raphael painted a fine representation of him, in the *Marriage of the Virgin*, now in the Brera Gallery, Milan (1504; no. 472); there are other notable examples by Zurbarán and Murillo. More extensive treatment of St Joseph will be found under 19 March.

See *O.D.S.* and *Bibl.SS.*, *s.v.* "Joseph"; M. Walsh, *A Dictionary of Devotions* (1993), pp. 146-8.

St Amator of Auxerre, *Bishop* (418)

Amator, or Amatre, is principally known as the immediate predecessor of the famous St Germanus of Auxerre (*c.* 378-448; 3 Aug.), who visited Britain twice to preach against the Pelagians. Amator was a priest of Auxerre in Burgundy, conspicuous for his zeal in building churches and converting the pagan country folk of the district. Consecrated bishop, he continued as beforehand, and miracles of healing were attributed to him. He helped to choose Germanus as his successor in spite of the latter's early attachment to pagan hunting rituals. Amator's Life is much embroidered with legends. These may retain a genuine tradition that he was married in early life and that Germanus was not in every respect an obvious choice as bishop. Amator's episcopate seems to have been long and fruitful: he died in his cathedral and was buried in the ancient cemetery outside the town. The church built over his tomb in the sixth century was destroyed in the French Revolution.

AA.SS., Mar., 1, pp. 50-60; *Bibl.SS.*, 1, 940-1.

St Brioc (Sixth Century)

Brioc (Brieuc or Briavel) was born of a noble pagan family, probably in Cardigan. After conversion to Christianity, he became a monk and a priest and founded a monastery. The fact that his cult is strongest in Britanny, where he died, and in Cornwall as well as Wales, points to his having been one of the many migrants who passed from one Celtic area to another in the fifth and sixth centuries.

Few details of his life are known, but there is no lack of implausible legends. One relates that he set sail with 168 monks in a ship, whose progress was impeded by a huge sea monster believed to be the devil. Another attributes his founding of the abbey of Saint-Brieuc to eighty-four monks who were his disciples; this is assigned to a period of his life after his return from Wales, where his prayers had arrested an outbreak of plague. The Breton ruler, Rigual, was assisted by Brioc on his death-bed, but the saint died soon afterward, at the age, it was claimed, of one hundred years.

It seems uncertain whether Brioc was ever a bishop, as the see which bears his name has its first recorded bishop some centuries after his death. He is rightly venerated as a notable monastic founder in a time of sparse historical evidence; his relics were translated to Angers (*c.* 850) for safety during Viking raids, but some of them were returned to Saint-Brieuc in 1210. Churches were dedicated to him in Cornwall (St Breocke), Cardigan (Llandyfriog), and Gloucestershire (St Briavels), as well as in Britanny. He was a patron of purse-makers because of his abundant charity.

See G. H. Doble, *The Saints of Cornwall*, 4 (1965), pp. 67-104; *Bibl.SS.*, 3, 534-6.

St Sigismund of Burgundy (524)

Sixth-century Burgundy comprised much of south-eastern France and south-western Switzerland. Its prince was a Vandal, Arian in religion, called Gundebald. His son and successor, Sigismund, was converted to the Catholic faith by St Avitus, bishop of Vienne. His conversion, however, seems to have been less than total. The few known facts of his life reveal incidents of violence, which are all too common in Gregory of Tours' *History of the Franks*. According to this and to a Life by a monk of Agaune (founded by Sigismund) he lost his first wife, by whom he had a son called Sigeric, and his second wife stirred up Sigismund with accusations that his son was plotting to dethrone him. She was so plausible that Sigismund had his son throttled by his servants. Overcome with remorse, Sigismund repented bitterly and prayed for pardon. His fate at the hands of three sons of Clovis, who defeated him in battle after a short reign and subsequently had him killed at Orleans and his body thrown down a well, was regarded as divine punishment. However that may be, Sigismund's relics were preserved at Prague and some even regarded him as a martyr. This, however, is not his title in the new Roman Martyrology. He is remembered rather as the founder of Agaune (Switzerland), whose monks chanted the office assiduously in the presence of the shrines of the martyrs. There a splendid reliquary survives.

See Gregory of Tours, *The History of the Franks* (1979), pp. 159-67; *M.G.H., Scriptores rerum Meroving*, 2, 333-40; *Bibl.SS.*, 11, 1043-7.

St Marculf, *Abbot*, (*c.* 558)

Born at Bayeux of noble Christian parents, Marculf (or Marcoul) gave away his fortune to the poor and retired to Coutances. There the bishop, Possessor, guided him, ordained him priest at the age of thirty, and sent him to evangelize the countryside. He attracted disciples, for whom he built a primitive monastery by the sea at Nanteuil, now Saint-Marcouf (Manche). One of these was St Helier (16 July), who settled on the island of Jersey. Marculf retired to another island for Lent and died there. In 898 his relics were translated to Corbeny (Aisne), between Reims and Laon. There a priory from Saint-Rémi of Reims was founded in 906. From this time onward, Marculf was invoked as a healer of skin diseases, and he was connected with the healings claimed for the kings of France. St Louis was not the first but was the best-known early king to visit Marculf's shrine and then to touch for the "King's Evil," a disease of the neck of tubercular origin. Kings of France up to Louis XVIII continued this practice, accompanied by the words, "The king touches you, God heals you." Some medieval kings of England also claimed this power. Marculf's relics, which were brought to Reims for the coronation of Louis XIV and his successors, were destroyed during the French Revolution in 1793 .

See the ninth-century Life in *AA.SS.*, May, 1, pp. 70–82, and short article in *H.S.S.C.*, 3 (1987), p. 279.

St Asaph, *Bishop* (*c.* 610)

Little is known for certain about this saint, whose name was chosen as that of a place formerly called Llanelwy, where the Normans established a bishopric, roughly coterminous with Powys, in 1143. There is no early Life of Asaph, but he is mentioned in the late Lives of St Kentigern (13 Jan.). When the latter departed for Scotland, Asaph was left in charge of his monastery in North Wales. Here, it was claimed by later writers, the praise of God never ceased, with a liturgy performed in relays. Asaph's main area of work was Flintshire; he became a bishop on the departure of Cyndeyrn to Cumbria in around 590. Several churches and wells are dedicated to Asaph, and a fair was held in his town on his feast; but written record of this survives only in late medieval calendars. There was also a cult in Scotland because of his link with St Kentigern.

A. W. Wade-Evans, *Welsh Christian Origins* (1934), pp. 191-4; D. R. Thomas, *History of the Diocese of St Asaph* (3 vols., 1908-13); E. G. Bowen, *The Settlements of the Celtic Saints in Wales* (1956).

St Theodard of Narbonne, *Bishop* (893)

Born at Montauriol, part of the present-day Montauban, Theodard studied law at Toulouse and was retained by the cathedral clergy in a suit brought by local Jews against an insulting religious pageant. Whatever may be thought of the custom complained of by the Jews, Archbishop Sigebold of Narbonne took him home with him, ordained him priest, and made him his archdeacon. In this office he excelled at charitable works of all kinds and was chosen as Sigebold's successor. He was prominent in redeeming captives from the Saracens and feeding the hungry in a long famine. This he achieved by spending his whole income and selling some church treasures. He also rebuilt his cathedral and restored the bishopric of Vich. Suffering from sleeplessness and continual fever, he returned to his native Montauriol, where the monks of St Martin received him joyfully, but he soon realized he had not long to live. After confessing his sins to the community he died peacefully, and the abbey was renamed St Audard in his honour.

St Mafalda of Portugal (1206–57)

The daughter of Sancho I, king of Portugal, Mafalda was married (presumably for dynastic reasons) to her cousin Henry I, king of Castile, in 1215. But in the next year the marriage was annulled for reasons of consanguinity, so Mafalda returned to Portugal. She then became a nun at Arouca, a convent which had adopted the Cistercian observance at her suggestion. She devoted her fortune to rebuilding Oporto cathedral and building a bridge over the river Tamega, as well as founding a hostel for pilgrims and a hospital for widows. The austerity of her life as a nun was expressed not only in the ordinary observance but also in sleeping on the ground or devoting the whole night to prayer. At the end of her life she chose sackcloth and ashes for her bed; her last words were "Lord, I hope in thee." When her body was exhumed in 1617, it was found to be both flexible and incorrupt. Her cult was confirmed in 1793.

See *Bibl.SS.*, 8, 490–1.

St Peregrine Laziosi (1265–1345)

Born at Forli (Romagna) of wealthy parents, Peregrine (Pellegrino) became active in local politics and supported the antipapal Ghibelline party. At one meeting tempers became very heated and Peregrine physically assaulted the Servite superior general, St Philip Benizi (23 Aug.), who had been sent as a peacemaker by the pope. Philip, however, literally turned the other cheek; Peregrine repented and then joined the Order of the Servite friars at Siena in 1292. There he practised assiduous prayer, sacred reading, penance, and almsgiving. One of his declared principles in the spiritual life was never to rest on one's laurels but always to press on toward higher things. In 1322 he founded a new house of Servites in his birthplace, Forli. Now a priest, he was especially fervent in the celebration of Mass, in preaching, and in spiritual direction. For many years he suffered from acute varicose veins in his right foot; at one time the pain was so severe that the surgeons decided to amputate it the next day. Pellegrino prayed for a very long time that night and woke up completely healed. He died at the age of eighty, and miracles were soon reported at his tomb. His cult was approved in 1609, and he was canonized in 1726.

See A. M. Serra, *Niccolo Borghese e i suoi scritti agiografici servitani* (1966); *Bibl.SS.*, 10, 468–80.

St Richard Pampuri (1897-1930)

Born at Trivolzio (near Pavia), the tenth of twelve children, he was well educated. He joined the faculty of medicine at Pavia in 1915; during the First World War he looked after the soldiers in the war zone, where the extent of injuries to their tortured bodies and suffering members made a deep impression on him. After the war he moved to Milan, where he continually acted as a good samaritan. Wishing to help further in a more organized way, he founded the Band of Pius X. This was a group of charitable people who made themselves available day and night to the suffering poor, whom they helped not only with medicine but also with food and clothing.

In 1927 he entered the Order of St John of God, taking the name of Richard. He was professed at Brescia in 1928. Conspicuous for his care of children, he was put in charge of all dental care under the Order's organization in that town. Only a year or so later he was taken ill with pneumonia, which developed into pleurisy. He died on 1 May 1930 in the hospital of his Order in Milan. He was buried in the cemetery of his home town of Trivolzio; his body was later transferred to the baptistery of the parish church. Following claims of miracles, which were seen as continuing and completing his work of healing in life, the process of inquiry began in 1949. His heroic virtue was declared in 1978; the miracles were approved and the beatification declared on 4 October 1981. Pope John Paul II said of him: "He was an extraordinary figure, close to our own times, but even closer to our problems and sensibilities. His short but intense life was of great value to the whole People of God, but specially to the young, to doctors and to religious." He was canonized on 2 November 1989.

See *Bibl. SS.*, Suppl.1, 1011-13; there are Lives by A. Montonati (1981), G. Radice (1982), and M. Soroldini (1983).

R.M.

St Andeolus of Viviers, martyr (third century)

St Bata of Persia, hermit and martyr (third century)

St Hippolytus of Avellino, martyr (fourth century)

St Isaac of Egypt, martyr (306)

St Orientius, bishop (440)

St Titianus, bishop in Liguria (476)

St Theodulph, abbot near Reims (sixth century)

St Arigius, bishop of Gap (Switzerland) (604)

St Romanus, monk and martyr in Syria (780)

St Aldebrand, bishop of Forsombrone in Italy (1219)

Bd Vivaldus, Franciscan hermit in Etruria (1320)

Bd Julian Cesarello, O.F.M. (1349)

Bd Petronilla, abbess of the Poor Clares, in Belloc (1355)

SS Augustine Scoeffler and Jean Louis Bonnard, martyrs (1851-2)—see "Martyrs of Vietnam," 2 Feb.

ST ASAPH (p. 4)
Keys as engraved in the seal of Robert Lancaster, bishop of
St Asaph (1411–33). Silver keys on black field.

ST ATHANASIUS (over page)
Symbols of his defence of othodoxy and episcopal office.
Gold triangle, white pallium with black crosses,
on blue field.

2

ST ATHANASIUS, *Bishop and Doctor* (295-373)

Born before the persecution of Christianity had ended, Athanasius in his life and teaching foresaw the problems of the next generation of Christians, who were to live under a civil power that no longer persecuted Christianity as such but used pressure and force to exact an imperially-led conformity. In Athanasius' lifetime one of the most important doctrinal conflicts ever also took place, over the true and proper divinity of the Son of God. He was utterly devoted to sharing and propagating the traditional belief in the identity of nature between Father and Son, expressed in the word "consubstantial" *(homoousios)*. In more simple language, Athanasius was the uncompromising protagonist that Jesus is the Son of God in the full and proper sense of these words; hence Jesus was truly God as well as truly man. Although it may seem surprising that it took theologians many years to work out the full implication of revelation, known through scripture and tradition, it is a matter of historical fact that orthodoxy became clearer and finally triumphed through error and heresy. Athanasius, its courageous champion, was repeatedly persecuted and exiled but finally vindicated. He was also important as a spiritual teacher of the ascetic and monastic life. Although not a monk himself, he had deep sympathy with them and wrote the Life of Antony of Egypt (17 Jan.), which became a classic of its kind.

He was born and died in Alexandria. He became its bishop (or more precisely, metropolitan patriarch) in 328, when in his early thirties. His see was comparable in prestige and power to those of Antioch and Jerusalem. How was he promoted to this office so young?

The short answer is that popular acclaim as well as the choice of his predecessor promoted him. He had already written important works on the Incarnation; above all he had been the secretary and companion to Alexander, bishop of Alexandria, at the Council of Nicaea in 325. Convoked by the emperor Constantine, this was attended by 320 bishops—mainly Eastern, as well as the papal legates—of whom 318 accepted the formulation of Christian belief which we now know as the Nicene Creed, including the all-important word "consubstantial."

Alexandria had for long been an important intellectual centre. One of its priests, Arius, well educated, austere, and eloquent, preached his ideas on the Word of God, which soon became suspect to Bishop Alexander. Arianism maintained that the Son of God was not eternal but was created out of nothing; therefore he was not God by nature but a creature. Although condemned by an Alexandrian synod as early as about 320, Arius ambitiously attempted to bring all the Eastern churches to accept his ideas and to propagate them through popular hymns.

Athanasius for his part was young and energetic but could sometimes be intransigent and difficult. He was warmly supported by monks and others; but some diocesan clergy, especially the followers of Meletus, would not accept the decisions of Nicaea. The situation was not helped when some extremist followers of Athanasius attacked and even killed some Meletians. Disorders of this kind led to denunciations to the emperor. Personal accusations, quite unfounded, followed. In all this controversy Athanasius gave as good as he got; but Constantine, prompted by the ambitious Eusebius of Nicomedia, exiled Athanasius to Treves (Trier) in 335. Exile, however, made him keep in touch with his flock by letter; he reminded them that his cause was the cause of the Christian faith. At this point St Antony wrote to the emperor in support of him but without result. Only when Constantine died in 337 was Athanasius restored to his see by the former emperor's two sons, Constantine II and Constantius.

Now a new problem arose in the shape of a rival bishop intruded into Alexandria by Eusebius of Nicomedia. Athanasius' reply was twofold. Eighty-five bishops of Egypt addressed a letter to the bishops of the whole Church, which denounced Eusebius' manoeuvres. In 339 Athanasius appealed to Rome. Pope Julius was soon convinced of the justice of Athanasius' cause and of the extreme danger of the "opposition's" attempts to impose the errors of Arius on the rest of the Church. The Roman council, to which Eastern bishops had been invited but which they refused to attend, recognized that Athanasius was right. Meanwhile, some Eastern bishops affirmed in a rival council at Antioch both their hostility to Arianism and the need to depose Athanasius. The subsequent Council of Sardica, at which Eastern and Western bishops refused to talk to each other, was largely inconclusive, but at least it enabled Athanasius to return to his diocese, this time in triumph. The next ten years (346-56) were among the most fruitful of his life.

Athanasius used this time to improve the spiritual life of his diocese. Huge crowds were present at the liturgy on feast-days. Vocations to the ascetic life (of monks and virgins) multiplied. The bishop sustained this revival both by preaching and by his substantial spiritual writings. He also appointed sound and mature men to bishoprics even if they were monks reluctant to leave their monasteries. He insisted that they could attain spiritual perfection in the episcopate and that their asceticism was most valuable exactly when in confrontation with worldly values. At this time of his life he left to others the pursuit of direct action at the court of the emperor, while he wrote *apologia* and other works to sustain his followers.

In 356 the emperor Constantius tried to overrule the Western bishops and then attempted to raise a revolt in Alexandria to eliminate Athanasius. Finally, he resorted to direct action. His army surrounded the church in which Athanasius held a night vigil. With the help of the monks Athanasius escaped, but there was now a price on his head. The faithful experienced a reign of terror by soldiers for eighteen months. Phaeno, a concentration camp of sinister memory, was reopened. Athanasius now ruled his diocese from the monastic cells of the Thebaid, encouraging resistance. But in 361 Constantius died and the repression ceased.

The new emperor was Julian the Apostate, who initially decided on a liberal policy of non-involvement in religious controversies. All the exiled bishops were allowed to go home, so in 362 Athanasius returned once more to Alexandria and invited the bishops to a council planned to bring reconciliation to the East. He took special care to appease the church of Antioch, often in history the rival of Alexandria. Unfortunately, once again his partisans' actions prevented any deep reconciliation. Furthermore, the emperor Julian abandoned his earlier policy of benevolent neutrality. Frightened by the success of Athanasius as a zealous apostle, he commanded him to leave Alexandria. An edict ordered him to be removed, dead or alive. Once more he returned to a monastery where (it seems) he neglected to take obvious precautions, thus risking capture by imperial police.

The sudden death of Julian in 363 led to another triumphant return to Alexandria by Athanasius. But once more he was in danger because the new emperor, Valens, resumed the religious policy of Constantius. Once again, in 365, Athanasius was exiled. This time he hid in the suburbs. Valens, unwilling to lose the support of Egypt, recalled him. Now, from 366 to his death in 373, he remained in peace in charge of his church. He gave himself to its pastoral care and wrote many letters, especially to St Basil (2 Jan.) and to St Damasus (11 Dec.). Only Antioch under Meletius was not reconciled.

Athanasius died in the night of 2-3 May 373 after forty-six years as a bishop, dedicated to the defence of the Church and its unity. Immediately after his death he was venerated as one of the first confessors (non-martyrs). In 379 St Gregory Nazianzen (2 Jan.) preached a fine commemorative sermon, associating Athanasius with the prophets, the apostles, and the martyrs. Since that time he has been venerated in the West as a champion of orthodox belief who suffered persecution and exile for the Church's doctrine. The Eastern Churches rightly complete this picture by seeing him as a spiritual teacher of ascetical and mystical life. He was regarded as a Doctor of the Church from early times. In the East his main feast-day is 18 January.

Athanasius had an outstanding perception of the Incarnation, the very heart of Christianity, both for what it tells us about God and God's care for humankind and for its consequences in the minds and hearts of the faithful. A few extracts from his writings reveal the quality of his thought:

"God the Word, by his union with humanity, restored to fallen man the image of God in which he had been created. By his death and resurrection he overcame death, the consequence of sin."

"There is one form of Godhead, which is also in the Word; one God the Father, existing by himself in respect that he is above all, and appearing in the Son in respect that he pervades all things, and in the Spirit in respect that he acts in all things in him through the Word. Thus we acknowledge God to be one through the Trinity."

"So (the monks') cells in the hills were like tents filled with divine choirs— people chanting, studying, fasting, praying, rejoicing in the hope of future good, working for the distribution of alms, and maintaining both love and harmony among themselves. It was as if one truly looked on a land all its own—a land of devotion and righteousness."

Early documents in *AA.SS.*, May, 1, pp. 1186-258; Lives by G. Bardy (1914), J.M. Leroux (1956). Works on his teaching include J. H. Newman, *The Arians of the Fourth Century* and *Select Treatises* against the Arians (1881); F. L. Cross, *The Study of St Athanasius* (1945); and the same author's edition of *De Incarnatione* (1939). Works ed. P. T. Camelot in *Sources Chrétiennes* 18 (1947). Recent studies include D. W. H. Arnold, *The Early Episcopal Career of Athanasius of Alexandria*; D. Brakke, *Athanasius and the Politics of Asceticism* (1995); A. Pettersen, *Athsansasius* (1995). Excellent articles in *Bibl.SS.*, 2, 522-47 and *H.S.S.C.*, 3, pp. 70-7.

St Waldebert, *Abbot* (c. 665)

Waldebert was a young nobleman who became a monk in St Columbanus' (23 Nov.) monastery of Luxeuil (Haute Saône). He was so exemplary that he was allowed to become a hermit about three miles from the monastery. There he remained for some years until the abbot, St Eustace, died. Another hermit, Gall, refused to accept the abbacy, so Waldebert was elected instead. His rule lasted forty years and was the most notable period in the abbey's history. He substituted the Rule of St Benedict (11 July) for that of Columbanus and obtained a papal privilege of exemption from the control of the local bishop. Thus Luxeuil enjoyed the same status as Lérins and Agaune. It was much enriched by lands including those which had belonged to Waldebert himself. In due course Luxeuil made foundations elsewhere in France, and Waldebert helped St Salaberga to found a large nunnery at Laon (Aisne). He was reputed to be a miracle-worker: his wooden drinking-bowl was believed to be the instrument of healing. In the church his weapons and military clothes hung from the roof for centuries in his memory.

Waldebert's life and miracles were written up from traditional sources about 300 years after his death. More recent studies include J. B. Clerc, *Ermitage et vie de S. Valbert* (1861), and J. Poinsotte, *Les Abbés de Luxeuil* (1900); *Bibl.SS.*, 12, 879-80.

St Wiborada, *Martyr* (926)

Born at Klingnau (Switzerland) of a Swabian noble family, Wiborada (also Guiborat or Weibrath) worked for some years for the monastery of Saint Gall, where her brother Hatto was a student, as a bookbinder for the abbey library. When her parents died, Wiborada joined Hatto, now provost of St Magnus' church. He taught her Latin so that she could say the offices with him, and she nursed the sick in their house. After both made a pilgrimage to Rome, Hatto decided to become a monk at Saint Gall, but Wiborada continued to live as a laywoman, becoming acquainted with St Ulric (of Augsburg; 4 July).

Whether a story that she underwent trial by ordeal to clear her reputation is true or not, it seems certain that she became a recluse, first near Saint Gall but later in a cell adjoining the church of St Magnus, where she remained from 915 to her death. Others settled close by, including Rachildis, a niece of Bd Notker the Stammerer

(6 Apr.), who suffered from an apparently incurable disease remedied by Wiborada. In the Hungarian invasion she is believed to have warned the clergy of Saint Gall and Saint Magnus to escape in time, but she remained in her cell by her own choice and was killed there by the intruders with a hatchet. Rachildis survived her for twenty-one years. Because she met a violent death as a witness to Christ against pagan enemies, she was venerated as a martyr and was canonized in 1047.

Early Life by Hartmann of Saint Gall in *AA.SS.*, May, 1, 284–308. More recent work stresses that Wiborada is mentioned in Lives of other saints; see *Bibl.SS.*, 12, 1072-3.

Bd Conrad of Seldenbüren (*c.* 1070-1126).

Born at Seldenbüren castle, Conrad, after his father's death, was the founder of the Benedictine abbey of Engelberg (Switzerland), from which were to be founded the American abbeys of Mount Angel (Oregon) and Conception (Missouri). He began the foundation in 1082 and it was completed in 1120. He then devoted the rest of his considerable princely fortune to founding a nunnery. He made a pilgrimage to Rome and obtained papal approval and recognition for his monasteries. He then entered Engelberg as a lay brother. A legal claim was made on some of the property he had given to the abbey, and when he went to settle the claim at Zurich, he was killed by his opponents without warning or provocation. His body was buried at Engelberg, where it was preserved incorrupt until it perished in the disastrous fire of 1729.

AA.SS., May, 1, pp. 309-10; Life by B. Egger (1926); *Bibl.SS.*, 4, 202-3.

Bd Nicholas Hermansson (1325-91)

Nicholas (Nils) Hermansson was an outstanding bishop and poet of medieval Sweden, closely associated with St Bridget (23 July). He was born at Skanninge (Ostergotland). Early in life he decided to be a priest. He studied at Paris and Orleans; on his return to Sweden in 1358 he became a canon of Linkoping and Uppsala. In 1361 he was appointed both archdeacon and vicar general of the ancient and important diocese of Linkoping, which he ruled firmly during the absence of its bishop. In 1374 he was elected bishop of Linkoping and confirmed by Pope Gregory XI, but the opposition of King Albert prevented him from taking possession of his see till 1375.

Nicholas' personal reputation has always stood high. Severe on himself, he devoted himself entirely to the Church and to the poor. Active in pastoral work, he energetically visited the parishes of his diocese, promoting the dignity of worship and the morality of the clergy. A tireless preacher, he was also accessible to the faithful. He was the friend of monasteries, especially St Bridget's foundation at Vadstena. Early in life he had been tutor to her sons, and later he helped draw up the Constitutions of the Brigettines. He had received her body for burial at Vadstena in 1374 and blessed the monastic buildings in 1384. He also helped substantially in her canonization process, which was completed in 1391. He was rightly a devotee

12

of Swedish saints: he revived the cult of St Anskar, the apostle of Sweden (3 Feb.), while he also had a special esteem for St Sigfrid (15 Feb.) and St Botwid (28 July). He was a liturgical poet, too, contributing hymns to the office of St Bridget, whose *Revelations* he used as a call to repentance and renewal. He helped subjects on occasion to withstand oppressive kings and even excommunicated both Albert and Haakon VI.

Nicholas died on 2 May 1391. The fame of his holiness spread over all Scandinavia, and miracles were soon reported at his tomb in Linkoping cathedral. These were registered in 1402. In 1414 the whole Swedish episcopate petitioned the antipope John XXIII for the canonizations of Brinolf of Skara, Ingrid of Skanning, and Nicholas. By now two Lives of him had been written with an account of his miracles. The Council of Constance authorized the opening of the canonization process. The formal inquiry into his life and miracles was held at Linkoping and at Vadstena: this provides insights of interest into both the character of Nicholas and the religious life in Sweden at the time of the Great Schism. This was ended in 1417 by the election of Martin V, who deposed his schismatical predecessors, after the previous legitimate pope had died. He confirmed the work of the commission for Nicholas' canonization, but at this point the pressure for the cause faltered owing to lack of money. Later the Swedish ambassador to the Holy See petitioned Alexander VI for the translations of the four Swedish *beati* to be accomplished. Presumably because of inaction, this petition was repeated in 1499, when the pope announced his intention of canonizing Nicholas. The solemn translation of his relics took place at Linkoping in 1515. This was followed by the bishop printing his Office and Mass in 1523. His cult and pilgrimage flourished in Sweden till the Reformation, which brought it to an end. His feast was formerly on 24 July but has recently been restored to his date of death, 2 May. If he has not yet been formally canonized, it would seem appropriate for more petitions to be made to this effect, both from Sweden and elsewhere. His memory and his cult must be an inspiration to the Catholic Church in Sweden, severely stricken by the Reformation and its consequences but now experiencing a relatively small but significant revival.

Excellent article by André Vauchez in *Bibl. SS.*, 9, 970-2; see also J. Gallen, "Les causes de Ste Ingrid et des saints suédois au temps de la Réforme," in *Archiv. Fratrum Praedicatorum VII* (1937), pp. 5-40; T. Lunden, *Sankt Nikolaus av Linkoping Kanonisationsprocess* (1963).

St Antoninus of Florence (1389-1459)

The son of a Florentine notary named Niccolo Pierozzi, Antonino (so-called because of his diminutive stature) became a Dominican under the reformer John Dominici at the church of S. Maria Novella in 1405. When he died as Florence's most famous archbishop, Pope Pius II described him thus in his memoirs: "He conquered avarice, trampled on pride, was utterly unacquainted with lust and most abstemious in food and drink; he did not yield to anger or envy or any other passion. He was a brilliant theologian, he wrote several books which are praised by scholars; he was a popular preacher though he inveighed against sin with the utmost energy; he reformed the morals of clergy and laity and strove earnestly to settle quarrels; he did his best to clear the city of feuds: he distributed the revenues of the Church to the poor, but to his relatives and friends (unless they were very needy) he gave nothing. He used only glass and clay dishes; he wished his household (which was very small) to be contented with little and to live according to the precepts of philosophy. When he died, he was given a splendid funeral. At his house was found nothing except the mule on which he used to ride and some cheap furniture: the poor had had everything else. The whole state believed that he had passed to a life of bliss—nor can we think their belief unfounded."

This almost unique eulogy can be completed from other sources. Antoninus was a man of diverse gifts and many achievements. His Dominican novitiate at Cortona was shared with the famous and saintly artist Fra Angelico (bd. 1982; 18 Feb.) and with Fra Bartolomeo, the future friend of Raphael. Initially assigned to Fiesole, Antoninus was appointed prior in turn to the houses of Cortona, Fiesole, the Minerva at Rome, Naples, Gaeta, Siena, and Florence. Here in 1436 he founded the famous convent of San Marco, formerly a Sylvestrine monastery, rebuilt by Michelozzi. It was decorated by Fra Angelico and his disciples with a fresco in each cell and the superb *Annunciation* on the main staircase. The late thirteenth-century church was rebuilt for the friars by Cosimo de'Medici.

Antoninus' most notable writings include a highly regarded summary of moral theology, various treatises on the Christian life (one of them had 102 early printed editions), and a world history. These titles indicate the breadth of his interests, while his specific contribution to the ethics of lending money at interest, which is not to be considered as usury, has been generally accepted.

In 1446 Eugenius IV appointed him archbishop of Florence. His way of life was very austere for the times. He owned no plate and no horses; his household had only six members; he gave audience to all comers and was lavish in alms for the poor, not only with food from the church's granaries but also with his furniture and clothes. Outbreaks of plague and earthquakes were special occasions for this abundant charity. He visited his diocese every year and preached tirelessly against both usury and magic. Pope Nicholas V (1447-55) declared that Antoninus was as worthy of veneration as the recently deceased Bernardino of Siena (20 May).

Toward the end of his life Antoninus acted as ambassador for Florence and was appointed by Pius II to a commission for reforming the Roman Curia. Thus was expressed the continuing confidence in him shown by Cosimo de'Medici, who attributed the preservation of the Republic of Florence to his example and prayers, and by several popes who saw him as an outstanding reforming bishop. Antoninus' life was inspired by his Dominican religious ideals and the example of other saintly pastors, but he was also a man of exceptional learning at a time when Renaissance humanism in scholarship and art was at its height. Like Francis of Assisi (4 Oct.) and John of the Cross (14 Dec.), he was small of stature but great in achievements. Contemporary artists recorded his likeness in a bust at S. Maria Novella and in a statue in the Uffizi gallery. Antonio del Pollaiuolo's painting of him at the foot of the cross can be seen at San Marco, with a series of scenes from his life which decorate its cloister. In this way outstanding artists of Florence have honoured appropriately their most famous and popular archbishop. He was canonized in 1523.

A contemporary Life written by one of his household survives in *AA.SS.*, May, 1, pp. 313-51; his *Summa Theologica* (ed. Ballerini) was republished in 1958 and his *Chronicles* (ed. J. B. Walker) in 1933. The best biographies are in French, by R. Morcay (1914) and A. Masseron (1926); but see also the more recent Italian work by C. C. Calzolai. Both Bede Jarret, O.P. (1914) and W. T. Gaughan (1951) have written on his economic and social importance. See also F. A. Gragg and L. C. Gabel (eds.), *Secret Memoirs of a Renaissance Pope* (1988); *O.D.S.*, pp. 24-5; *Bibl.SS.*, 2, 88-105.

Bd Joseph Mary Rubio Peralta (1864-1929)

This Spanish Jesuit is known principally as one of the apostles of Madrid. He was born at Dalias (Almería) in 1864 to a devout merchant family, six of whose twelve children survived. He was educated at Almería, then in a junior seminary, and from 1878 in the major seminary of Granada. In 1886 he completed his studies at Madrid with a licentiate in theology and a doctorate in canon law. He was ordained priest in 1887 and wished to become a Jesuit. At this time he was not allowed to do so, but nineteen years later he was able to follow this path. After two parochial appointments he was recalled to Madrid in 1890 to teach Latin, metaphysics, and pastoral theology in the seminary besides being a diocesan examiner and chaplain to the monks of St Bernard. Following a pilgrimage to the Holy Land he entered the Jesuit novitiate in 1906 and made simple, perpetual profession in 1908. No doubt the diocese of Madrid was sorry to lose him, but he was able to help the apostolate in a different way. This was in the Jesuit house at Seville (1908-10) until he took his tertianship at Manresa. He was then assigned to their house in Madrid, where he remained until his death at Aranjuez on 2 May 1929.

Joseph was an exemplary priest of deep spiritual life built around devotion to the Holy Eucharist and the Sacred Heart. His apostolate was expressed in long hours in the confessional and frequent, simple preaching devoid of rhetoric but able to touch souls, as the Curé d'Ars had done. He was also a director of religious communities and of lay sodalities. He would frequent the poorest and most neglected parts of Madrid, to whose spiritual renewal he contributed powerfully. Toward the end of his life numerous extraordinary events gave him the reputation of a miracle-worker. The cause of his beatification was introduced in 1963, and his heroic virtue and the genuineness of the miracles were approved with his beatification in 1966.

Lives by C. M. Staehlin (1953) and T. Ruiz del Rey (1957); see also *A.A.S.*, 56 (1964), 703-5, and especially *Bibl. SS.*, 11, 452-3; also J. N. Tylenda, *Jesuit Saints and Martyrs* (1983), pp. 123-4.

R.M.
SS Hesperus and Zoë, martyrs in Pamphylia (second century)
St Felix, martyr in Spain (fourth century)
St Daniel, monk in Syria (439)
St Vindemial and Companions, martyrs in Africa (483)
St Boris, king and monk in Bulgaria (907)
St Joseph Nguyen Van Luu, martyr (1854)—see "Martyrs of Vietnam (Tonkin)," 2 Feb.

ST PHILIP
Gold cross, silver roundels (representing loaves of bread), on red field.

ST JAMES THE LESS
Saw with silver blade and gold handle, on red field.

3

SS PHILIP AND JAMES, *Apostles* (First Century)

The principal reason why these two saints are venerated on the same day is that the basilica at Rome, later known as that of the Twelve Apostles, was dedicated to both of them, as an early inscription indicates. If the reason for this dedication is sought, the answer is probably that their supposed relics were brought there for veneration and the church built up around them. Virtually all our information about these apostles can be found in the New Testament; they can be seen as representing respectively Greek and Jewish elements in the early Church.

Philip, whose name is Greek and seems to mean etymologically "lover of horses," came from Bethsaida (John 1:43-51) and obeyed the call of Jesus before introducing Nathanael to him. Later, in the same Gospel (6:5-7), Jesus appealed to Philip before the feeding of the five thousand; Philip answered that six months' wages would not buy enough bread for them. Again, shortly before the passion (John 12:20-2), some Hellenistic Jews asked Philip if they could see Jesus. This request elicited Jesus' answer about the grain of wheat falling into the ground, dying, and subsequently bearing much fruit, followed by the prayer that the Father would glorify his name.

A little later, at the Last Supper, it was Philip who asked Jesus, "Show us the Father." Once more, this was the occasion for a deeper revelation, that of the unity of the Father and the Son. From all this it will be seen that Philip was of Greek origin, accessible to the Greeks desirous of knowing Jesus, and that he was both practical and earnest in his devotion to Jesus.

Like the other apostles, Philip received the Holy Spirit at Pentecost. Where he went after this is uncertain. Polycrates of Ephesus connects him with Phrygia and Hierapolis, where he is said to have preached and died.

In art he is represented either with a loaf, to commemorate his share in the feeding of the five thousand, or else with a long cross, interpreted either as a symbol of his supposed death on a cross, or else as a symbol of the weapon with which (according to the medieval *Golden Legend*) he routed a dragon from the temple of Mars. Such uncertainty, like the confusion in other legends between Philip the Apostle and Philip the Deacon (Acts 8:26-40), show how little, unfortunately, can be known about him with certainty.

There is also some uncertainty about James, for different reasons. First, he is not St James the Great (25 July), but James the Less. Second, he seems to be identical with James the son of Alpheus and James the "brother" (*i.e.*, cousin) of the Lord, (Matt. 10:3 and 13:5), who subsequently ruled the church at Jerusalem, where,

17

according to the usually reliable Josephus, he was martyred in the year 61. Whether and in what sense he should be called the author of the Epistle of James will be discussed below.

All the apostles were witnesses who had seen the risen Christ, but James had been favoured with a personal apparition (1 Cor. 15:7). Apparently he rose rapidly in the Church, and he summed up the conclusion of the "Council of Jerusalem" in 49/50, allowing Jewish and Gentile Christians to remain unified without forcing the Gentiles to accept circumcision but asking them to abstain from the meats sacrificed to idols, from impurity, and from blood (see Acts 15:13-16). St Paul also provides evidence for the authoritative position of James in the letter to the Galatians (2:9-12). He was seen especially as the spokesman of the Jewish Christians who observed the details of the Mosaic Law and its traditional interpretation.

The Epistle of James is a literary composition rather than a personal one, written in good quality Greek and known at Rome by the end of the first century. Scholarly opinion is divided both about the person of the author and its date. The Epistle claims to come from James, the brother of Jesus, but this may well be a literary convention which cloaks the work of an editor of a text which may have come from James or another of the apostles. The content and context of the Epistle are full of interest. In the context of hostile discrimination and economic pressure, the author is concerned both about people adopting the outlook and practices of the oppressors and about disunity in the community through gossip and criticism. His first theme is the importance of testing. Patient endurance will be rewarded by God, but not the attitude of the double-minded person, whose real trust is in human solutions. The second theme is wisdom, known through gentleness in speech and action. The third theme is wealth, seen by James as the possessions of the oppressors, while the Christians are mostly poor. Throughout the Epistle emphasis is also placed on prayer in joy and expectation of the coming of Christ and eternal reward.

Some famous difficulties of terminology between Paul and James have long caused controversy. James' Epistle seems to have been written without knowledge of Paul's doctrine, except perhaps through distortions. In fact, their use of key words differs considerably; they understood the terms "justification" and "works" in a different way. For Paul works are ritual acts such as circumcision; for James they are deeds of charity. For Paul faith is a commitment to God, which produces good works; for James faith is merely an intellectual belief. For Paul "justified" means the pronouncement of a sinner to be righteous; for James it means a declaration that the person did in fact act justly. Such being the case, the contradictions can be seen to be more apparent than real. The emphasis is different: one doctrinal, the other practical; overall, the teaching is the same. A reasonable compromise position on the date of the Epistle of James is that it was finally edited a few years after 61 (when James died) but before the fall of Jerusalem in 70. This makes it an important early writing in the New Testament canon.

In art James' principal emblem is a fuller's club, believed to have been the instrument of his death after he was condemned by the Sanhedrin. His soubriquet of James the Less made him a less popular patron of churches than James the Great of Compostela fame. The feast of Philip and James was formerly 1 May (as it still is in the Book of Common Prayer), but the Roman Calendar moved it first to 11 May (1955) and then to 3 May (1969).

Entries on these two saints can be found in *O.D.C.C.* and *O.D.S.* Both the *Jerome Biblical Commentary* and the *Oxford Companion to the Bible* provide useful insights into the Epistle of James. See also P. H. Hartin, *James and the Q Sayings of Jesus* (1991).

SS Timothy and Maura, *Martyrs* (*c.* 286)

In the East there was a notable cult of these martyrs, who suffered in Upper Egypt under the prefect Arrian. Timothy was a reader of the church at Penapeis near Antinoe, and with Maura, his wife, he was an ardent student of the Bible. Only twenty days after they were married, Timothy was taken to the governor and ordered to deliver up the sacred books. This he refused to do. For her part Maura also refused and declared she was ready to die with her husband. They were both executed soon afterward. Their Acts claim, not very convincingly, that Timothy was tortured with red-hot instruments in the ears and Maura had her hair pulled out. Both were then nailed to a wall, where they lingered for nine days.

St Juvenal of Narni (*c.* 376)

The oratory and tomb of St Juvenal, first bishop of Narni in Umbria, are still venerated today. Not much is known of his life; even the Bollandists' compilation contains legendary material. This makes Juvenal a priest and doctor who came from the East to Narni, where he enjoyed the hospitality of a lady named Philadelphia. Pope St Damasus I (366-84; 11 Dec.) is said to have consecrated Juvenal a bishop. It is said that a pagan priest, who struck Juvenal for refusing to sacrifice to the gods, cut his own throat in trying to withdraw his sword blade from between Juvenal's teeth. On another occasion he saved the city from Ligurian invaders by climbing the city wall and singing Psalm 34, which implores divine help against powerful and dangerous enemies. When the people answered Amen to a prayer for the city's safety, a sudden thunderstorm broke out and killed three thousand of the attacking army, and Narni was saved. The bishop died in peace after ruling his diocese for only seven years. His feast since the fifth century has been on 3 May; the diocese of Fossana claims him as its patron.

See *AA.SS.*, May, 1, pp. 386-7; *Bibl.SS.*, 6, 1069-70; P. Grosjean in *Anal. Boll.* 54 (1936), pp. 168-91.

St Conleth of Kildare (*c.* 520)

This hermit of Kildare, a skilled metalworker, is known mainly through the Lives of St Brigid. He lived at Old Connell (Co. Kildare) on the river Liffey, and to him has been ascribed the fine crozier of St Finbar, now in the Royal Irish Academy. Two legends concern him. One is that he became bishop or even archbishop. This must be placed in the context of Kildare's claim to episcopal or even metropolitan status. The other is a curious gloss in the martyrology of Oengus that he was eaten by wolves while on a journey to Rome against St Brigid's wishes. This is probably amateur etymology, as the two syllables of his name, "coin" and "leth," mean "half to wolves."

See D. Pochin Mould, *The Irish Saints* (1964), p.132, and the article on St Brigid in the present work under 1 Feb.

St Ansfrid of Utrecht, *Bishop* (1010)

The principal source for the life of this saint is the reliable Benedictine Albert of St Symphorian (Metz), whose chronicle *De diversitate temporum* ("On the different ages") was written as early as 1022. This recounts how Ansfrid, a notable soldier of Flanders, had considerable success in suppressing piracy and armed robbery. For this reason he enjoyed the favour of the emperors Otto III and Henry II. In view of his military success as count of Brabant, Henry wished to reward him with the see of Utrecht, the principal see of Flanders, founded by the English apostle St Willibrord (7 Nov.) in the early eighth century.

Unlike a number of other bishops, appointed by emperors for military prowess rather than spiritual excellence, Ansfrid was a devout and successful bishop from his appointment in 994 to the end of his life. He founded two religious houses: one for nuns in 992 at Thorn near Roermond, and the other for monks at Heiligenberg (or Hohorst) a few years later. Ansfrid became blind in 1006 and retired to Heiligenberg, where he died four years later. During his funeral some townsmen of Utrecht took possession of his body and carried it off to their cathedral for burial while the people of Heiligenberg were extinguishing a fire, started at just this time, perhaps not by accident. However that may be, the abbess of Thorn mediated between the two claimants and prevented a forceful restitution by the monks. So Ansfrid was buried in his cathedral of Utrecht.

See *AA.SS.*, May, 2, pp. 428-32; Albert of Metz in *M.G.H.*, *Scriptores*, pp. 705-9; *Bibl.SS.*, 2, 39.

Bd Mary Paradis (1840-1912)

Marie-Léonie was born at L'Acadie (Quebec); at the age of seventeen she was professed as a Marianite Sister of the Holy Cross. She taught in Canada for five years, but in 1862 she was invited to the United States, where she taught for some years in the orphanage of St Vincent (New York). Some years later she founded the Little Sisters of the Holy Family, officially recognized as an independent

Institute in 1880 and given definite status as a diocesan Congregation in 1896. In 1904 she was given the highest mark of personal confidence by her appointment as superior general for life. Eight years later she died at the mother house of Sherbrooke (Canada), where she is buried. The diocesan process in her regard was begun in 1952; she was beatified in 1984.

See E. Nadeau, *Mère Léonie* (1952) and *Montre-moi tes chemins* (1974); T. Lelièvre, *100 Nouveaux saints et bienheureux de 1963 à 1984* (1985).

R.M.
SS. Eventius, Alexander, and Theodulus, martyrs of Rome (*c.* 300)
St John of Sanhut, martyr (*c.* 303)
St Peter the Wonderworker, in the Peloponnese (922)
St Theodosius, abbot of Kiev (1074)
Bd Emilia Bicchieri, Dominican nun (1314)

PALM
Symbol of martyrs' triumph over death.
(over page)

4

BB MARTYRS OF ENGLAND AND WALES (1535-1680)

Today's feast is distinct from that of the Forty Martyrs of England and Wales, canonized by Pope Paul VI in 1970 and venerated on 25 October. It is more general in character and includes not only those beatified by Pope John Paul II in 1987 (whose names will be found listed under the date of their beatification, 22 Nov.) but also those beatified by earlier popes, numbering some two hundred in all. Here a historical outline will be provided with the principal names and dates.

The earliest martyrs of this period were the Carthusian monks from London and elsewhere, who suffered in 1535, even before SS John Fisher and Thomas More (9 July). They and others were victims of a law, recently changed, which made it high treason to deny that "the King is the only Supreme Head on earth of the Church in England." This not only defied traditional teaching about the pope being the successor of St Peter but also directly contradicted (as More said at his trial) the declarations of councils and the age-old belief of the Church. This had followed the legislation which made it a capital offence to reject or deny the validity of Henry's marriage to his mistress Anne Boleyn during the lifetime of his wife, Catherine of Aragon. This extension of the concept of treason was followed in the first legislative year of the reign of Elizabeth I (1559) by the Act of Supremacy, which made it high treason to deny the queen's spiritual authority—but only on the third offence (changed to the second offence in 1563). A further act of 1571 covered "seditious words" against the queen, and in 1581 it became treason to reconcile or be reconciled to the Catholic Church or even to induce others to be so reconciled. Four years later (1585) another act made it high treason for a Catholic priest ordained abroad after 24 June 1559 to enter or remain in the realm. This act also made it a felony for anyone to harbour or assist him.

No fewer than seventy-five out of the eighty-five martyrs beatified in 1987 were condemned under this act. The penalty for a priest was that he should be hanged, drawn, and quartered, while for a layman it was that he should be hanged. When the hunt for priests was on, the hiding-holes built by St Nicholas Owen and others were often instrumental in saving them; but the priests' hosts and hostesses also risked their lives by helping them. The will of the sovereigns had been decisive in defining the nature of, and the penalty for, the so-called crimes. It is fair to add that there were no martyrdoms during the first twelve years of Elizabeth's reign, but the intervention of Pope St Pius V (30 Apr.) excommunicating Elizabeth in 1570 persuaded the government to move more forcefully against Catholics. Eight were martyred between 1570 and 1578, followed by a respite to 1581. But from 1581 to

1603 not a year passed without the deaths of several martyrs, most of whom suffered for the fact of their priesthood.

During the first sixteen years of James I's reign (1603-25) over twenty martyrs died, but none from 1619 to 1628. Meanwhile the severe recusancy laws (against those who refused to receive the Sacrament at the local "church of England") took a heavy toll of the property of Catholics. However, they were not rigorously enforced to the letter in several regions. In London, too, conditions had changed. The marriages of both Charles I (1625-49) and Charles II (1660-85) led to less violent and more sporadic persecution of Catholics under the Stuarts, while the need for the government to foster good relations with Catholic foreign powers led to embassy chapels being open to Catholic worship. Some of these, such as those in Warwick Street and Maiden Lane, survive as Catholic churches to this day. Persecution revived at critical times like those of various alleged seditions such as the Gunpowder Plot and the Popish Plot. Sometimes it was extreme and led to executions; at other times it was less apparent but no less effective. During the Civil War (1642-52), many known Catholics supported King Charles I, which made them more unacceptable to Cromwell and his followers, though only Catholics suffered martyrdom during the Commonwealth and Protectorate periods (1649-60). At the Stuart restoration Catholic loyalty remained unrewarded in legislative terms, as was made clear in the last outbreak of persecution caused by Titus Oates' so-called Popish Plot of 1678.

The English martyrs of the Reformation were privately venerated, often from the time of their deaths. But official recognition came when Pope Gregory XIII (1572-85) allowed the martyrs who had already suffered to be included in the series of frescoes by Circiniani for the English College in Rome, which this pope had founded. These paintings represented English martyrs: St Alban, St Boniface, St Edmund, St Alphege, St Thomas of Canterbury, and others who had given their lives for Christ and been venerated as martyrs by the Church. This was a clear, authoritative indication that the English martyrs of the Reformation should be regarded in the same way. In 1642 Urban VIII, important in the history of canonization, initiated a formal inquiry, but this was shelved owing to the Civil War.

During the eighteenth century Bishop Challoner (1691-1781) kept the martyrs' memory alive with his *Memoirs of Missionary Priests* (1741), while in other circles Catholic interest in them tended to wane through a distrust of anything that resembled "enthusiasm" as well as the need to live in peace with Protestants as good neighbours.

The next official steps in promoting the cause of the martyrs were not taken till 1874. Earlier negotiations over the various Relief Acts and Catholic Emancipation (1829), to say nothing of the anti-Catholic outbursts that sparked the Gordon Riots (1780) and accompanied the restoration of the hierarchy (1850), had seemed to make further movement inopportune. But Cardinal Manning began the "ordinary process" by sending to Rome a list of 360 names for beatification. Twelve years later the Holy See, having carefully sifted the evidence, acknowledged that Gregory

XIII had "equipollently" beatified fifty-four, so these cults were now confirmed by Leo XIII. Forty-four cases were referred back for further information. Of the 253 cases pending, the beatification of a further 136 was granted by Pius XI in 1929. From Manning's original list 116 remained, but this had been increased by another 242 added in 1889, including the Franciscan Matthew Atkinson, who had died in prison at Hurst Castle as late as 1729 after thirty years' detention.

In 1960 Cardinal Godfrey petitioned the Holy See to proceed further in the canonization of selected martyrs who were already beatified, well known, and established in the devotion of the faithful. The canonization of the Forty Martyrs in 1970 was the first result. From the same long list were taken the eighty-five beatified in 1987. The Holy See scrutinized the many applications, admitting only those who suffered for religious rather than political causes. Those commemorated in today's feast include men and women, priests and laypersons, rich and poor alike, from many professions and walks of life. They came from many regions of England and Wales. If some seem less attractive or charismatic than some of the Forty, they are equally deserving of our veneration because they too gave their lives for Christ.

In considering the survival of Catholicism in England through the long "penal times," it is important to note that persistent and praiseworthy loyalty prevented its virtual disappearance, as in Scandinavia. Second, in this process, the witness of the martyrs was paramount, as it has been in other places and other periods of history. In the second century Tertullian had called the blood of the martyrs the seed of the Christians (often rendered "the seed of the Church"), and such it has been both in missionary expansion and in more settled societies. For example, in comparatively modern times France, China, Japan and Vietnam, Uganda and Spain, England and Ireland, have all provided martyrs. In England persecution was the work of the government, aided, abetted, and executed by members of the established Church. Comparisons are often understandably made with the persecution of Protestants under Queen Mary. This, largely confined to London and Essex and of short duration, targeted mainly (but not exclusively) Anabaptists such as John Lambert, in whose trial and execution both King Henry VIII and Archbishop Cranmer had taken part, and other nonconformists suspect to Catholic and Anglican alike. Few or none would nowadays defend, however, a policy that resulted in the fires at Smithfield and the deaths of some 278 people—more than the number of Catholics executed under Elizabeth. It is also a fact that "English law, from the sixteenth to the eighteenth century, piled up more than 200 capital crimes, ranging from high treason to the theft of property worth a few shillings.... These were reduced to four in 1861" (D. R. Campion, "Capital Punishment" in *N.C.E.*, 3, p.80). Human life seemed cheaper; public executions were enjoyed as a spectacle by many; all sorts of penalties were much more severe in the sixteenth and seventeenth centuries than in our own. On the other hand, the gruesome barbarity of Tudor regimes has been matched by modern dictatorial governments of both Right and Left.

In the ecumenical climate of today the comment of the British Council of Churches in 1970 was most welcome: "The martyr tradition is one in which all have shared and from which all may draw strength, even across ecumenical boundaries." And in 1987 Dr Runcie, archbishop of Canterbury, hoped that "these beatifications will indeed prompt all the Christians of England, Wales and Scotland to pursue the path of reconciliation and reunion with greater understanding and effectiveness.... Today we can celebrate their heroic Christian witness and deplore the intolerance of the age which flawed Christian convictions."

The English and Welsh martyrs, both local and national, have a continuing claim to our veneration. Like St Thomas More, they were by no means lacking in patriotism and were the king's good servants, but God's first. Among those commemorated today are George Haydock, priest, and his companions, executed at Tyburn in 1584, also Hugh Taylor, a seminary priest executed at York in 1585. On the next day (27 Nov.) suffered Marmaduke Bowes, "an honest gentleman wonderfully beloved" who had for some time attended Protestant services while remaining a Catholic at heart; he was hanged for sheltering Hugh Taylor. His temporary reluctance to reveal his true convictions did not deprive him of a martyr's crown. In current revisionist views of recusancy, it is suggested that those who were less heroic also contributed not a little to the survival of Catholicism in England and Wales.

See P. Caraman, "Martyrs of England and Wales" in *N.C.E.*, 9, pp. 318-33 (with full lists of names; illustrations from Cardinal Allen's *Briefe History of the Glorious Martyrdom of Twelve Reverend Priests*, Macerata [1583]); also J. Jukes in *N.C.E.*, 18, pp. 144-8; B. C. Foley, *The Eighty-Five Blessed Martyrs* (1987). Older works include: R. Challoner, *Memoirs of Missionary Priests* (ed. J. H. Pollen, 1924); B. Camm, *Nine Martyr Monks* (1931) and *Lives of the English Martyrs* (2 vols., 1904-5); L. E. Whatmore, *Blessed Carthusian Martyrs* (1962); J. H. Pollen, *Acts of the English Martyrs* (1891); J. Morris, *The Troubles of our Catholic Forefathers* (3 vols., 1872-7); T. P. Ellis, *The Catholic Martyrs of Wales* (1933). Recent surveys of the Reformation in England include J. J. Scarisbrick, *The Reformation and the English People* (1984); P. Hughes, *The Reformation in England* (3 vols., 1950-4); C. Haigh, *The English Reformation Revised* (1987) and *English Reformations* (1993).

St Florian, *Martyr* (304)

There is solid evidence that Florian was a martyr in the last and most violent of the persecutions in the Roman Empire, that of Diocletian, and that he suffered at Lorch (Lauriacum). He was an army officer and civil administrator at Noricum (Austria), who gave himself up to the soldiers of Aquilinus, the governor. His Acts claim that he was scourged, flayed, and thrown into the river Emms with a stone tied round his neck. His body was buried by a pious lady and then moved to the Augustinian abbey called St Florian's, near Linz. At least some of his relics were translated to Rome, where Pope Lucius III gave them to King Casimir of Poland and to the bishop of Cracow. From that time onward Florian was invoked as patron of Poland as well as of Linz and Upper Austria. Many healings were attributed to his intercession, and he is also invoked against dangers from fire and water. The tradition that he was martyred near the place where the river Emms flows into the Danube is both ancient and dependable.

His Acts were written in the eighth century, but it seems agreed that they have a sound historical basis. See *M.G.H., Scriptores rer. meroving.*, 3, 68-71; *Bibl.SS.*, 5, 937-8.

Bd Gregory of Verucchio (?1225-1343)

The cult of Gregory Celli was formally confirmed by Clement XIV in 1769; hitherto local, it was based more on miraculous cures than on substantial contemporary sources. The most important of the latter was a document attested by a public notary of the Celli family. According to this, Gregory lost his father at the age of three and was brought up by his mother. When he was fifteen, he entered the Order of the Hermits of St Augustine, while his mother founded and endowed a house of the same Order at Verucchio. After she had died and he had lived in the monastery for ten years, the community expelled him from the house. Homeless and destitute, he was kindly received by the Franciscans of Monte Carnerio (near Reati), and remained with them for the rest of his long life, estimated by some at 118 years. The mule which bore his coffin to the cemetery at Reati suddenly changed direction and went instead to Verucchio, where bells greeted its arrival. When rain is needed locally, Gregory is invoked to provide it.

Bibl.SS., 7, 1115-6; *Studies for the Sixth Centenary of His Death at Verucchio* (1950).

Bd Michael Giedroyc (1485)

Born at Giedroyc Castle, near Vilnius (Lithuania), the only son of noble parents, Michael was physically and permanently very handicapped from an early age. He was a dwarf, very delicate, and lost the use of one foot. Both he and his parents desired a life in the Church for him. When his studies were interrupted by illness or lack of teachers, he made sacred vessels for the altar. He joined the Augustinian Canons in the church of Our Lady of Metro (Cracow) but was soon authorized to become a hermit in a cell adjoining the church. He spent the rest of his life in a very austere regime of fasting and abstaining from all meat. Sometimes he lived on bread and salt alone. It is said that he suffered much physical and mental torment but was also consoled by visions. Miracles and prophecies were also attributed to him.

Bd Ladislas of Warsaw (1440-1505)

Apostle of Lithuania and patron of that country as well as of Galicia and Poland, Ladislas was born at Gielniow in 1440. He was educated at Warsaw University and entered the Franciscan convent of the reform of St John of Capistrano (23 Oct.) there. After some years he was elected provincial and held this office several times. He also revised the Constitutions, which were approved by the general chapter of Urbino in 1498. He sent a carefully chosen team of friars to evangelize Lithuania, warning them that personal holiness must precede the preaching of the gospel. As a consequence of this mission, many schismatics were reconciled and pagans converted.

Ladislas was an eloquent and ardent preacher and was in much demand when he was guardian at Warsaw. These years were especially notable for his preaching on the passion of Christ, as the new Roman Martyrology reminds us, and his celebration of it in devout hymns. These were sung mainly at evening services.

In 1498 Poland faced an invasion of Tartars and Turks combined, with an army estimated at 70,000 men. Ladislas initiated a campaign of prayer based on hope in God's deliverance. The invaders were trapped by extraordinary floods of the rivers Pruth and Dniester, between which they were camped; these were followed by intense frost and snowstorms. Thousands were thus killed by natural disaster, and more by the Polish army led by Prince Stephen. Ladislas' reputation stood very high as a man of prayer. He experienced levitation in his monastery, and on his last Good Friday he was raised in the air while preaching and was suspended there as though crucified. He sank gently to the ground but was so weak that he was carried to the infirmary and died a month later. He was beatified in 1586, and his cult was confirmed in 1769.

Bibl.SS., 7, 1067-8.

Bd John Martin Moye, *Founder* (1730-93)

A missionary in China and founder of two Congregations of nuns, John was born at Cutting (Moselle), the sixth of thirteen sons of a devout peasant family. He studied under the Jesuits at Strasbourg, entered the seminary of Metz, and was ordained priest in 1754. He was known for his piety and austerity but also for a certain rigidity of character. His life can be divided into three parts: parochial ministry from 1754 to 1767, apostolate in China from 1771 to 1783, and then more parochial ministry from 1788 to his death in 1793.

He worked first as a curate in several parishes of Metz, during which he found time to write a treatise on grace against the Protestants. To provide for the somewhat neglected needs of rural Catholicism, he founded two schools staffed by his Sisters of Divine Providence (founded 1762) to provide for the education of the poor. To support this venture he wrote a book on schools and nuns, following it up with a vigorous campaign in favour of baptizing newly-born infants. In 1767 he was denounced to the bishop but continued to found new schools. In 1771, however, he volunteered for the foreign missions and left for Macao.

He encountered various difficulties, such as adjusting to different food and clothes as well as learning a new language. Again he planned to found schools as before, but adapted to Chinese conditions. These led him to found the Institute of Christian Virgins, both to care for the sick and to give instruction to mothers and children in their own homes. Once again, too, he insisted on the baptism of infants at the first possible opportunity. Once more opposition to his methods arose, and complete exhaustion sent him home in 1784.

Again he worked in Lorraine, this time giving special help and counsel to priests and others affected by the troubles of the decade of the French Revolution. He moved his nuns to Trier in 1791, but they were suppressed by the French armies in 1792. In the next year John died of typhoid fever. After his death his Sisters were

27

revived in 1816. The Congregation grew to 116 convents by 1900, including a foundation at San Antonio (Texas) in 1866. Its success probably contributed to the progress of his cause. This was introduced in 1891; the heroic character of his virtues was declared in 1945, and in 1954 he was beatified by Pope Pius XII.

Life in English by M. G. Callahan (1964); in French by R. Plus (1947); see *N.C.E.*, 10, pp. 56–7; *Bibl. SS.*, 9, 660–5. Moye's works were published in 1858 and in 1874.

R.M.
SS Agapius and Secundinus, martyrs in North Africa (*c.* 259)
St Antonina, martyr at Nicaea, Turkey (third-fourth century)
SS Aphrodisius and Companions, martyrs in Palestine (third-fourth century)
St Silvanus and Companions, martyrs in Palestine (304)
St Nicephorus, abbot in Bithynia (813)

5

St Maximus of Jerusalem, *Bishop* (350)

Very little is known about this saint. He confessed the faith under Diocletian and Maximian (*c.* 303) but was first crippled by torture and then condemned to the mines. After the Peace of the Church under Constantine, he became bishop of Jerusalem, following Macarius. During the Arian controversy his simplicity betrayed him into false positions in theological matters, but he made amends afterward. Eventually he died in peace.

St Hilary of Arles, *Bishop* (400-49)

Hilary of Arles, not to be confused with his more famous namesake of Poitiers (13 Jan.), came from an aristocratic family related to St Honoratus of Arles (16 Jan.). He was probably educated at a school of rhetoric and describes his conversion by Honoratus in terms that are based on St Augustine's *Confessions*. Endowed with great natural ability, he decided to become a monk at Lérins. He was not left there long, however, because Honoratus was elected bishop of Arles and took Hilary with him. There he remained until Honoratus died, after which he planned to return to Lérins. Messengers followed him from Arles, and he was chosen their bishop at the age of twenty-nine.

As a bishop he aimed at combining the characteristics of a monk with those of a cleric. He undertook manual work at stated times, giving the proceeds in alms. On occasion he sold sacred vessels to redeem captives. He also built and visited monasteries in his diocese. However, he was also overzealous in his treatment of other bishops, over whom, like some of his predecessors, he claimed metropolitan jurisdiction. He even deposed one bishop, Chelidonius, who immediately appealed to St Leo the Great (10 Nov.). Hilary had also nominated a successor to a bishop who was very ill, but did not die. Hilary too went to Rome, but Leo found him somewhat intractable. He left him in office but forbade him to consecrate any more bishops and gave his metropolitan rank to the bishop of Fréjus.

Little is known of Hilary's last years. He died at the age of forty-nine, after working indefatigably for his diocese. It seems likely that he was reconciled with St Leo, who referred to him as "of blessed memory." Hilary seems a good example of someone with considerable talent and piety who was promoted too young by an influential relative and was never subjected to the normal pressures of monastic and ecclesiastical life.

AA.SS., May, 3, pp. 24-34; S. Cavallin, *Vita SS. Honorati et Hilarii* (1952). See *H.S.S.C.*, 2, p. 276, and *Bibl.SS.*, 7, 713-5.

St Maurontius, *Abbot* (634–702)

Maurontius was born into a holy family. His father, St Adalbald, was an official at the court of Dagobert I. His mother, St Rictrudis (12 May), was in her later years abbess of Marchiennes. Three sisters are also venerated: Clotsinda, Eusebia, and Adalsinda.

When Maurontius was only fifteen, his father was killed on an expedition to Gascony, so he went to live at the court of Clodovis II. He became engaged to a girl named Ermengarda but broke off the engagement in order to serve God in the religious life. Ordained a deacon, he founded a monastery at Breuil-sur-Lys on a family estate. Later he was recalled to court as chancellor by Theodoric I, who also ordered him to invite St Amatus (13 Sept.), an exiled bishop of Sion (Switzerland), to rule his monastery. In 690, however, Maurontius regained possession of it.

During the last years of his life he ruled two monasteries, his own abbey of Breuil and the nunnery of Marchiennes, left vacant by the death of his mother. He also built a church in honour of Our Lady, consecrated by the bishop of Thérouanne.

Maurontius died at Marchiennes and was buried in the abbey church beside his mother. In 870 Viking raiders obliged the monks to transfer his relics to a safe place. They chose Douai, of which town he became the patron. His name was also given to the town of Merville *(Maurontii villa)*, built beside his own monastery. His cult was strong in the areas of Lille and Cambrai.

AA.SS., May, 2, pp. 53–4; *Bibl.SS.*, 9, 235.

St Gothard of Hildesheim, *Bishop* (*c.* 960–1038)

The famous pass of St Gothard over the Alps takes its name from a chapel dedicated to this saint, built on its summit by the dukes of Bavaria. Gothard, or Godehard, was born at Reichersdorf (Bavaria). He was educated by canons who occupied the abbey of Nieder-Altaich and attracted the patronage of the archbishop of Salzburg, Frederick. Together with the bishops of Passau and Regensburg he restored the Rule of St Benedict to this abbey. Gothard, now a priest, along with several canons, became first a monk and then eventually abbot. During his rule of twenty-five years he reformed the monasteries of Tegernsee (Freising), Hersfeld (Thuringia), and Kremsmunster (Passau) and provided nine abbots for several houses.

On the death of St Bernwald, bishop of Hildesheim (20 Nov.), St Henry the Emperor (13 July) nominated Gothard in his place. Although sixty years old, he showed the energy of a much younger man. He built and restored churches, provided schools, reformed the cathedral chapter, and built a hospice for the sick and the poor. While deeply caring for the destitute, he was less favourable to professional tramps, whom he called "peripatetics," and would allow them to stay there for only two or three days. Gothard was canonized in 1131. Notable representations of him survive from the thirteenth to seventeenth century.

Two versions survive of the Life of Gothard written by his disciple Wolfher. Both are printed in *M.G.H., Scriptores*, 11, 167–218. Gothard's Letters survive in *M.G.H., Epistolae Selectae* 3, 59–70 and 105–10. See also *Bibl.SS.*, 7, 134–40.

St Angelo, *Martyr* (1220)

In the new Roman Martyrology as in the old, Angelo is commemorated today as a martyr. The details of his life are known only through Carmelite sources. According to these, Angelo was born of Jewish parents who had been converted to Christianity by a vision of Our Lady. Angelo was a twin, but the name and destiny of his brother are unknown. Both entered the Carmelite Order at the age of eighteen, already polyglot, and Angelo became a hermit on Mount Carmel for five years. In obedience to a vision of Our Lord, we are told, he went to Sicily, where he converted many by his teaching and miracles, including two hundred Jews at Palermo. In Leocata he enjoyed similar success but also aroused the fury of one Berengarius, whose evil life he had denounced. While Angelo was preaching, a gang of thugs headed by Berengarius broke through the crowd and stabbed him. Mortally wounded, Angelo fell to his knees and prayed for all the people, especially his murderers.

See *D.H.G.E.*, 3, 6–9; *B.H.L.*, pp. 77–8.

Bd Nuntius Sulprizio (1817–36)

Nunzio's short life was defined by suffering at almost every turn. Born at Pescosansonesco (Pescara) but orphaned at an early age, he was brought up by his aunt, until she too died prematurely when he was only nine years old. He then joined the household of a blacksmith and helped in his work at the forge. A serious illness developed in his left foot, which required a three-month stay in the hospital of S. Salvatore of Aquila, when he was only fourteen.

After a painful return to the workshop, he moved to Naples the next year at the request of his uncle, Francesco Sulprizio. At this stage a Colonel Wochinger, who "loved him like a son," wished to adopt him and live with him at the Castel Nuovo of Naples, a royal palace then used as a barracks. But after a new and very painful illness, heroically endured, the doctors decided in 1835 to amputate his leg. Nunzio, however, was in too weak a state to undergo an operation, so it was postponed. He never recovered normal health and died at the age of nineteen. In character he was very precise in everything he did; he carefully observed a rule of life and took great care not to fall into the slightest sin.

When his body was placed in the church of S. Maria Avvocata at Naples, the artist Maldarelli painted his portrait. In 1859 he was declared venerable; in 1891 Leo XIII promulgated the decree of heroic virtue and recommended him as a patron of working young men, contrasting with the patronage of St Aloysius Gonzaga (21 June) for schoolboys. In 1963 John XXIII approved his miracles and later Paul VI beatified him, inviting all believers to make a friend of him and "follow his heavenly way of life on our earthly pilgrimage."

There are several popular lives in Italian, the most recent being those by D. Rossio (1964) and A. Macena (1965); see also *Bibl.SS.*, 8, 66–7.

R.M.

St Jovinian, martyr of Auxerre (third century)

St Euthymius, martyr of Alexandria (*c.* 305)

St Britto, bishop of Trier (386)

St Nicetus, bishop of Vienne (fifth century)

St Geruntius, bishop of Milan (*c.* 472)

St Sacerdos, bishop in Aquitaine (720)

St Athanasius, bishop of Corinth (tenth century)

St Avertinus, deacon of Tours (1189)

Bd Benevenutus Mareni, Franciscan lay brother near Loreto (1289)

6

St Evodius of Antioch, *Bishop* (*c.* 64)

"At Antioch, where Evodius had been the first bishop, Ignatius was becoming famous at this time." Thus Eusebius, the first historian of the Christian Church, described today's saint. Evodius was presumably chosen by St Peter himself, but he left no writings, and his memory has been understandably overshadowed by the writings and martyrdom of his successor, Ignatius of Antioch (17 Oct.). Origen mentioned Evodius as the predecessor of Ignatius also, and some writers regarded him as one of the seventy disciples sent out to preach by Our Lord. At Antioch the disciples of Jesus were first called Christians; it may be that Evodius was responsible for this name, mentioned by Luke in Acts 11:26. If, as the sixth-century writer Malalas claimed, St Peter passed through Antioch when Evodius died, this event must be dated to the year 64 or earlier.

For further information see under Ignatius of Antioch (17 Oct.).

SS Marian and James, *Martyrs* (259)

These martyrs from Numidia in North Africa are of special interest both because of the authentic record of their deaths and because they were neither priests nor bishops but respectively a reader and a deacon. They suffered in the persecution of Valerian, shortly after the more famous St Cyprian of Carthage (16 Sept.); their Acts were known to St Augustine, who made use of them in his Sermon 284. The place where they were condemned was Cirta Julia (later called Constantina); that of their martyrdom is now known as Tazoult (Algeria). Much later their relics were translated to Gubbio (Umbria), where Guido Palmerucci painted a fine cycle of scenes from their lives in about 1350. These are now in the museum of Nancy.

Like other persecutions in the Roman Empire, that of Valerian was local and sporadic but very severe for a time in the places most affected. The author of these martyrs' Acts was their companion, but he was not martyred himself. He tells of a visit by Bishops Agapius and Secundinus, both of Numidia, to a farm called Muguas, where they met and encouraged Marian and James. (The bishops were in fact themselves martyred soon afterward.) A large force of soldiers surrounded the farm and made several arrests. Marian and James openly confessed their faith under interrogation and were imprisoned after the torture of the rack. Now they experienced various visions, recorded in the Acts and doubtless read to the assembled believers as part of the record of their martyrdom, like those of SS Perpetua and Felicity, who suffered at Carthage in 203 (7 Mar.). By now Agapius had been martyred (with two young girls); he appeared in the vision telling James that with Marian he would join him next day in his enjoyment of the heavenly banquet. On the following morning the Christians were brought to a river valley with high banks on each side resembling an amphitheatre. There they were placed in lines, blindfolded, and executed by swords piercing their throats. Marian's mother, called Mary, was present and rejoiced in his triumph. By their deaths, said the author of their Acts, they were "at last restored to the patriarchs in glory and delivered from the distress of this world." Their bodies were thrown into the river Rummel, and an ancient sculptured inscription recorded their memory at the spot.

See *A.C.M.*, pp. xxxiii–iv and 194–213; *H.S.S.C.*, 2, 217–21; for the inscription, Y. Duval, *Loca Sanctorum*, 1, fig. 126.

St Edbert of Lindisfarne (698)

Everything we know about Edbert comes from Bede's *Ecclesiastical History*. Edbert was a biblical scholar who, however, left no works. He was very generous to the poor and would give them a tenth of livestock, grain, and fruit. This did not prevent him from re-roofing with lead the large wooden church of Lindisfarne built by St Finan about forty years before (see 17 Feb.). Edbert was the immediate successor of St Cuthbert (20 Mar.) and was consecrated bishop in 688. Bede stressed this connection and told how Edbert authorized the examination of Cuthbert's body in 698. When this was found to be unexpectedly incorrupt, Edbert authorized a reburial in a shrine in the church. This was the contemporary equivalent to canonization. Like Cuthbert, Edbert used to retire to an island twice a year for forty days' solitude and prayer, and it is likely that the island he chose was the little one called St Cuthbert's Isle, just off Lindisfarne. After Cuthbert's translation, Edbert was taken ill and asked to be buried in Cuthbert's original grave outside the church. This was done, and Edbert's relics shared the many travels of Cuthbert's relics in 875 and afterward until both came to rest at Durham.

See Bede, *H.E.*, 1, 25; 4, 27–8.

Bd Bartholomew of Montepulciano (1330)

Bartholomew Pucci-Franceschi, in the words of the new Roman Martyrology, was a priest of the Order of Friars Minor, who "renounced wife, children and wealth for the love of God and became a little poor man of Christ." Not much more can be added to this owing to lack of historical record, beyond stressing that Bartholomew had been married for many years before joining the Franciscans, that his wife also took a vow of chastity, that Bartholomew experienced visions of Our Lady and the angels, but that he sometimes tried to become a "fool for Christ's sake," which led him to be ridiculed by children in the streets. He died at Montepulciano at a very advanced age.

His cult was confirmed by Leo XIII in 1880.

See *Bibl.SS.*, 10, 1239–40.

BB Edward Jones and Antony Middleton, *Martyrs* (1590)

Edward Jones came from North Wales and Antony Middleton from Yorkshire. They were both educated at Douai College (then at Reims), ordained priests, and chosen for the English mission. Middleton arrived in 1586, and his youthful appearance and small stature enabled him to work for some years as a priest without raising suspicion. Jones, who arrived in 1588, was soon identified through his eloquent fervour and was captured and tortured. Under torture he confessed that he was a priest, then a capital offence. Middleton also was tracked down by spies; his trial contained several irregularities and he was refused permission to address the people. Nevertheless he was able to call God to witness that he died simply and solely for the Catholic faith and for being a priest and a preacher. He then prayed that his death might expiate his sins, advance the Catholic faith, and convert heretics. He was then thrown off the ladder, cut down and disembowelled while still alive. The tradition is that they were executed in Fleet Street and Clerkenwell at the doors of the houses where they were arrested, with the explanatory placard "For treason and foreign invasion."

The persecutions of the English Catholics, like those of the early Christian martyrs, were sporadic, not continuous; Jones and Middleton incurred the fury that followed the Spanish Armada of 1588.

See J. H. Pollen, *Acts of English Martyrs*, pp. 308-9 and 315-7. The narrative of their martyrdom is in *Catholic Record Society*, 5, pp. 182-6; for the general background see C. Haigh, *English Reformations* (1993), pp. 251-67.

Bd Francis of Quebec (1623-1708)

Born at Montigny-sur-Aure (Eure), François Montmorency-Laval was a member of one of the most distinguished families of France. He was educated at the Jesuit school of La Flèche, received the tonsure at the age of twelve, and was named a canon of Evreux by its bishop, his uncle. Wishing to become a priest, he entered the college of Clermont in Paris but in 1645 had to interrupt his studies to attend to family business on the death of his two elder brothers.

As often happened in seventeenth-century France, clerics of noble families were destined for high office, and Francis was no exception. He was ordained priest in 1647 and was soon appointed archdeacon of Evreux. Still in his late twenties, he at once undertook the journeys necessary for effective visitations. These were interrupted only when, at the age of thirty, he was appointed vicar apostolic of Tongking (Indochina, now Vietnam). He was unable to take up residence there owing to difficulties caused by both geography and wars, and once again necessary care of his nephews and nieces interrupted his ecclesiastical career.

In 1654 he resigned his post at the still inaccessible Tongking and retired for four years to the Hermitage at Caen, a school of spirituality directed by Jean de Bernières. In 1658 Pope Alexander VII appointed him vicar apostolic of New France. He reached Canada in May 1659 and Quebec in the following month.

There could be no doubt of his commitment to the Church, sorely tested by the pioneer conditions of Canada, well away from the settled prosperity of France. For the next thirty years of his life he was prodigiously active, founding many parishes, fighting against the exploitation of the Indians by the merchants, and opposing the Gallicanism of successive governors. During a visit to France in 1662 he obtained many privileges for the church in Canada from Louis XIV. On his return to Quebec he founded a seminary in the same year. About ten years later he erected the see of Quebec and was appointed its first bishop in 1674. Ten years of active episcopate remained to him, but age and ill health (and very likely overwork) took their toll, and he resigned the see. He spent the last years of his life in retirement at the seminary he had founded, dying there at the age of eighty-five.

The diocesan or ordinary process was begun in 1878 and the apostolic process in 1890. The decree of heroic virtue was issued in 1960, and he was beatified in 1980.

See *AA.SS.*, 52 (1960), pp. 788-91; G. E. Demers in *Rapports du Congrès de la société canadienne d'Histoire de l'Eglise Catholique* (Ottawa, 1958), pp. 13-32; especially, L. Boyle in *Bibl.SS.*, 9, 576-7.

Bd Mary-Catherine of Cairo (1813-87)

Born at Giuliano (Rome), Constanza Troiani was educated by the Franciscan nuns at Ferentino, entered their novitiate in 1829, and made her profession the following year. She developed a strong desire to be a missionary and to spread the kingdom of God in Islamic lands, especially Egypt. There she hoped to found a school with the help of her Franciscan Sisters. She left for Cairo in 1859 amid general sympathy. She made a start in difficult conditions, but the community at Ferentino refused to help further. The result was that the convent at Cairo became the motherhouse of a new Congregation of Franciscan Missionary Sisters of Egypt, with Mary-Catherine as superior.

As the years passed, her enthusiasm did not diminish. Her initiative in Egypt bore fruit in Palestine and other countries with the spread of her ideals and her Congregation. This numbered over 1,250 Sisters in 1975. Mary-Catherine was especially devoted to St Joseph, the patron of happy death. She died on 6 May 1887. Her cause was introduced in 1944, and she was beatified by Pope John Paul II in 1985.

See *Bibl.SS.*, 8, 103-4; Italian Lives by P. P. Paoli (1929) and A. Pierotti (1952).

R.M.

St Venerius, bishop at Milan (409)

St Gaudentius, confessor in Rhetia (fourth-sixth century)

Bd Falco, abbot of Cava in Campania (1146)

7

ST JOHN OF BEVERLEY, *Bishop* (721)

Bede and Alcuin in the eighth century, King Athelstan in the ninth, the biographer Folcard in the eleventh, the anchoress Julian of Norwich, King Henry V at Agincourt, and St John Fisher (22 June), who was born at Beverley, all declared their admiration for this saint. Calendars from early times witness to the official cult in his honour, while a famous shrine-list from the eleventh century also reveals the existence of pilgrimage to his tomb. The fullest and most articulate witness to his life was Bede.

John was born at Harpham (Yorkshire) and studied in St Theodore's (19 Sept.) famous school at Canterbury under Abbot Adrian (9 Jan.). On returning to Yorkshire he became a monk in St Hilda's (17 Nov.) double monastery at Whitby, where he was distinguished for his care for the poor as well as for his learning. He was consecrated bishop of Hexham in 687; he used to retire for periods of prayer to a chapel of St Michael nearby; he ordained Bede both deacon and priest, and Bede recounted several miracles of him when he was bishop. One of these is an interesting early example of speech therapy: little by little, under John's guidance, a formerly dumb boy advanced from the letters of the alphabet to words and sentences. Then a physician was asked to cure the scabs on his head, and the bishop took him into his household.

In 705 John was appointed bishop of York, and St Wilfrid (12 Oct.) was restored to Hexham. Little is known of John's episcopate. He consecrated at least one church and founded the monastery of Beverley, to which he eventually retired and where he died; he cured a nun of Watton who was destined to succeed her mother as abbess. In old age, when his infirmities prevented him from fulfilling all his duties, he consecrated his priest Wilfrid (called the second) to the see of York and gracefully retired to Beverley where he died.

The reference to him by Julian of Norwich is full of interest. In chapter 38 of her *Revelations* she wrote: "And St John of Beverley our Lord shewed him full highly, in comfort to us for homeliness and brought to my mind how he is a dear neighbour and of our knowing. And God called him Saint John of Beverley plainly as we do . . . shewing that he is a full high saint in Heaven. . . . And with this he made mention that in his youth and tender age he was a dear worthy servant to God, greatly God-loving and dreading, and yet God suffered him to fall, mercifully keeping him that he perished not, nor lost no time. And afterward God raised him to manifold more grace, and by the contrition and meekness that he had in his living, God hath given him in Heaven manifold joys, over passing that which he would have had if he had not fallen. And that this is sooth, God sheweth in earth with plenteous miracles doing about his body continually." Miracles were also claimed when some of his relics were discovered in 1644. Henry V invoked him at Agincourt because it was his feast-day: he used to choose the days of his battles (as far as possible) on the feasts of English saints. At his request a synod in 1416 ordered his feast to be kept throughout England.

See Bede, *H.E.*, 4, 23 and 5, 2-6; Alcuin, *The Bishops, Kings, and Saints of York* (ed. P. Godman, 1982), lines 1084 ff., 1120-35, 1210-5; Julian of Norwich, *Revelations of Divine Love*, ch. 38; J. Raine (ed.), *Historians of the Church of York* (R.S.) 1, pp. 239-91; *O.D.S.*, p. 259.

St Flavia Domitilla, *Martyr* (*c.* 90)

Flavia Domitilla, a niece of the consul Flavius Clemens, was a Roman martyr in the persecution of Domitian (81-96). Her penalty for witnessing to Christ consisted in exile to the island of Pontia (Ponza, in the Gulf of Gaeta). Thus states the new Roman Martyrology, basing its entry rightly on Eusebius. In the fourth century Jerome described the journey of St Paula (26 Jan.) in the East to the place where "Domitilla had undergone a long martyrdom." Legendary Acts were written in the fifth century which linked her in life to SS Nereus and Achilleus, both real historical people, but whose only connection with Domitilla was to be buried in the cemetery called Domitilla's (see 12 May). Domitilla has also been sometimes confused with her aunt of the same name, who also suffered with her husband Flavius in the same persecution. He was executed, but she was exiled to the island of Pandataria, according to the historian Dion Cassius.

See *H.S.S.C.*, 2, p. 273; Eusebius, *The History of the Church* (ed. G. A. Williamson, 1965), pp. 125-7.

St Domitian of Maastricht, *Bishop* (560)

French in origin, Domitian became bishop of Maastricht and is known to have taken a prominent part in the synod of Orleans (549), refuting the errors of heretics. He evangelized the valley of the Meuse, making many converts, building churches, and founding hospitals. When charitable almsgiving flagged, he exhorted his flock to greater efforts by prophesying a plentiful harvest. Legends concerning Domitian include one of him killing a dragon which had somehow poisoned the water supply of Huy. In modern times his relics are still venerated in the church there and a procession to a spring commemorates his care for fresh water.

The Lives of this saint are late and unreliable. See *AA.SS.*, May, 3, pp. 146-53, and *M.G.H., Scriptores*, 7 (ed. G. H. Pertz), pp. 178, and 25, pp. 26-7.

St Serenicus (669)

"At Le Mans in France, St Serenicus, monk and deacon of the church at Rome, who after visiting the tombs of St Martin of Tours and of St Julian of Le Mans, passed his life in solitude and austerity." This is how the new Roman Martyrology describes this saint; a not very convincing narrative makes him and his brother young patricians from Spoleto, directed to Rome by an angel. There they became monks (perhaps in St Paul's Outside the Walls) but, again under angelic guidance, migrated to France. Serenicus sought solitude near the river Sarthe but was joined by disciples. He ruled the monastery until he died in extreme old age. Meanwhile his brother Serenus remained in solitude until he died, also in old age, when he was summoned to heaven by celestial music. The entry in the new Roman Martyrology seems to imply that there was but one saint instead of two and that he was a hermit.

See *AA.SS. OSB* (ed. J. Mabillon), 2, pp. 572–8.

Bd Giselle of Bavaria, *Abbess* (1060)

Giselle is known to history principally as the wife of St Stephen of Hungary (d. 1038; 16 Aug.), who was the first effective Christian king of his people, whom he united into a single State (more extensive than at the present day) by strong legislation and limited feudalism. Giselle's share in this, as well as the king's almsgiving and church building, is likely to have been considerable, but the sources are scarce.

She was the daughter of Henry II of Bavaria and his wife Giselle of Burgundy, who was the sister of St Henry II the Emperor (d. 1024; 13 July). Today's Giselle married Stephen in 996 shortly before he became king. Over nearly forty years she collaborated with him in the work of conversion, founding and endowing churches and monasteries with generous gifts. Her eldest son Emeric died in 1031 and her husband Stephen only seven years later. His successor was hostile to Stephen's policy and to Giselle's wealth. He rejected the one and confiscated the other. His name was Peter Orseolo. Giselle realized that she was no longer wanted and retired to the Benedictine nunnery of Niedenburg (near Passau), where she became the abbess. She died in 1060 and was buried in this monastery. Her tomb was venerated for centuries as a place of pilgrimage, revealing an immemorial cult. There is also strong martyrology evidence from Benedictine abbeys and from Hungary and the diocese of Passau, both of which kept her feast on 7 May. In 1908 her relics were exhumed and official recognition made.

See *Bibl.SS.*, 6, 1149.

Bd Rose Venerini (1656-1728)

Born at Viterbo, the daughter of a doctor, she entered a convent on the death of her fiancé. After a few months she returned home to look after her widowed mother and used to invite the women of the neighbourhood to say the rosary in her house. Directed by a Jesuit, Fr Ignatius Martinelli, she chose to be a teacher in the world rather than a contemplative in a convent. In 1685 she opened a free school for girls in Viterbo and was soon recognized as a "born teacher."

In 1692 Cardinal Barbarigo invited her to advise on and organize the training of teachers and the administration of schools in the diocese of Montefiascone. Here she became the friend and confidante of St Lucy Filippini (25 Mar.). Rose organized many schools in different parts of Italy, culminating in a foundation at Rome in 1713. In these tasks she was undeterred by opposition, which sometimes resulted in arson and physical attacks on the teachers. She died in 1728 in Rome, where a cult began after miracles were claimed. She was beatified in 1952. Only after her death was her sodality raised to the rank of a religious Congregation, and today the Venerini Sisters are found in the U.S.A. and elsewhere working among Italian immmigrants.

See the decree of beatification in *A.A.S.*, 44 (1952), 405-9.

R.M.

St Flavius and Companions, martyrs in Bithynia (third-fourth century)
St Domitianus, bishop in Flanders (*c.* 560)
St Peter, bishop in Lombardy (743)
Bd Frederick, abbot in Suabia (1071)
St Antony, hermit of Kiev (1073)
Bd Albert of Cremona, or of Bergamo, Dominican tertiary (1279)

8

St Victor the Moor, *Martyr* (303)

This famous martyr and patron of Milan was very probably black, like the more widely venerated soldier-saint Maurice of the Theban Legion. St Ambrose of Milan (7 Dec.) venerated him with Milan's other patrons, SS Felix and Nabor (12 July). Victor was a native of Mauretania, a Christian from his youth who served as a soldier in the Praetorian Guard. In the persecution of Maximian (with that of Diocletian the most severe in the Church's history) he was martyred at Milan (then a very important military and civic centre) in 303. His body was buried outside the town near a small wood, and a chapel was built over his tomb. Many miracles were claimed there from an early time. In 1576 St Charles Borromeo (4 Nov.) translated his relics to a new church in Milan, which still bears his name. This saint's Acts (of later date) accumulate the torments with little plausibility. It is better to dwell on the fact of Victor's martyrdom and early veneration at Milan.

See *C.M.H.*, p. 238, and F. Savio, *I santi Martiri di Milano* (1906), pp. 3-24 and 59-65; also *Bibl.SS.*, 12, 1274-5.

St Acacius, *Martyr* (303)

Mucius (13 May) and Acacius are the only early martyrs of Byzantium. Acacius was from Cappadocia and a centurion in the Roman army. He died alone for the Christian faith during the persecution of Diocletian and Maximian. At least two ancient churches in Constantinople were dedicated to Acacius, one of them built by Constantine. This one was called "the Walnut" because a walnut tree on which the saint was hung up to be scourged was built into its structure. The later Acts ascribe numerous companions to him as well as improbable tortures.

This saint's Acts survive in Greek and Syriac (*AA.SS.*, May, *s.d*); see H. Delehaye, *Origines du Culte des Martyrs* (1933), pp. 233-6, and, for the churches dedicated to him, *Echos d'Orient*, 11, pp. 105 ff.

St Gibrian (*c.* 515)

What little is known of this Irish saint is compatible with historical fact, insofar as many Celtic people from the British Isles did migrate to Brittany in the late fifth century. Furthermore, the Irish practice of voluntary exile for Christ is well documented. The story of Gibrian is that of an Irish family which emigrated in this way. It consisted supposedly of seven brothers and three sisters, of whom Gibrian was the oldest and a priest. They settled as hermits in the forest near the Marne, com-

41

paratively close to each other for easy access. Gibrian's hermitage was at the junction of the Coole and the Marne. He died after a life of prayer and penance, and a chapel was built over his grave. In the time of the Viking invasions, his relics, like those of countless other saints, were translated to a place of comparative safety, in this case to the abbey of St Remigius at Reims. There they remained until they were destroyed in the French Revolution. Although the historical character of these saints has been widely doubted, they were venerated both at Châlons-sur-Marne and at Reims, and their memory is retained in the new Roman Martyrology.

See *AA.SS.*, May, 3, 903-5; *Bibl.SS.*, *s.v.* "Elano," 4, 981-2.

St Desideratus of Bourges, *Bishop* (550)

The historical existence and admirable achievements of Desideratus cannot be questioned, even if all the details claimed about him are not worthy of credence. It seems safe to assert that he was born at Soissons of devout parents who were prominent in caring for the health of the poor. Desideratus served King Clotaire at his court and rose to the office of keeper of the king's seal. This implied considerable executive power, exercised in ecclesiastical as well as civil matters, as was usual under Merovingian kings. On the one hand Desideratus lived a quiet and mortified life in the midst of palace splendour and corruption; on the other, though still a layman, he tried to stamp out heresy and simony. In 541 he was chosen as bishop of Bourges, and in a nine-year episcopate he was reputed to be both a peacemaker and a miracle-worker. He took part in synods at Orleans and in the Auvergne, which aimed to restore orthodoxy of doctrine and daily church discipline. Another of his achievements was to enrich his churches with relics of the martyrs.

See *Bibl.SS.*, 4, 578; *D.H.G.E.*, 14, 343.

St Boniface IV, *Pope* (615)

Boniface was the son of a doctor and was born in Valeria (L'Aquila). By 591 he was a deacon and treasurer to St Gregory the Great (3 Sept.). He was elected pope in 608 and followed the ideals and policies of Gregory, making his house a monastery, encouraging monks in spite of the famine and plague which affected Rome at this time. He enjoyed good relations with the emperors Phocas and Heraclius; thanks to the first of these he transformed the Pantheon into the church of St Mary and the Martyrs, transferred numerous relics there, and thereby provided a significant example of how the Christian Church aimed at retaining and transforming the good elements of pagan culture. It is now often called Santa Maria Rotonda.

In 610 he held a synod of Italian bishops to regulate the life and discipline of monasteries. Mellitus, bishop of London, was present, and he returned to England with letters to Laurence, archbishop of Canterbury, Ethelbert, king of Kent, and his people, as well as the decrees of the synod. Bede mentions this as well as transcribing the letter of Laurence, Mellitus, and Justus to the Irish on the subject of church unity. St Columbanus (23 Nov.) was referred to in this letter. He in turn wrote a letter to Boniface in 613, which combines expressions of devotion and loyalty to the Holy See with accusations of heterodoxy, which were apparently without foundation. It seems likely that in requesting a repudiation of the "Three Chapters" condemnation, Columbanus was instigated by the Arian Lombard king Agilulf at his monastery of Bobbio in the Apennines. Boniface's answer to this letter has not survived. On his death he was buried in St Peter's, first in the portico and then in the church itself. This probably indicates an early cult, but it has documentary proof only from the late thirteenth century.

See *O.D.P.*, p. 69; *Bibl.SS.*, 3, 331-3. Bede, *H.E.*, 2,4; B. Mondin, *Dizionario Enciclopedico dei Papi* (1995), p. 75.

St Benedict II, *Pope* (685)

Roman by birth, Benedict had served the Church in the choir-school and as a priest when he was elected pope in July 683. The *Liber Pontificalis* described him as gentle, charitable to the poor, and energetic in restoring and improving Roman churches such as St Peter's, St Laurence's, and St Valentine's as well as Santa Maria Rotonda. Although he had to wait several months before receiving imperial confirmation, he successfully obtained the emperor's agreement to delegate this power to the exarch of Ravenna, thus ensuring that consecration took place with the minimum of delay. The emperor Constantine IV then sent to Benedict locks of his sons' hair, thereby signifying that Justinian and Heraclius would be the pope's spiritual sons.

Little information survives about Benedict's short reign of less than two years, but it reveals energetic activity on his part. His first aim was to secure the acceptance of the Church in the West to the sixth general council (680-1) and its condemnation of Monothelitism under Pope Agatho. To this end he sent a notary to Spain, where the council of Toledo accepted them, but with certain reservations by the metropolitan. Benedict, like his predecessors, supported the restoration of St Wilfrid (12 Oct.) to the see of York, with little immediate effect. He also tried unsuccessfully to persuade the deposed patriarch of Antioch (then in a monastery in Rome) to abandon his heretical views. At his death Benedict bequeathed thirty pounds of gold to the Roman clergy, to the diaconal monasteries for charitable relief, and to the lay sacristans of churches. While essentially a Roman by birth and interests, he was also energetic (like Gregory the Great) in caring for the needs of other churches.

See *O.D.P.*, pp. 79-80; *Liber Pontificalis* (ed. L. Duchesne), 1 (1886), 363-5; B. Mondin, *Dizionario Enciclopedico dei Papi* (1995), pp. 83-4.

St Indract of Glastonbury (Seventh-Eighth Century)

Historical information about this saint is extremely sparse. The best starting-point is the account of his death, possibly at Huish Episcopi, and burial at Glastonbury by its re-founder, King Ina of Wessex. The historian William of Malmesbury

(d. 1143) mentioned his relics among the many saints claimed by Glastonbury, a monastery of unique antiquity with a splendid library. Using a vernacular source now lost William described him as the son of an Irish king, of wonderful mildness and sanctity, who with his seven companions was killed by brigands, so that "credulous antiquity venerated them as martyrs." Indract was buried beside the high altar of the famous Old Church there, which was destroyed by fire in 1184. In 1478, however, William Worcestre said that his body lay at Shepton Mallet, by which time his companions had grown in popular estimation to the number of one hundred. In the seventh and eighth centuries many Irishmen accepted voluntary exile and were called pilgrims, so there is nothing impossible about the bare facts of Indract's story. It is noteworthy that the Irish martyrology of Tallaght (*c.* 800) describes him as a martyr for the Faith at Glastonbury, and his name occurs in a litany of the eleventh century, presumably of Glastonbury origin. All in all, there seems no reason to doubt his existence, but the claim that he was in any sense a martyr must be considered dubious.

William of Malmesbury, *Gesta Pontificum* (*R.S.*, 1870), pp. 196-8; J. Scott, *The Early History of Glastonbury* (1981), pp. 61, 69, 71; M. Lapidge, "The cult of St Indract at Glastonbury," in *Ireland in Early Medieval Europe* (ed. D. Whitelock, 1981), pp. 179-212; *O.D.S.*, p. 244.

St Wiro of Utrecht, *Bishop* (*c.* 753)

Wiro or Wera was a Northumbrian, who like his compatriot St Willibrord (7 Nov.) became an apostle of Frisia; he was one of a comparatively numerous group of Englishmen who took part with Willibrord and Boniface (5 June) in the Anglo-Saxon mission to the Continent. He was a monk, and it is possible (as his biographer claimed) that he also was consecrated a bishop at Rome. In 741 Boniface appointed him bishop of Utrecht, but he was not a metropolitan. Before or after this event he built a monastery and church at Roermond together with his English companions Pleghelm and Otger on land donated by Pepin of Herstall. The favour of this friendly ruler was most important for the success of this mission. In 746 Wiro joined Boniface in writing a letter of reproof to Ethelbald, king of Mercia, for the irregularity of his life and the oppression of the Church. Wiro was English and died in Holland; his cult is centred on Roermond and Odilienberg, while his relics are claimed by Utrecht. A ninth-century Life makes him an Irishman who died in Ireland. The new Roman Martyrology does not support this latter claim.

See W. Levison, *England and the Continent in the Eighth Century* (1956), pp.82-8; *E.H.D.*, 1, 751-6; L. Van der Essen, *Etude critique et litéraire sur les Vitae des saints mérovingiens* (1907), pp. 105-9; *O.D.S.*, p. 502.

Bd Mary Catherine de Longpré (1632-68)

She was born at Saint-Sauveur-le-Vicomte (Manche) on 3 May 1632. Early in her life she was professed as a nun, a Hospitaller of Mercy of the Order of St Augustine. In the course of her duties she tended the sick with exceptional care and was well known for her skill in caring for them as well as in comforting and counselling. She was invited to the convent of her Order in Quebec, where she zealously performed these duties for the rest of her comparatively short life. She died on 8 May 1668 at the age of thirty-six. She was beatified by Pope John Paul II on 23 April 1989, another example of an impressive series of holy men and women from French Canada of the seventeenth century.

T. Lelièvre, *100 Nouveaux Saints et Bienheureux* (1990); F. Holböck, *Die neuen Heiligen der katholische Kirche*, 3 (1994), pp. 118-9.

Bd Frances Nisch (1882-1913)

Frances came from south-eastern Germany, became a nun, and spent much of her short life working in various kitchens. She may perhaps be destined one day to become the patron saint of cooks.

She was born at Oberdorf-Mittelbiberach (in the diocese of Rottenburg-Stuttgart). Her father was a groom and her mother a domestic servant in the village inn. They bore ten children in acute poverty, and Frances was brought up by a maternal aunt. She made her First Communion at thirteen after an exemplary childhood. When she left school, she worked to contribute to the upkeep of the family. From the age of sixteen she worked as a maid in various places, including the canton of Saint Gall (Switzerland). After being ill with erysipelas in 1903, she was nursed back to health by the Sisters of Charity of Holy Cross of Ingenbohl.

This experience led her to become a nun in the same Congregation, first (in 1904) in the provincial house of Baden-Wurttemberg (in the diocese of Freiburg-im-Breisgau), then, (in 1906) for her novitiate, in Zell-Weierbach, where she was professed in 1907. For the rest of her life she worked in the kitchens of this predominantly nursing Congregation, first at Buhl, then at Baden-Baden. Even in the kitchen, she lived in a state of continual union with God, but with patience and charity to her neighbours and always in humility and joy. A surviving photograph of her, however, with firm, unsmiling mouth and determined chin, shows a different facet of her personality from the rather conventional summary of her virtues.

She was taken ill with tuberculosis in May 1912 and died just a year later, on 18 May 1913, aged only thirty. The fame of her holiness spread quickly. The faithful flocked to her tomb, attracted by stories of favours attributed to the "little sister's" intercession. The archbishop of Freiburg initiated, in response to this special interest in her, the judicial examination of her life and virtues. By 1963 as many as 100,000 people were visiting her tomb. In 1987 Pope John Paul II approved the introduction of her cause and beatified her in the same year.

See *Bibl. SS.*, Suppl. 1, 980-2; Lives by B. Baur (1963), M. Eckhardt (1976), and E. Giorgetti (1983).

R.M.

St Helladius, bishop of Auxerre (fourth century)

St Arsenius, hermit of Egypt (fourth-fifth century)

St John, bishop of Autun (*c.* 475)

St Martin, abbot in Aquitaine (sixth century)

St Metro, hermit of Verona (eighth century)

Bd Amatus Ronconi, lay brother at San Giuliano, near Rimini (late thirteenth century)

Bd Angelo of Massatio, Camaldolese martyr (*c.* 1458)

Bd Aloysius Rabata, Carmelite friar (1490)

9

St Pachomius, *Abbot* (*c.* 292-346)

Recent work on this saint has underlined his great importance as the founder of Christian community (cenobitic) monasticism, whereas Antony (17 Jan.) was the founder of solitary (eremitic) monasticism. Both came from Upper Egypt and were contemporaries, but Antony embarked on the monastic life as a young man, while Pachomius came to it after being conscripted into the Roman army and becoming a Christian when he was demobilized in 316. His parents were comparatively wealthy peasants. He had learned to read and write Coptic when young; much later he learned some Greek. He was a disciple of the hermit Palamon from 316 to 323, when he moved to Tabbennesi and was joined in his venture by villagers from the neighbourhood. As they could not accept discipline, he sent them away.

Pachomius was an exceptional organizer, and numerous recruits soon joined his monastery; his basic aim was to build up houses of up to forty monks, each devoted to the practice of basic crafts to ensure their subsistence. These included agriculture, weaving, mat making, and pottery. In addition, one house (with kitchen attached) was set aside for the care of the sick from the whole establishment; in time this became very large. Each house was ruled by a dean and his assistant, who was in practice the organizer of work and sales. Thirty or forty houses of this kind constituted a monastery, but each unit may not always have been at full strength. Weekly assignments to both church and kitchen resulted in the smooth performance of the liturgy and the provision of meals. These were simple and austere: Wednesdays and Fridays were fast days, when only one meal a day was eaten, while on other days a midday meal was served and an optional supper. Pachomius himself, who was superior general of the whole institute, fasted always and had but three meals a week in winter and often spent the whole night in work and vigils. His (and others') method of meditation was to learn by heart and frequently repeat the Psalms and other passages of the Bible. This occupation filled the intervals between the liturgical Hours and work; it inspired both the written rule (with 2,500 biblical texts quoted) and the living regime of the monastery. This indeed was a centre where the word of God "reigned supreme." By Pachomius' death his monasteries numbered nine for men and three for women.

As spiritual director of his monks, Pachomius was credited with knowledge at a distance and penetration of the secrets of the heart. He also showed a readiness to transfer his monks from one monastery to another. A particular case of his methods concerns his successor Theodore. This gifted young man came to the monastery and was given a series of charges which he fulfilled satisfactorily. In 336-7

Pachomius moved to his second monastery of Pboou, leaving Theodore in charge of the first monastery of Tabennesi. A few years later Pachomius was taken ill, and Theodore was indiscreet enough to tell the other abbots that he was quite ready to rule the whole institute if Pachomius should die. Pachomius recovered and deposed Theodore from all his charges; Theodore did penance for two years.

Every year there were two important meetings for the superiors: one at Easter, the other in August. These were held both for liturgical reunion and for the inspection of accounts. Remarkable unity was achieved inside the monasteries and with regard to the local bishops, who were strongly supported when the imperial police were hunting St Athanasius (2 May).

The story of the succession to Pachomius on his death is interesting. Just before he died, Pachomius nominated Petronios, but the latter died two months later, a victim of the plague like Pachomius himself. Petronios nominated Horsiesis, a good man but not a forceful one. He was unable to cope with the rebellion of several monasteries, resigned, and nominated as his successor the rejected Theodore, who ruled until his death in 368. Horsiesis then became superior general once more and died in 387. After this time (*c.* 450) the monasteries seem to have fallen into obscurity, but at least in 391 a foundation had been made at Canope, where St Jerome (30 Sept.) found and translated the Rule and the Letters of Pachomius in 404. This ensured Pachomius' fame in the West, where his influence on other monastic founders, including St Benedict (11 July), was considerable. In the East, however, his teaching was known largely through the writings of Theodore the Studite (759-826; 11 Nov.). Cassian provided a glimpse of Pachomian liturgy in Book Two of his *Institutes*. His regime and ideals, however, were too austere and too specialized to be generally popular, although reformers like Benedict of Aniane (750-821; 11 Feb.) were quite ready to use his writings in their study of pre-Benedictine monasticism.

Rule and Letters of Pachomius translated by St Jerome in *P.L.*, 23, 61-99; Greek Lives edited by F. Halkin (1932) and Coptic Lives by L. T. Lefort (1943). A. de Vogüé, "Etudes récentes sur S. Pachome," *R.H.E.*, 69 (1974), 425-53; F. Halkin, "Une vie inédite de saint Pachome," *Anal. Boll.* 87 (1979), pp. 5-55 and 241-79; P. Rousseau, *Pachomius* (1985). A. J. Festugière, *Historia monachorum in Aegypto* (1981) and *Les Moines d'Orient* (1981). D. J. Chitty, *The Desert a City* (1977) provides a very good account of Pachomius and his communities.

St Gerontius, *Bishop and Martyr* (501)

Very little is known about this saint. He was bishop of Cervia in the province of Ravenna and was murdered by "ungodly men" at Cagli, near Ancona, on the Flaminian Way, as he was returning from a synod at Rome held by Pope Symmachus. On the site of his death a Benedictine abbey was built later to help preserve his memory. His local cult is strong and comparatively well documented, but the claim that he was a martyr seems weak. Like all the other evidence, its only written witness is a tenth-century Life, which survives in only one manuscript.

See *AA.SS.*, May, 2, pp. 461-4; *Bibl.SS.*, 6, 71-3.

Bd Thomas Pickering, *Martyr* (1620–79)

Thomas Pickering, a Benedictine lay brother, was one of the victims of the so-called Popish Plot, the fictitious revelations by the impostor Titus Oates that the king, Charles II, would be assassinated and the French king would re-establish Catholicism. Thomas, born at Skelsmergh near Kendal (Cumbria) of a junior branch of the Pickerings of Westmoreland, was professed at St Gregory's, Douai, in 1660. He had been sent to London in 1665 as procurator to the small Benedictine community who performed the liturgy in the chapel of Queen Catherine of Braganza. This was at St James' Palace from 1660 and from 1671 at Somerset House in the Strand. Although the other monks had been banished in 1675, he was allowed to remain in the hope of better days to come.

Three Jesuits (William Ireland; Thomas Whitebread, the provincial; and William Harcourt) and a layman, John Grove, nominal owner of the house where they lived, and Thomas Pickering were charged together for conspiracy to kill the king. Oates and an accomplice swore that Grove and Pickering were to be the assassins, that they had been seen loitering suspiciously in St James' Park armed with pistols, and that three times a mishap such as a loose flint in the pistol had saved the king's life. Fr Ireland had plenty of witnesses to prove that he was absent in the Midlands and Wales during the critical time, but one witness swore she had seen him in Fetter Lane, and he was found guilty. So too was Thomas Pickering, although he rightly denied the charge and had never fired a pistol in his life. Part of the allegation was that he would receive "30,000 Masses" (though as a lay brother he could not say Mass and so could receive no Mass offerings) for his share in the alleged plot.

Ireland and Grove were executed at Tyburn on 24 January, but Pickering was reprieved to 9 May, when he also suffered at Tyburn. As he went to execution, he was called on by a bystander to confess his guilt. Raising his cap, he answered, innocent and cheerful: "Is this the countenance of a man who dies under so gross a guilt?" It was, in fact, that of "of all men living the most unlikely and the most unfit for that desperate undertaking."

The new Roman Martyrology describes him as a man of ancient simplicity and innocent life who went to his execution most serenely because of his fidelity to the Church of Rome. The whole persecution took place in the reign of Charles II, who seems to have done little to help its victims. Pickering's father had fought and died for Charles I in the Civil War. However, it seems certain that Charles II became a Catholic on his death-bed in 1685. Thomas Pickering was buried in the cemetery of St Giles in the Fields, London.

See B. Camm, *Nine Martyr Monks* (1930) and M. V. Hay, *The Jesuits and the Popish Plot* (1934); N. Birt, *Obit Book of the English Benedictines, 1602–1912* (1912), p. 53; H. Bowler, "Blessed Thomas Pickering: Some New Facts," *Downside Review* 58 (1940), pp. 292–300; D. Lunn, *English Benedictines* (1980), pp. 135–6.

Bd Mary-Teresa Gerhardinger (1797-1879)

Born in Stadtamhof, a suburb of Regensburg (Bavaria), the daughter of a boatman, she was christened Caroline, and was educated by the Canonesses of Our Lady, founded by St Peter Fourier (9 Dec.) and Bd Alix Le Clerc (22 Oct.). This Congregation was suppressed in Germany under Napoleon but revived by a local priest, Fr Wittmann, under whose direction Caroline finished her studies and then taught in the school from 1816 to 1833. Fr Wittmann's plan was to send Sisters, two by two, into rural schools, but he and his colleague Fr Francis Job, confessor of the empress of Austria, both died in 1833-4. Bereft of money and other support, the Congregation soldiered on. In this difficult situation Caroline made her profession to the bishop of Regensburg, taking the name of Maria-Theresa. Her character was said to be rigid, and this may well have been an advantage in surmounting the varied obstacles which faced a Congregation with an insecure future.

It was a tribute to her ideals and ability that she was chosen to be the superior in 1839. She continued in office till her death some forty years later. In 1847 she accepted an invitation to send five Sisters to the American mission. In spite of initial difficulties she founded an orphanage at Baltimore and schools at both Pittsburgh and Philadelphia with the help of St John Nepomucene Neumann (5 Jan.). These were foundations for Czech immigrants similar to those initiated by St Frances-Xavier Cabrini (22 Dec.) for Italians. By 1850 foundations had also been made in Germany, Hungary, and England. In this situation of international expansion some of the bishops found it difficult to accept the idea of a single motherhouse and superior general; but in 1859 the Holy See strongly supported Mary-Teresa Gerhardinger and she was confirmed as superior general for life.

Twenty years of fruitful activity remained to her, during which she was highly esteemed by the parents of her schoolchildren and by both ecclesiastical and civil dignitaries. In 1877 she had seemed to be at the point of death, but she lingered on to 1879, when she had foretold she would die. Her last words were, "My death will be a consolation for my whole life." In 1952 her cause was introduced, and she was beatified in 1985 by Pope John Paul II.

There are Lives in German by M. L.Ziegler (1950) and E. Kawa (1958); see especially *Bibl.SS.*, 6, 217-9.

R.M.

St Denis, bishop of Vienne (fourth century)

St Beatus, hermit in Normandy (seventh century)

Bd Fortis Gabrielli, hermit of Camalduli (1040)

St Mainard, bishop of Urbino (1088)

Bd Benvenuti Mareni, Franciscan lay brother (1289)

St Joseph Do Quang Hien, Dominican martyr (1840)—see "Martyrs of Vietnam (Tonkin)," 2 Feb.

10

SS Gordian and Epimachus, *Martyrs* (*c.* 250)

For these two martyrs the liturgical and archaeological evidence is strong, but the biographical evidence is sparse. They have been venerated on 10 May since the fifth century, and their bodies were buried in a crypt on Rome's Latin Way, over which a church was subsequently built.

Although their tombs are in the same church, the origins of these martyrs appear different. The church is dedicated to Epimachus, who was buried there first; later the better-known Gordian was buried beside him. The persecution of Decius is the most likely setting.

It has been conjectured that Epimachus was an Alexandrian martyr, mentioned by Eusebius, whose relics were supposedly translated to Rome. Gordian is mentioned in an epitaph by Pope St Damasus (fourth century; 11 Dec.) as a martyr who suffered while still young. His later Acts added these details: that in the reign of Julian the Apostate Gordian was a minister of the emperor (very unlikely) who was converted while visiting a prisoner and subsequently baptized a persecutor with his mother and household. Gordian was killed by the sword. After his body (we are told) was exposed to the dogs for five days, it was buried in the crypt on the Latin Way.

Whatever we may think of these details, martyrologies from the sixth century onward are almost unanimous in recording these martyrs. Parts of their relics were given by Charlemagne's wife, Hildegard, to the abbey of Kempten (Bavaria). Possibly as a consequence of this, some fifteenth-century paintings of the two saints survive on the high altar of the church at Dietersheim (near Bingen). Gordian is painted in military uniform, holding the palm of martyrdom and a sword as the instrument of his death. Epimachus, however, holds a book and (anachronistically) a crucifix, both of which seem unrelated to his martyrdom. This uncertainty reflects the limitations of any detailed knowledge of these two martyrs.

See *Bibl.SS.*, 7, 117–20. Eusebius, *H.E.*, 6, 41 (pp. 275-9); *Propylaeum*, p. 182; the Acts are in *AA.SS.*, May, 2, pp. 549-53.

SS Alphius and Companions, *Martyrs* (*c.* 251)

These very ancient martyrs of Sicily had a considerable cult. They are patrons of Vaste (near Otranto, in the "heel" of Italy), where they were born, and of Lentini (south of Catania, Sicily), where they died.

They suffered in the persecution of Decius. They were interrogated at Messina, imprisoned at Catania, and martyred at Lentini. Their cult soon spread through Sicily and in south-eastern Italy, but about a hundred years after their deaths their Acts were written in Greek by Byzantine monks in southern Italy. This diffused their cult, especially when Sicily was conquered by the Byzantines. These Acts, however, have little historical value. They abound in hagiographic romance with miraculous elements unduly multiplied and with the original three martyrs (Alphius and his brothers Philadelphus and Cyrinus) increased to about a dozen. If few details are certain about these martyrs, there can be no doubt about their popularity. They occur in the Roman and other martyrologies; in 1517 bodies believed to be theirs were discovered, identified, and translated at Lentini. Popular representations were numerous, especially in a mystery play performed in the marketplace of Acireale with audience participation and beautiful stage scenery and decorations. This was called "The Tragedy of St Alphius." This feast has been constant on 10 May.

AA.SS., May, 2, pp. 502–20 and 772–88; *Bibl.SS.*, 1, 832–4.

St Comgall of Bangor, *Abbot* (516–602)

Information about this important and influential abbot is comparatively abundant. He was the founder of the abbey of Bangor, on Belfast Lough, from which St Columbanus (21 Nov.), his disciple, left for Gaul in about 590. If Columbanus was his disciple, Columba of Iona (9 June) was his friend, and the biographers of both these saints provide us with much of what we know of Comgall. He is also mentioned in the annals of Ulster and of Innisfallen.

He was born in Dal Araide (Antrim), founded Bangor in about 558, and died at the age of over eighty. His father, Sethna, was a soldier and hoped his son would follow a military career. Instead, he went to study, first with a cleric, who reputedly kept a mistress, and then in a monastic school, probably that of Finian of Moville (10 Sept.). After the usual temptations of boredom and instability as well as homesickness, he revealed all to his abbot, who prayed specially for him. Comgall prayed, too, at the foot of one of the fine sculpted crosses. After this he settled in monastic life, was ordained priest, and founded a small monastery on Lough Erne (Inis Cometa). His extreme asceticism had to be modified because of the danger to the health of his disciples. It had included praying standing up in the cold rivers.

It was the foundation of Bangor, strategically placed for expansion into Scotland and Gaul, that was the principal achievement of Comgall's life. Here were formed some of the principal examples of the Irish monastic apostolate overseas, often called "pilgrimage (or voluntary exile) for Christ." The number of monks there has been claimed to be as high as three or four thousand; but perhaps (as elsewhere in Ireland) the number includes laymen attached to the monastery, or else it is an estimate of the total number of monks who passed through his hands in the course of about forty years. Whatever the numbers involved, Comgall's importance in the whole movement was considerable. Although he never went to the Continent, he influenced the monastery of Saint Gall (Switzerland). But he did travel in Scotland in Columba's company to obtain authorization for his foundation on the island of Tiree (Inner Hebrides) and for his monks to preach in parts of Scotland ruled by King Brude of Inverness. There are various stories about the two saints recounted to display the prophetic ability of Columba, including the prediction that there would be a battle between the kindred of the two holy men, identified as that of Dun Cethirn in 629. In a lighter vein, the introduction of milk into the Bangor monks' diet is attributed to a visit by Finian of Moville in his extreme old age. We are on more certain ground in quoting from the Rule attributed to Comgall, which is metrical and survives in Irish, and from the Antiphonary of Bangor, written in Latin, taken to Bobbio and now in Milan.

From the first comes the "essence of the Rule: love Christ, hate wealth: piety . . . toward the king of the sun and smoothness toward men." Again: "These are your three rules, have nothing else dearer: patience and humility and the love of the Lord in your heart." And in particular: "Though great injuries come to you, do not lament at this, because they are not more abundant than those of the King who sent them."

From the Antiphonary comes this praise of the Rule: "Good the rule of Bangor, correct and divine: strict, holy and constant, excellent, just and admirable. Happy the family of Bangor, founded on a sure faith; graced with the hope of salvation and made perfect in love." It also reveals interesting details of Bangor's liturgy: this had three night offices (Vespers, Vigils, and Lauds) and three day offices (Terce, Sext, and None). A century later, Prime and Compline were added. A number of canticles and hymns, found elsewhere in the monastic office of the West, are found here, as well as the earliest Eucharistic hymn in the West, *Sancti venite*. This is translated "Come, you who are holy, receive the body of Christ, drinking (also) the holy blood by which you are redeemed."

Two other memorials of Comgall should be recorded here. One is a little bronze bell, dug up in Bangor graveyard, which with the mention in his life of a house-shaped reliquary reminds us of the famous Irish skill in metalwork. The other is a saying often attributed to him: "My soul-friend has died and I am headless; you too are headless, for a man without a soul-friend is a body without a head." Comgall himself died after a long illness, sometimes attributed to his austerities. The last word may be left to Jonas, the biographer of Columbanus: "Comgall was the outstanding father of the monks in Ireland, and was known for his insistence on study and strict discipline." His relics at Bangor were scattered by the Vikings in 822.

See A. Gwynn, "The Irish Monastery of Bangor" in *Irish Ecclesiastical Record* (1950), pp. 388-97; for the Rule, J. Strachan in *Eriu* 1 (1904), pp. 191-208; 2, (1905), pp. 58ff. For the Latin Life see P. Grosjean, "S. Comgalli Vita Latina," *Anal. Boll.* 52 (1934), pp. 343-56. The evidence is well resumed in D. Pochin Mould, *The Irish Saints* (1964), pp. 125-32. See also R. Sharpe (trans.), *Adomnán of Iona: The Life of St Columba* (1995). The Life of Columbanus is in G. M. S. Walker, *Sancti Columbani Opera* (1957).

St Catald (Seventh Century)

Catald, an Irish pilgrim believed to have been bishop of Taranto (Basilicato), is the object of a widespread cult in southern Italy, Sicily, and Malta. Unfortunately, detailed information about his life is almost non-existent, but there are interesting archaeological and artistic data. His relics were discovered at Taranto in 1071. Buried with him was a cross in Irish style, believed to have come from a pastoral staff. This was inscribed with his name and probably dates from the seventh century. From the late eleventh century, following the discovery of his tomb, came a series of miracles claimed at Taranto, including cures from the plague. He was also widely invoked against natural disasters such as drought and storms. The cult, spread by both Norman and Benedictine influence in the twelfth century, found artistic expression in mosaics at Palermo and Cefalu (Sicily) as well as at Taranto. Apart from his cult the only firm evidence about him is his Irish name, inscribed on his cross. He was very probably an Irish "pilgrim" who died at Taranto. He may have been a bishop in Ireland or an Irish centre in mainland Europe. He is also believed to have been a monk who taught in the schools of Lismore.

The best account of him is by J. Hennig, "Cathaldus Rachau," in *Medieval Studies* (1946), pp. 217-44; see also D. Pochin Mould, *The Irish Saints* (1964), pp. 61-2; *Bibl.SS.*, 3, 950-1.

St Solangia (880)

At Villemont, near Bourges, where she was born, and in the neighbouring province of Berry, Solangia is widely invoked as a special patron. There are a number of devotional brochures in her honour which contain frequent clichés of hagiography. According to these she was a poor vine-dresser's daughter who worked as a shepherdess and had taken a vow of chastity at an early age. She was often able to cure her father's sheep, and a guiding star used to shine over her when the time of prayer approached. One Bernard, a son of the count of Poitiers, having heard of her beauty, rode on horseback to woo her when she was alone with her flock. When she resisted, he lifted her on to the saddle in front of him, but she slipped off the horse and was seriously injured when she fell. Bernard then killed her with his hunting-knife. The legend completes the account by claiming that the dead girl walked to the cemetery of Saint-Martin-du-Cros, carrying her head in her hands. An altar was built there in her honour in about 1281, while a field near her home is called "Le champ de Sainte Solange." The details of the story lack credibility and therefore inspire little confidence, but behind the cult there is possibly some genuine story of a young girl who, like St Mary Goretti (6 July), preferred death to dishonour. Solangia's relics were prominent in procession at Bourges in the seventeenth century in times of severe drought.

See O. P. de la Villeon, *Sainte Solange, protectrice du Berry* (1948); J. Goubert and L. Christiani, *Sainte Solange* (1954); *Bibl.SS.*, 11, 1287.

Bd Beatrice d'Este (1206-26)

There are three women of this name and family who have enjoyed a reputation for holiness. Today's Beatrice was the daughter of the Marchese Azzo d'Este but was orphaned at the age of six. She was brought up by her stepmother and her aunt, but from her father's death she refused to wear fine dresses and jewellery suitable for one of her aristocratic standing. When she was fourteen she secretly left home and became a Benedictine nun at Solarola, near Padua. There, in spite of family opposition, she received the religious habit. In 1221 she was sent with ten other Sisters to their foundation at Gemmola, where she died at the age of only twenty. Her incorrupt body was translated to the church of S. Sophia at Padua in 1578. Her cult was formally approved in 1763.

Contemporary Life by Albert was printed by G. Brunacci (1767); that by Bishop Thomasini is in *AA.SS.*, May, 2, pp. 598-605; *Bibl.SS.*, 2, 995-6.

Bd Nicholas Albergati (*c.*1375-1443)

The unlikely achievement of a Carthusian monk being chosen to preside at a council of the Church as papal legate provides an outline of Nicholas' life. He was born in Bologna of a wealthy family and studied law at its famous university, but at the age of twenty became a Carthusian monk. He thus joined the most austere and the most solitary Order in the Church, but one which, with its emphasis on mystical prayer as well as austerity, made considerable appeal to men of the later medieval period. After some years he was appointed prior of several charterhouses in succession. In 1417 his efforts were successful in reuniting his Order, which had been divided into two "obediences" by the Great Schism.

In the same year the clergy and people of Bologna chose him as their bishop. As in similar cases (see St Hugh of Lincoln, 17 Nov.), only the express command of his religious superiors secured his consent. Unlike some of his peers he lived very simply in a small house in monastic austerity; he would also visit the poor in their own homes. The times in which he lived were difficult ones for the Church, not only because of widespread corruption but also because the Church had been deeply divided by the conciliar movement, not to mention the long-standing schism of the East. Nicholas proved an effective reformer. He began with his own cathedral chapter. He continued by reforming several religious Congregations and also worked effectively in the fields of education and welfare work. In spite of Bologna's revolt against the Papal States, Pope Martin V chose Nicholas for important diplomatic missions to France, Milan, Florence, and Venice, appointing him a cardinal in 1426. Foreign courts and Italian city-states appreciated his mediation; they called him "The Angel of Peace."

Pope Eugenius IV also esteemed Nicholas highly. First he appointed him chief penitentiary. Even more important, he made him papal legate for the opening of the Council of Ferrara-Florence. This council reconciled the Eastern Churches as their representatives agreed to the doctrines of papal primacy, purgatory, the

Eucharist, and even the *filioque* clause in the Nicene Creed. Moreover, most of the members of the Council of Basle now abandoned it and joined in at Florence instead. Eugenius' reign thus resulted in the triumph of the papacy over the council, but the agreement with the Greeks was disowned by their clergy at home who had not attended the council. This was no fault of Nicholas' but was an example of how appointed delegates do not always satisfy those who sent them. Eugenius still consulted Nicholas, visiting him on his sick-bed even when he was near death. Nicholas died at Siena when visiting a house of Augustinians whose protector he had been for some years. Eugenius defied precedent to take part in both the Requiem Mass and the burial at Bologna. Another, less famous skill of Nicholas' was to be both writer and a patron of writers: if he had lived in less difficult times, this aspect of his achievements would have been better known. His cult was confirmed in 1774.

Life and panegyric in *AA.SS.*, May, 2, pp. 467-90, and in "Encomium B. Nicolai Albergati," *Anal. Boll.*, 7 (1888), pp. 381-6. See also C. le Couteulx, *Annales Ordinis Cartusiensis*, 7; *Bibl.SS.*, 1, 662-8; P. Partner, *The Papal State under Martin V* (1958), pp. 50-3, 89-90.

St John of Avila (1500-69)

This holy priest, mystic, and writer was highly esteemed in sixteenth-century Spain and was the friend of St Ignatius Loyola (31 July) besides being an adviser of St Teresa of Avila (15 Oct.) and other saints. His principal biographer was Luis de Granada. After some centuries of comparative obscurity, his canonization in 1970 led to a well-deserved revival of interest.

He was born at Almodóvar del Campo in the province of Ciudad Real (some seventy miles south of Toledo) of wealthy parents of Jewish extraction, who sent him to Salamanca University to study law. This career, however, had no attraction for him, and he gave himself to a regime of prayer and penance at home for three years. At the suggestion of a Franciscan he studied philosophy and theology at Alcalá under Domingo de Soto from 1520 to 1526. Meanwhile both his parents died, and he was ordained priest in 1525. He now gave away most of his inheritance to the poor, and, with a remarkable gift for preaching, he desired to join the missions in Mexico. The archbishop of Seville, on the other hand, wished him to remain in Spain and to preach in Andalusia.

This he did for nine years with remarkable success. People of all ages and every class were brought both to initial conversion and subsequent progress by him. John's work in Andalusia was part of a decades-long effort to convert Muslims and Jews following the conquest of the area by Ferdinand and Isabella. John preached with conspicuous success there from 1529 to 1538. The success, however, was threatened by his being denounced to the Inquisition, which imprisoned him for a time on the grounds that his preaching was rigoristic and excluded the rich from the kingdom of heaven. He was acquitted of the charges, which could not be substantiated, and was widely acclaimed on his release. He then preached in several other Spanish towns such as Córdoba, Granada, and Seville.

His preaching was completed by spiritual letters, and though the latter can be read as he wrote them, the sermons survive only in extracts made by some of the hearers. During the years 1554-69 he was in constant pain but continued his preaching and writing to the end. He is a comparatively rare example of a saint of Catholic-reformation Spain who did not belong to a religious Order. Although he helped to convert St Francis Borgia (10 Oct.) and St John of God (8 Mar.) and wished at one time to join the Society of Jesus, he was dissuaded by their provincial of Andalusia, but he was buried in the Jesuit church of Montilla.

Aspects of his teaching can be studied in his systematic treatise *Audi filia* ("Hear, O daughter") or in his spiritual letters (English edition, 1914) or glimpsed in extracts such as this one on the difference of one soul from another: "Men's bodies are of very various temperaments, and there is just as great a dissimilarity in the constitution of their minds, for God bestows very different gifts on different individuals. He does not lead all by the same path, therefore it is impossible to specify one particular devotion as the most suitable. Some have no special attraction to any one form of devotion and they ought to consult someone ... so as to know whether they should allow themselves to be led by motives of love or fear, of sadness or joy; and how to apply the remedies most suitable to their needs." This extract seems like an updating of the teaching of St Gregory the Great's *Pastoral Care*, and John insisted that the one way, which was indeed for all, was the way of Christ himself: "Christ tells us that if we wish to join him, we shall travel the way he took. It is surely not right that the Son of God should go his way on the path of shame while the sons of men walk the way of worldly honour." Elsewhere he prayed that his correspondent would see "what hidden treasures God bestows on us in the trials from which the world thinks only to flee." In similar vein he emphasized that those who "imagine they can attain to holiness by any wisdom or strength of their own, will find themselves after many labours and struggles and weary efforts only further from possessing it, and this in proportion to their certainty that they have gained it by themselves."

The early Life by Luis de Granada (1588) is ed. L. Sala Balust (1964), who also edited his works (2 vols., 1952-3); his *Spiritual Letters* are ed. V. García de Diego (1912), trans. by the Benedictines of Stanbrook (1914). See also *O.D.C.C.*, p. 745, and *Bibl.SS.*, 2, 649-56. In recent times renewed interest in his teaching has led to the publication of a specialist review, *Maestro Avila* (Montilla, 1946-).

R.M.
St Dioscoris, martyr at Mara (second-third century)
SS Quartus and Quintus, martyrs of Rome (fourth century)
St Mocius, martyr of Constantinople (*c.* 300)

11

St Mamertus of Vienne, *Bishop* (*c.* 475)

Mamertus is remembered principally as the bishop who in a time of crisis instituted the penitential processions, which we call the Rogations, on the three
days immediately preceding the feast of the Ascension. Not many details are
known about his life. He was the brother of the poet Claudian, whom he ordained priest. We do not know how or when he became bishop of Vienne, an
ancient bishopric in Isère, just south of Lyons. In 463 Mamertus seems to have
exceeded his powers in consecrating a bishop of Die (Drôme), when the
bishopric had been transferred by St Leo the Great (10 Nov.) from the province of Vienne to that of Arles in Provence. Pope Hilarius reproved Mamertus,
but a council at Arles sent a report to Rome, as a result of which the new bishop
retained his see after confirmation from Arles. Less controversial than this was
Mamertus' action of translating to Vienne the relics of St Ferreolus (16 June),
a martyr of the third century who suffered close to Vienne.

Mamertus' role in establishing the Rogation processions is witnessed by St
Avitus of Vienne (5 Feb.). In his homily on the Rogations he said that these
ceremonies were instituted by Mamertus at a time when disasters were prevalent.
At one time, these included frequent earthquakes and the consequent presence of
savage packs of wolves and stags which came in through the gates and ranged
throughout the city, fearing nobody. This disaster lasted for about a year and was
crowned by the burning of the king's palace during the Paschal Vigil. Mamertus
implored God's mercy with prayers and lamentations. As Ascension Day approached, he told the people to fast, go to a special service, and give alms to the
poor. Gregory of Tours (17 Nov.) commented: "All the horrors came to an end.
The story of what had happened spread through all the provinces and led all the
bishops to copy what this particular prelate had done in faith. Down to our own
times these rites are celebrated with a contrite spirit and a grateful heart in all our
churches to the glory of God."

If the fact of Mamertus' intervention is well founded, the details of his liturgy are
less clear. According to Edmund Bishop: "So far as the original testimonies go, the
substance of the devotion of the Rogations was psalm-singing with the prayers or
collects which in some quarters accompanied the psalms." The litanies, as we
understand them, were apparently added later. Mamertus' example was indeed
followed by other churches, as at the First Council of Orleans in 511, which even
prescribed fasting and abstinence from servile work. In time the observance (but
without the fasting) became general in the West.

Mamertus, in short, was a devout pastor who also showed both courage and tact in propagating this observance to officials and the people. He was buried at St Peter's, Vienne; later his relics were translated to the church of Holy Cross, Orleans, where they were burned by the Calvinists in 1563.

See *AA.SS.*, May, 2, pp. 629-31; E. Bishop, *Liturgica Historica* (1918), pp. 128-30; *Bibl.SS.*, 8, 614-5.

St Gengulf (760)

Gengulf was a layman, a knight who faithfully served Pepin the Short, the mayor of the palace of Merovingian kings. He was a victim of a disastrous marriage and a revenge killing which could have happened in any other age, our own included. His wife was notoriously unfaithful and deaf to all remonstrances and correction. Gengulf accordingly left her and went to live at his castle of Avallon, near Vézelay, dedicated to penance and almsgiving. There he was supposedly assassinated by his wife's lover as he lay asleep. Later his relics were distributed following the report of miracles, and the widespread cult flourished in present-day France, Germany, and the Low Countries.

AA.SS., May, 2, pp. 644-55; W. Levison, *M.G.H., Scriptoresrer. meroving.*, 1, 142-74, for the legendary Life; verse account by Hroswitha of Gandersheim in the late tenth century, in her *Opera* (ed. Winterfeld, 1902), pp. 32 ff. (and in *P.L.*, 137, 1083-94); *Bibl.SS.*, 6, 127-8.

St Majolus of Cluny, *Abbot* (906-94)

Born at Avignon and the heir to large estates at Riez in Provence, then overrun by Saracen invaders, Majolus (Maieul in French) went to live with his relatives at Mâcon, studied philosophy at Lyons under a famous master, Antony, and became archdeacon of Mâcon. Although still young, pressure was put on him to be bishop of Besançon, but he refused and became a monk at Cluny, of which some of his family were notable benefactors. Eventually he was given the offices of librarian and bursar; in this way both the organization of copying and collecting monastic books and the whole temporal administration were in his hands. In the course of journeys he made on behalf of the monastery, his wisdom and prudence became well known.

When the abbot, Aymard, became blind, Majolus was appointed his coadjutor, and on Aymard's death he became abbot of Cluny in 965. Majolus was a handsome man with a fine presence who inspired both respect and affection. His aristocratic background helped him in his dealings with the rulers of both Church and State. He improved Cluny's already close relationship with the papacy, which entrusted to fourteen bishops of Burgundy, Provence, and the Auvergne the special care of Cluny and its abbot as well as its monastic dependencies. This also implied the restoration to Cluny of alienated lands and care for its general security at a time of disorder and violence, when civil government was notoriously weak. At the same time, Majolus was highly esteemed by the emperors Otto the Great and Otto II.

The former asked him to oversee the monasteries in the empire, while the latter with his wife, the empress Adelaide, enabled Majolus to found monasteries in Italy, notably at Pavia, where San Salvatore was a new foundation (971), and he reformed San Pietro Ciel d'Oro in 983. Besides these, he re-founded several monasteries in France, notably that of Saint-Bénigne of Dijon.

As with his series of saintly successors, it is difficult to strike a balance between the internal and external achievements of Majolus. On the one hand, Otto II wished him to become pope, but he refused, saying that he and the Romans would not be able to agree. He was convinced that his most important mission was for Cluny itself. Here he was a notable builder, and the fine church nowadays called Cluny II owes its origin to him. In the final assessment, the words of the Cluniac historian Noreen Hunt are impressive: "[Majolus] was one of the most attractive figures of his age and the warmest of all the abbots of Cluny, striking everywhere an authentic note of holiness. He is considered to have been the most contemplative of all the abbots. He was the first to be given the title of saint and was referred to as such in a papal bull of Gregory V within a few years of his death. Unfortunately he has left no writings."

See *AA.SS.*, May, 2, pp. 657–700; N. Hunt, *Cluny under St Hugh* (1967); H. E. J. Cowdrey, *The Cluniacs and the Gregorian Reform* (1970); K. J. Conant, *Cluny* (1968); J. Leclercq, "Pour une histoire de la vie à Cluny," *R.H.E.* 7 (1962), pp. 385–408, 783–812.

St Walter of L'Esterp (1070)

Walter (or Gautier) was born at Conflans Castle on the river Vienne. This was the principal residence of his family, which was one of the most notable in Aquitaine. He was educated by the Austin Canons at Dorat, where he entered the novitiate and was professed in due course. For a time he had to retire to Conflans, supposedly owing to divisions in the community, but after some years he was elected abbot of L'Esterp, an office he held for thirty-eight years. His influence spread far and wide, and contemporary chroniclers refer to him as a man of outstanding holiness whose enterprises seemed specially blessed by God. His special gift was that of reconciling sinners. For this purpose Pope Victor II gave him special faculties, including wide-ranging rights both to excommunicate and to absolve from this penalty.

His biographer relates stories of him that reveal his character when young. On a pilgrimage to Jerusalem a strange bird dropped a huge fish on a desolate shore, opportunely proviving a meal for Walter and his companions. Another time, we are told, his companions had inadvertently prepared a meal of meat on a Friday. Walter allowed them to eat it in honour of St Martin (11 Nov.), whose feast it was that day; he himself shared in this meal. One of his companions, rigorist and scandalized, vigorously denounced this concession but soon afterward lost all the money he was carrying in his purse. For the last seven years of his life Walter was blind, but he continued his various activities as abbot until his death at L'Esterp on 11 May 1070. The Martyrology recalls his reputation for gentleness to his community and charity to the poor. His cult seems to have been initially restricted to the Canons Regular; it dates back to 1090, shortly before his biography was written.

Life by Bishop Marbod (*c.* 1100) in *AA.SS.*, May, 2, pp. 701-6; *Bibl.SS.*, 7, 426.

St Francis di Girolamo (1642-1716)

Born at Grottaglie, near the port of Taranto in south-eastern Italy, the first of eleven children, Francis spent most of his life in Naples, whose apostle he became. From the age of twelve he was educated by priests of the Theatine Congregation. After some years he studied canon and civil law at Naples University. In 1666 he was ordained priest, and for the next four years he taught in the Jesuit Collegio dei Nobili, again in Naples. Only in 1670 did he become a Jesuit. He underwent a very strict novitiate and was then sent to work under the famous preacher Fr Agnello Bruno in mission work among the peasants of Otranto. This new experience (1671-4) gave him a change both of place and environment. He then made his profession, completed his theological studies, and was appointed preacher at the Gesù Nuovo church in Naples.

At this time, shortly after the ruthless persecution of Christians in Japan, there was much talk about sending out new groups of missionaries. Francis greatly desired to go but was told that the kingdom of Naples must be considered his India and Japan. This was so for the next forty years. His preaching attracted large congregations in Naples and the neighbourhood. Men and women flocked to his confessional; it was said that four hundred "hardened sinners" were reconciled by him each year. Prisons, hospitals, and even the galleys experienced his ministry, and in these last he converted twenty Turkish prisoners. He would go to the most neglected and dangerous parts of the town, where sometimes he was physically attacked. Occasionally he would preach in the streets on the spur of the moment. Once a prostitute overheard him at her window and came to confession the next day. His penitents came from all classes. One was a Frenchwoman, Marie Alvira Cassier, who had murdered her father and then served in the Spanish army disguised as a man. Under Francis' direction she attained holiness after repenting. Another exercise of his apostolate was the training of other missionaries, and in this work his own desire for the mission field was sublimated. Cures were claimed through his ministry, but he always attributed them to St Cyrus (31 Jan.), to whom he was deeply devoted. Toward the end of his life he experienced much physical suffering; he died in Naples at the age of seventy-four and was buried in the Jesuit church. There his tomb can still be visited. He was canonized in 1839. After World War II his relics were translated to the Jesuit church in Grottaglie.

Francis' notes on his first fifteen years of apostolate were printed by Fr Boero in *S. Francisco di Girolamo e le sue missioni* (1882). There is a French Life by J. Bach (1867), an English one by A. M. Clarke (1891), and good articles in the *Catholic Encyclopedia* (A. Van Ortroy) and J. N. Tylenda, *Jesuit Saints and Martyrs* (1983), pp. 120-2.

St Ignatius of Laconi (1701-81)

Ignatius was one of a family of nine children. His parents were Matthew and Ann Peis, who lived at Laconi, then a large village, in the middle of Sicily. Little is known of his early years except that he worked in his father's fields and that he was physically thin and pale. During a serious illness he decided to join the Franciscan Order, in which he was encouraged by his mother but discouraged by his father. One day when he was riding a horse in pursuit of his father's cattle, it bolted out of control but then suddenly pulled up and resumed its previous gentle pace. Ignatius regarded this as a sign from God and joined the Capuchins at Buoncammino (near Cagliari), about forty miles to the south. This was in 1721.

In spite of his father's opposition, he received the habit in the small but beautiful friary. Initially he met with approval, but his second novice-master thought him physically weak and insincere in character. Ignatius, however, redoubled his efforts to give satisfaction, and he was duly accepted for profession. Still attached to the small friary of St Benedict, he was also sent for short periods to neighbouring houses in Cagliari and Iglesias. For fifteen years he worked as a lay brother in the weave shed at Cagliari. In 1741 he was sent out as questor (begging for alms) from St Antony's friary at Buoncammino; this was to be his principal occupation for the rest of his life. Like others who filled this difficult office, he sometimes met rejection and abuse, but he was also greatly esteemed as a counsellor by others.

He was especially devoted to the sick and to children. A contemporary nun described him as of medium height with slight features, white hair, and beard. He carried a forked stick, walked uprightly, had an easy manner, and was "gentle and caressing" with children. Calm serenity was his dominant characteristic. A surviving portrait at Cagliari confirms most of these details. Another contemporary told how he was sometimes lifted off the ground in prayer (like St Joseph of Copertino, 18 Sept.) but moved slowly down to the ground when it was time for the night office. Many healing cures were attributed to him in life as well as after death. He disclaimed medical skill and just recommended simple remedies, trust in God, and steady prayer.

A picturesque legend tells of an unscrupulous moneylender of Cagliari who complained that Ignatius never called at his house for alms. The Franciscan guardian told Ignatius to call there, and he returned with a sack of food. When it was opened, it dripped with blood. The guardian was astonished, but Ignatius said, "This is the blood of the poor. That is why I ask nothing from that house." In 1781 Ignatius' health began to fail. He visited his sister, a Poor Clare, and told her that they would not meet again on earth. In the morning of 11 May he went into his last agony and died soon after. Ignatius was canonized in 1951. Like the later St Thérèse of Lisieux (1 Oct.), he seems to have done nothing extraordinary but did ordinary things extraordinarily well.

There are Lives of Ignatius by S. da Chiaramonte (1940) and F. Majella (1946); letters about him were edited by J. Fues (1899); see also *O.D.S.*, pp. 241-2, and *Bibl.SS.*, 7, 672-4.

R.M.

St Anthimus, martyr of Rome (second-third century)

St Maiulus, martyr of Byzema (Libya) (*c.* 200)

St Philip of Celles, hermit of Worms (*c.* 770)

St Matthew Le Van Gam, martyr (1847)—see "Martyrs of Vietnam (Tonkin)," 2 Feb.

12

SS Nereus and Achilleus, *Martyrs* (Second Century)

The most ancient and important source for these Roman martyrs is an inscription written in their honour by Pope St Damasus (11 Dec.) during the fourth century. Travellers describe its content before it was broken, and the archaeologist G. B. de Rossi restored it from fragments in the nineteenth century. Translated, this reads as follows: "The martyrs Nereus and Achilleus had enrolled themselves in the army and exercised the cruel office of carrying out the orders of the tyrant, being ever ready through the constraint of fear to obey his will. O miracle of faith! Suddenly they cease from their fury, they become converted, they fly from the camp of their wicked leader; they throw away their shields, their armour and their blood-stained javelins. Confessing the faith of Christ, they rejoice to bear testimony to its triumph. Learn now from the words of Damasus what great things the glory of Christ can accomplish."

So it seems certain that they were Praetorian soldiers who were more or less suddenly converted to Christianity and paid with their lives for their faith. The same G. B. de Rossi discovered their empty tomb with a contemporary sculpture in 1874 in the underground church built by Pope Siricius in 390. Their tomb was a family vault in what was later known as the cemetery of Domitilla. In about 600 St Gregory the Great (3 Sept.) preached on them in the same way: "These saints, before whom we are assembled, despised the world and trampled it under their feet when peace, riches and health gave it charms." This church was rebuilt about 800 by Leo III, but it was in ruins when Cardinal Baronius, the learned Oratorian of the sixteenth century, restored it yet again and translated afresh the relics of these saints, which had been moved to the church of St Adrian.

Their legendary acts deserve little credence and seem to have been written to explain their presence in the cemetery of Domitilla, herself a Christian martyr (above, 7 May). According to this, they were exiled together to the island of Terracina, where today's martyrs were beheaded and Domitilla was burned because she refused to sacrifice to idols. It must also be remembered that there were two Domitillas, related to each other, and that it was not unusual for martyrs to be buried in private vaults.

See *C.M.H.*, pp. 249-50; P. F. de Cavalieri, *Note agiographice* 2 (*Studi e Testi*, 22, 1909); A. Guerrieri, *La chiesa dei SS. Nereo ed Achilleo* (1951); *Bibl.SS.*, 9, 813-20. Acts are in *AA.SS.*, May, 3, pp. 4-16. See also U. Fasola, *La Basilica dei SS. N. e A. e la catacomba de Domitilla* (1967), with bibliography; S. G. A. Luff, *The Christian's Guide to Rome* (n.e. 1990), pp. 217-8, 288.

St Pancras, *Martyr* (? 304)

There was a strong cult of Pancras at Rome from the fifth century or before and in England from the time of Augustine (d. 604; 26 May). His tomb was near the second milestone along the Via Aurelia, above which Pope Symmachus (498-514) rebuilt the basilica, later restored by Pope Honorius (625-38). The cemetery in which he was buried was called the cemetery of Calepodius but was later renamed the cemetery of Pancras. St Gregory the Great (3 Sept.) dedicated one of his monasteries to Pancras; this may explain why St Augustine dedicated a church in Canterbury to him also. Early Canterbury, indeed, in its church dedications was like a miniature Rome, with the cathedral of Christ (= St Saviour's at Rome), the monastery of SS Peter and Paul, the suburban see of Rochester dedicated to St Andrew, and other churches in Canterbury dedicated to the Four Crowned Martyrs (8 Nov.) and to Pancras. About sixty years later Pope Vitalian sent relics of this saint with other gifts to King Oswiu of Northumbria. Pancras is mentioned in the martyrology of Bede, in the Old English martyrology, and in most medieval English calendars, including that of Sarum. Six ancient churches were dedicated to him in England, including the one in north London, from which the cemetery, the railway station, and the hotel take the name.

The Roman Acts, as so often, tried to build up the image of this saint, since the faithful were dissatisfied with knowing nothing more than his name. According to this source Pancras was a Syrian or Phrygian orphan who was brought to Rome by his uncle; there they were both converted to Christianity and suffered martyrdom under Diocletian. At this time Pancras was aged only fourteen. This last point may help to explain in part why his cult was so strong. It provided an example of a comparatively young boy who suffered martyrdom at about the same age as Agnes (21 Jan.) and other young women.

AA.SS., May, 3, pp. 17-22; Bede, *H.E.*, 3, ch. 20; P. Franchi de Cavalieri, *Hagiographica* (1908), pp. 77-105; *O.D.S.*, p. 377.

St Epiphanius of Salamis, *Bishop* (*c.* 310-403)

He was born into a Jewish family near Eleutheropolis in Palestine but became convinced of the truth of the Christian faith and was baptized, together with his sister, Callithrope. At the age of twenty-six he became a monk in the monastery of St Hilarion (21 Oct.), in the desert south of Gaza. He then left Palestine for Egypt in order to study but also to stay with some hermits who were devoted partisans of Athanasius (2 May, above) and defenders of the term "consubstantial." On his way to Egypt he met St Paphnutius "the Great" (11 Sept.), a noted opponent of Arianism, who is said to have prophesied that he would one day become a "hierarch in Cyprus." An intransigent supporter of orthodoxy himself, Epiphanius found, in the course of his monastic travels in Egypt, some unorthodox Gnostic monks and nuns whose way of life was dissolute. He denounced them and had them expelled. He then returned to Palestine and founded a monastery, which he directed for thirty years. During these years he visited Eusebius of Vercelli (2 Aug.) and Paulinus of Antioch, both also champions of orthodoxy.

In 367 he was indeed appointed bishop in Cyprus, in apparent fulfillment of Paphnutius' prophecy, to the see of Salamis, previously known as Constantia, situated six miles north of Famagusta. There he devoted himself to the needs of the diocese for thirty-six years. He was also involved in controversies, including those over the date of Easter, the Schism of Antioch, the criticism of images, and above all, the deviations of Origenism. In all of these he displayed vast erudition (he knew four Eastern languages as well as Latin) but also limited understanding of his opponents' positions and excessive zeal. Nevertheless his writings in support of orthodoxy and against errors make him the saint whose works tell us most about unorthodox movements in the Church during its first four centuries.

Toward the end of his life he became even further embroiled in controversy, with John, bishop of Jerusalem, and even with St John Chrysostom (13 Sept.). The emperor Arcadius and his wife, Eudoxia, invited him to Constantinople to take part in the synod of bishops, which they forced to condemn Chrysostom and have him removed from the see of Constantinople in 403. This was the Oak Tree Synod, held in a suburb of Constantinople known as "the Oak." Learning that Epiphanius was siding with the emperor and empress against him, Chrysostom is reputed to have written to him with a prophetic threat: "My brother Epiphanius, I hear that you have advised the emperor that I should be banished: know that you will never again see your episcopal throne." To this Epiphanius apparently replied with another prophecy: "John, my suffering brother, withstand insults, but know that you will not reach the place to which you are exiled." Both "prophecies" came true: Chrysostom died on his way into exile in Armenia; Epiphanius took ship to return to Cyprus, but died on the voyage.

The principal of his many works are the *Panarion*, or "medicine-chest (or box of remedies) against heresies," and the *Ancoratuus*, or "good anchor of the faith"; others include treatises on gems and on weights and measures. An eighth-century fresco of him from Nubia survives in the national museum of Poland in Warsaw.

See *H.S.S.C.*, 3, p. 270, and *O.D.C.C.*, pp. 464-5; his works were ed. by Patavius (2 vols., 1622, rp. in *P.G.*, 41-3); critical text of the two major works ed. K. Holl in *G.C.S.* (3 vols., 1915-33). See also H. Delehaye, "Saints de Chypre," *Anal.Boll.* 26 (1907), pp. 161-301. His "Homily on the Burial of Christ" has been trans. by the Holy Transfiguration monastery in Boston, Mass. (1981).

St Modoaldus, *Bishop* (640)

Modoaldus (also called Modoald, Modowald, and Romoald) was born in Aquitaine of an aristocratic family. Most of his life was spent in close association with Merovingian kings, whose deficiencies, such as those described by Gregory of Tours (17 Nov.), both hindered and helped Modoaldus' career. He served at the court of King Dagobert I, who appointed him bishop of Trier at an early age. This did not prevent him from reproving Dagobert for his own and his court's immoralities. Not at once, but eventually, Dagobert repented and tried to make amends. He took Modoaldus as his spiritual adviser and gave him generous grants of land and money for the foundation of monasteries. Few details of Modoaldus' achievements have survived, but he took part in the Council of Reims in 625. He also ordained the future martyr St Germanus of Grandval (21 Feb.), whom he had educated, and was associated in friendship with St Desiderius of Cahors (15 Nov.). Modoaldus' episcopate probably lasted about twenty years.

AA.SS., May, 3, pp. 50-78; *Bibl.SS.*, 9, 528-9

St Rictrudis, *Abbess* (612-78)

Born in Gascony of wealthy and devout parents, Rictrudis in early life was directed by St Amand (6 Feb.), then in exile from the court of King Dagobert, whose licentious conduct he (like Modoaldus, above) had reproved. Amand then lived in Rictrudis' house, from which he, a Frank, evangelized the Gascons. Another Frankish nobleman, Adalbald, later arrived in their house. He enjoyed the favour of King Clovis II. In spite of the opposition of Gascon nobles, he wooed and married Rictrudis. They went to live at Ostrevant (Flanders), where four children were born to them and where Amand used to visit them. Their devout and contented lifestyle was described by her biographer with relish. However, it was not to last. Adalbald was murdered by Gascons, supposedly because they still could not accept his marrying Rictrudis, even after sixteen years.

At this juncture she wished to become a nun, but Amand advised her to wait until her son Mauront (Maurontius, 5 May) was old enough to join the court. Clovis II, however, had other plans for her and wished her to marry one of his favourites. Only Amand was able to persuade the king to allow her to go, and she left joyfully for Marchiennes, where she had founded a double monastery. This she ruled as abbess for many years, where first her daughters Adalsind and Clotsind joined her, followed later by her son, Mauront. Adalsind died young, but Clotsind succeeded her mother as abbess when Rictrudis died at the age of seventy-six. Her remaining daughter Eusebia lived with her grandmother. Husband, wife, and all four children were venerated as saints. Flemish and Gascon dioceses kept her feast.

Life by Hucbald of Elnone in *AA.SS.*, May, 3, for which see L. Van der Essen in *R.H.E.* 19 (1923), pp. 543-50, and the same author's *Etude critique des Saints mérovingiens* (1907), pp. 260-7; *Bibl.SS.*, 11, 181-2.

St Germanus of Constantinople, *Patriarch* (*c.* 634-732)

Germanus was the son of a senator of Constantinople and was educated as a cleric, becoming first a priest and later dean of the clergy of Santa Sophia. He enjoyed an exceptionally long life, but most of what we know about him concerns his life after the age of sixty. He was one of the promoters of the Trullan Synod (692), largely concerned with consolidating the decisions of previous councils and adding some disciplinary decrees; soon afterward he became archbishop of Cyzicus (Kapidagi,

Turkey, in the Sea of Marmara). Some say that he subscribed under imperial threat to a synod of 712 which aimed to restore the Monothelite heresy, but if he did, he soon retracted and returned to orthodoxy. In 715 he was chosen as patriarch of Constantinople; shortly afterward he convoked a synod which proclaimed the Catholic faith and explicitly rejected the Monothelite teaching. Even so, he was by no means free of the interference of Byzantine emperors in doctrinal matters. In 725 the emperor Leo III (the Isaurian) issued his first edict against the veneration of images and icons. This was a topic of great importance to all the churches of the East at every level, and controversy over it lasted for about a century. Germanus for the next five years was the heart of the resistance to the emperor's iconoclasm and appealed to the pope for help. But in 730 he was forced to resign by imperial pressure and retired to Platonium for the rest of his life.

He was a notable writer, but several works were suppressed by the emperors. The extant ones include four dogmatic letters, mainly on images and iconoclasm, and seven homilies on the Blessed Virgin, whose universal mediation in the distribution of supernatural blessings is repeatedly stressed, as is her personal purity, in a way that almost seems to prefigure the doctrine of the Immaculate Conception. His orthodoxy with regard to icons, of which those of the Virgin and Child have always been considered the most important, was recognized by Pope Gregory II's appreciation of his vindication of Catholic teaching. "Pictures are history in figure and tend to the sole glory of the Heavenly Father. When we show reverence to representations of Jesus Christ, we do not worship the colours laid on the wood; we are venerating the invisible God who is in the bosom of the Fathers. Him we worship in spirit and in truth." Another surviving work is a historical one on heresies and synods, and his also is a very influential interpretation of the Byzantine liturgy, to which he contributed several fine hymns. Among his lost works is a defence of St Gregory of Nyssa (10 Jan.).

Life from various and uneven sources in *AA.SS.*, May, 3, pp. 155-61; works in *P.G.*, 98, 9-454; see also F. E. Brightman in *J.T.S.* 9 (1907-8), pp. 248-67 and 387-98, and articles in *O.D.C.C*, p.561, and *Dict. de Spiritualité*, 6 (1967), 309-11; *Bibl.SS*, 6, 243-53. See also P. Meyendorff, (ed. and trans.), S*t Germanus of Constantinople on the Divine Liturgy* (1984).

St Dominic of the Causeway (1109)

A native of Villoria in the Spanish Basque country, Dominic (Domingo) tried unsuccessfully several times to become a Benedictine monk, but he was repeatedly rejected because of his ignorance, deformity, and generally uncouth appearance. Instead, he went to live in a hermitage which he built himself, complete with a garden on whose produce he lived. He is said to have accompanied St Gregory of Ostia, a Benedictine cardinal who was a legate in northern Spain and is still venerated in Navarre and Rioja on 9 May, but the chronology of the two saints makes this nearly impossible. After the death of Gregory (1044?), Dominic again sought his vocation. He moved to a forest of Bureba, which was on the route for the many pilgrims to the shrine of St James (25 July) at Compostela. There he built himself a little house and oratory of wood, and cut down trees and made a safe road. Helpers gathered round him, and together they built both a bridge and a hospice for the pilgrims. He was buried in the grave he had made for himself, where a little town grew up as a consequence of the miraculous cures that took place. The town eventually grew large enough to have a bishop of its own; it is still known as Santo Domingo de la Calzada, St Dominic of the Causeway.

AA.SS., May, 3, pp. 167-80; *Bibl.SS.*, 4, 682-3.

Bd Imelda Lambertini (1322-33)

The cult of this child saint was confirmed by the Holy See in 1826, nearly 500 years after her death. Imelda was born in Bologna, the daughter of Count Ergano Lambertini and his wife. Like some other children, she delighted in adorning a quiet corner of the house with flowers and holy pictures. She wished to be brought up by the Dominican nuns in Val di Pietra, from the age of nine. While there, she developed great devotion to the Eucharist and a longing to receive Holy Communion, in those days not permitted to small children. On the feast of the Ascension, in the presence of the nuns, what appeared to be a sacred host hovered in the air above Imelda, as she knelt in prayer before the tabernacle. The chaplain approached with a paten and gave her Communion. This proved to be her first and last, as she died almost immediately afterward. During the early years of this century, when Pope St Pius X (21 Aug.) wisely encouraged early and frequent Communion, the cult of Imelda received fresh impetus as the patron of first communicants. Her relics have been in the church of S. Sigmund, Bologna, since 1582.

See M. C. de Ganay, *Les bienheureuses Dominicaines* (1913), pp. 145-52; and J. Procter, *Lives of Dominican Saints* (1900), pp. 259-62; also R. Zeller, *Imelda Lambertini* (1930); *Bibl.SS.*, 7, 1067-7; L. Boyle in *Doctrine and Life* 6 (1957), pp. 48-56.

Bd Jane of Portugal (1452-90)

The life of this princess is an excellent example of the difficulties and achievements of one who consistently sought the religious life in spite of strong family opposition. She was born in Lisbon, the daughter of King Alphonsus V of Portugal. Her mother died young, her brother was delicate, and it seemed likely that she would one day become queen. Although there was strong pressure on her to prepare for marriage, from the age of sixteen she practised austerities such as fasting and the hair-shirt, with long prayer at night. Her father refused to allow her to become a nun but allowed her to live a secluded life in the palace.

In 1471 King Alphonsus and Prince John led a military expedition against the African Moors, leaving Jane as regent. When they returned after a successful campaign, Jane again asked to retire to a convent. She gave away her personal possessions and passed through the Bernardine convent of Odivellas on her way to her true goal, which was the Dominican priory in the more important town of Aveiro (Beira Litoral, between Coimbra and Oporto). This she entered in 1472, but her family did not allow her to take vows or give up control of her properties. For some time she did not even take the Dominican habit but lived in simplicity as one of the Sisters. She devoted much of her income to the redemption of Christian slaves from the Moors, but her family repeatedly suggested marriages for her—to Maximilian, king of the Romans, or to Richard III, king of England. They were also worried about her health, insisting that she leave Aveiro during the plague. Eventually she took her religious vows in 1485, by which time the succession to the throne of Portugal was assured, and lived out the remaining five years of her life as the Dominican nun she had long wanted to be. She died of a fever supposedly contracted from poisoned water given on her return from a visit to the court by a woman she had banished from Aveiro. Jane's cult was confirmed in 1693.

Life by Margaret Pineira, one of her ladies-in-waiting, in *AA.SS.*, May, 7, pp. 719-62; see also M. C. de Ganay, *Les bienheureuses Dominicaines* (1913), pp. 279-304; J. Procter, *Lives of Dominican Saints* (1900), pp. 122-6; *Bibl.SS.*, 6, 557-8.

R.M.
SS Cyril and Companions, martyrs of Axiopolis, Romania (*c.* 200)
St Philip, priest of Sicily (fifth century)
Bd Jutta, widow and solitary of Prussia (1260)

13

St Servatius, *Bishop* (384)

Supposedly of Armenian birth, Servatius, or Servais, is known to history as one of the most constant supporters of Athanasius (2 May) during his long struggle for Christian orthodoxy. At the councils of Sardica (343) and Rimini (359) he valiantly supported the cause of orthodoxy. There, however, he was tricked into signing an ambiguous formula, which made Jerome complain that the whole world had "gone Arian." Servatius was later enlightened by St Hilary (14 Jan.) on its true meaning.

The date of Servatius' consecration as bishop of Tongres, in Belgium, is not known, but it must have preceded his active part in the councils mentioned above. Toward the end of his life he undertook a penitential pilgrimage from Tongres to Rome, according to Gregory of Tours, in connection with his supposed prophecy that Attila the Hun would invade Gaul. In fact Tongres was plundered and partly destroyed in the same year that Servatius died, either just before or just after the see was removed to Maastricht. There his relics are kept in a fine ancient shrine together with his staff, drinking-cup, and silver key, made as a papal gift and containing filings from St Peter's chains. The cup is believed to help cure fever. The cult of Servatius was widespread and lasting and it gave rise to numerous legends about him.

For the earliest Lives see *Anal. Boll.* 1 (1882), pp. 88–112, and G. Kurth, *Deux biographies de S. Servais* (1881), and the same author's *Nouvelles Recherches sur S. Servais* (1884). More recent work includes a Life by G. Gorris (1923), and see *Anal. Boll.* 55 (1937), pp. 117–20.

SS Mel and Sulian (Sixth Century)

These saints, according to the Roman Martyrology, were monks and disciples of Cadfan (1 Nov.). They died at Bardsey island, called the Island of the Saints. To-day's commemoration reminds us of the many holy monks who died at this island, still rather inaccessible and still the abode of at least one hermit. Cadfan (or Gadfan) seems to have been of Breton origin and to have founded the church of Towyn and the monastery of Bardsey island. His cult at Towyn (Gwynedd) was ancient and strong enough to survive the Reformation. Nothing is known of Mel and Sulian except their names.

See *O.D.S., s.v.* "Cadfan."

SS Argentea and Wulfram of Córdoba, *Martyrs* (931)

These martyrs lived in the extreme south of Spain at a time when it was ruled by the Moors and eventually suffered at their hands. Some of the details of their lives are of considerable historical interest; the manuscript that is the principal source is kept in the British Library in London.

Argentea was born toward the end of the ninth century to a noble Mozarabic family. Descended from a Spanish count, Adefonsus, her father was Omar-ben-Afcoun, a Christian who lived in a castle called Robestro in Moorish territory between Antequera and Málaga. From this fortress he waged war energetically against the Moors and held their forces in check for nearly fifty years. After his death his four sons vainly tried to continue the fight, but had to come to terms. Before this happened Omar had built churches in the small territory he had ruled.

Argentea, on her mother's death, expressed the wish for a life of solitude and silence away from the warlike environment of the castle. She lived with her brother Hafs, who had surrendered honourably in 928 and retired to Córdoba with all the inhabitants of Bobastro. Another of her brothers, Abderahman, was described by an Arab as a fine scribe, but one with little intelligence.

In 931 Wulfram arrived in Córdoba from Frankland hoping to preach the Christian religion. Although the Moors could be privately tolerant, this was regarded as an outrage, because public preaching could lead to the defection of Muslims from their faith and way of life. Wulfram found Argentea but was soon imprisoned. She had not previously publicly declared her faith, but now she did so and was imprisoned with him. Soon afterward they were executed: Wulfram was buried in the cemetery and Argentea eventually in the church of the Three Martyrs, now San Pedro at Córdoba. All this information comes from a Life written in the tenth century but not published till 1719. It occurs in a manuscript book of saints' Lives written at different points of the tenth century and kept in the British Library as MS Add. 25,600. The precise details about Argentea's childhood have led some scholars to conjecture that it was written by Abderahman, the saint's brother. Their feast-day has always been 13 May.

See *D.H.G.E.*, 4, 20-21, and *Bibl.SS.*, 2, 404.

Bd Gerard Meccati (*c.* 1174-*c.* 1276)

There are conflicting opinions about the life and death of this saint but not about his life as a hermit. He was born at Villamagna, and his life as a hermit included penance and contemplation. On Mondays he prayed especially for the souls in purgatory, on Wednesdays for the remission of his own sins, and on Fridays for the conversion of the infidel. Some claim that he was a Franciscan tertiary, which is possible only after 1220 (because that is the date of their inception), others that he was a pilgrim to the Holy Land who settled at the hospital of St John of Jerusalem, where he worked for some years receiving other pilgrims and nursing the sick in what is often regarded as the finest hospital of its time. Then, according to the

Roman Martyrology, he went home and led the eremitical life until his death.

Opinions differ about his death, with dates proposed of 1242, 1245, 1254, and 1276. This last date seems to be the most probable. But when one finds that an alternative day for his death (13 or 25 May) has been proposed, one may ask if there were not two hermits of the same name, approximately contemporary. A life-span of over one hundred years is not impossible and seems certain for two English saints of the same epoch, Gilbert of Sempringham (4 Feb.) and Godric of Finchale (21 May), so it should not be ruled out as impossible. Whatever may be the details of his life, his cult was confirmed by the Holy See in 1833. Part of the evidence for his cult is a fine illumination of him as a haloed figure standing outside his hermitage with a young man and his donkey, who seem to offer money to an elderly lady. It is in MS 643 of the Pierpont Morgan Library in New York (fol. 34).

AA.SS., May, 3, 246-51; *Bibl.SS.*, 9, 257-8.

Bd Gemma of Solmona (1439)

Gemma was a recluse at Goriano Sicoli (L'Aquila). Her life is known from an ancient manuscript of this church, first published in 1673. Brief memorials of her are also found in other authors. Her regime was austere and penitential, lasting for over forty years. She occupied a cell in the church of St John Baptist with a window looking onto the altar. After her death miracles were soon reported. In 1440 the bishop of Solmona exhumed her body, which was found to be incorrupt.

The legend makes her a shepherdess who was pursued by a local count, Roger. But she withstood his evil designs so well and with such eloquence and determination that he built her this cell in the church. It may well be that the story was brought forward to explain an unusual feature of the church. However this may be, her cult was approved in 1890.

AA.SS., May, 3, p. 182; *Acta S. Sedis* 23 (1890), p. 48; *Bibl. SS.*, 6, 105.

Bd Madeleine Albrici (*c.* 1400-65)

The daughter of Niccolo Albrici, a nobleman of Como (Lombardy), Madeleine (Maddalena) entered the Augustinian convent of Brunate, close by. Professed in due course, she excelled in humility, obedience, and mortification. After some years a vacancy occurred and she was elected abbess. Under her rule the monastery experienced new life and became a model of religious observance, recognized as such for the other houses in Lombardy.

A surviving privilege granted by Pope Pius II exempted her convent from the jurisdiction of the Chapter of the Chiesa Maggiore of Como, placing it under the sole jurisdiction of the Visitor of the Augustinians of the province of Lombardy. With the help of Bianca Visconti, duchess of Milan, Madeleine founded a new convent in Como in 1455. This became independent three years later.

She died of tuberculosis, borne with great fortitude and self-sacrifice, in 1465.

Her body was first buried at Brunate but was translated to the church of St Julian in Como in 1595. The immemorial cult was confirmed in 1900.

See *AA.SS.*, May, 3, pp. 252-62; *Bibl. SS.*, 1, 728-9; Life in Italian by A. M. Confalioneri (1938).

St Andrew Fournet, *Founder* (1752-1834)

For those who are tired of hearing of the preternatural piety of saints in their childhood, the story of Andrew Fournet will come as some relief. He was born at Maillé (near Poitiers) of a comparatively wealthy family, and through reaction against his too-pious and insistent mother, he declared himself bored by religion. He wished neither to pray nor to to learn; all he wanted was to amuse himself. He even wrote in one of his books, "This book belongs to Andrew Hubert Fournet, a good boy, though he is not going to become a priest or a monk." At school he had a reputation for idleness and frivolity; once he ran away and was brought back to receive a thrashing. Later (1772) he went to study law and philosophy at Poitiers but in fact pursued a life of pleasure. He even enlisted in the army but was bought out. Then his mother tried to make him a secretary, but his handwriting was too bad. In despair, his parents sent him in 1774 to an uncle who was a parish priest in an obscure rural area.

In this new environment the boy did far better away from an overbearing and pious mother. His uncle skilfully drew out his good qualities, and Andrew undertook the study of theology. In 1776 he was ordained priest, first becoming his uncle's curate in the country and then taking another appointment in a town. Eventually he was appointed parish priest in his native town of Maillé, in 1781. Here his generosity to the poor, as well as his transformed character, made him many friends. His simplicity now extended from his way of life to the style of his sermons, which were much improved in consequence. One of his hearers said that formerly no one understood him, but now "we can follow every word you say." At this time of his life he gave away surplus furniture and silver; his mother and sister, as well as his curate, shared a frugal life in the presbystery.

The French Revolution drastically affected their way of life. Andrew refused to take the oath the revolutionary government required from all priests and was consequently outlawed. The severity of this persecution is seldom realized. Andrew could minister to his flock only in danger of his life. In 1792 his bishop sent him into Spain for safety, but in 1797 he returned in secret, by night. Pursuivants tracked him constantly. Once he was saved by a housewife who boxed his ears and told him to go off and mind the cattle; another time, he pretended to be a corpse and was covered with a shroud and surrounded by candles and kneeling women. When Napoleon came to power, he brought an end to this situation. He made peace with the Church, enabling it to return to unity, but at the cost of alterations to a number of bishoprics and other sacrifices.

Andrew regained control of his parish and his presbytery and preached tirelessly to revive the Christian life wherever he could. He worked at missions as well as spending long hours in the confessional. Also at this time of his life he became a founder of a religious Congregation, the Daughters of the Cross. He had become the director of St Elizabeth Bichier des Ages, whose group of women, pledged to teaching as well as to the care of the sick and the poor, formed the nucleus of the new Congregation. St Elizabeth (26 Aug.) preferred to call them the Sisters of St Andrew.

At the age of sixty-eight Andrew resigned his parish from illness and fatigue; he then retired to La Puye, where he devoted himself to the new Congregation besides helping in the neighbouring parishes, especially through acting as spiritual director to a number of clergy and laypeople. One well-attested miracle (similar to one attributed to the Curé d'Ars) involved multiplication of grain and other food needed by the nuns for themselves and the children in their care.

Andrew was beatified in 1926 and canonized in 1933.

The Bull of canonization, with useful biographical summary, is in *A.A.S.*, 25 (1933), pp. 417-28; see also the Life by J. Saubat (1925) and further material under St Elizabeth Bichier (26 Aug.); *Bibl.SS.*, 1, 1174-5.

R.M.
St Marcellianus, bishop of Auxerre (337)
St Agnes, abbess of Poitiers (588)
St Pausacus, bishop in Phrygia (606)
St Sergius of Constantinople (820)
St Euthymius the Younger, monk of Mount Athos (1028)

ST MATTHIAS (over page)
Battle axe with silver head and tawny handle, inscription black,
except red "M," in white book, on red field.

14

ST MATTHIAS, *Apostle* (First Century)

The Acts of the Apostles relate that after the death of Judas the apostles met to choose another to succeed him. The qualifications required were that he should have been a follower of Jesus from the baptism to the ascension and to have seen the risen Lord (Acts 1:15-26). Two candidates were presented, Joseph Barsabas (of whom we know nothing) and Matthias (of whom we know very little beyond this passage). Matthias was chosen by lot as the new twelfth apostle. Like the others, he received the gift of the Holy Spirit at Pentecost, but after this authentic details about his apostolate are hard to find. He is said to have preached first in Judaea, which seems very likely. Later, the Greeks claimed that he preached in Cappadocia and near the Caspian Sea.

Another tradition links him with Ethiopia, and fictitious Acts of Andrew and Matthias in the city of the Cannibals, which survive in several languages, were very popular. Sometimes these stories were related about Andrew and Matthew, as in the Old English poem "Andreas." Compared to these, the testimony of the early Christian writer Clement of Alexandria that Matthias was one of the seventy-two disciples mentioned in the Gospel and that he was remarkable for his insistence on the importance of mortification seems much more credible.

The manner of Matthias' death is not known for certain. Some of the legends assert that he was crucified, but artistic representations give him an axe or a halberd as the instrument of his martyrdom. His relics were claimed by Jerusalem, and these, at least in part, were translated to Rome by the empress St Helena (18 Aug.). Matthias' feast was formerly on 24 February but since 1969 has been on 14 May.

AA.SS., Feb., 3, pp. 431-54; J. Renié, L'Election de Mathias, *Rev. Biblique* 54 (1948), pp. 43-53; *O.D.S.* and *Bibl.SS.*, 9, 150-4.

St Boniface of Tarsus (Early Fourth Century)

This martyr has been venerated from the ninth century, but his Acts are riddled with fiction. According to this source Boniface was the chief steward of a wealthy young woman of Rome called Aglae, beautiful and dissolute. Boniface was her paramour, but liberal, hospitable, and generous. One day (for reasons unknown) she asked him to go to the East and fetch some relics of the martyrs, saying: "I have heard that those who honour people who have suffered for Jesus Christ will share in their glory. In the East his servants daily suffer torments and lay down their lives for him." He answered that he would not fail to bring back the relics, and added,

"What if my own body should be one of them?" Henceforward he was a changed man; he prayed and fasted much and abstained from meat and wine.

At this time the West enjoyed peace, but in the East persecution continued under Maximian and Maximinus, especially in Cilicia under the governor Simplicius. Boniface arrived in Tarsus and found Simplicius presiding over the torture of twenty Christians. Boniface interrupted the proceedings, crying out: "Great is the God of the Christians!... Servants of God, pray for me that I may join with you in fighting the devil." Simplicius angrily had him arrested and tortured and on the next day executed by the sword. The body was embalmed and returned to Italy. Half a mile from Rome it was met by Aglae, who built a church there on the Latin Way to house the relics. She herself led a penitential life for fifteen years before she was buried beside him. In 1603 their relics, together with those of St Alexius, were found. The church, formerly St Boniface, is now Sant'Allessio. This story is summarized here to give readers some idea of the fictional stories which often accompanied the cult of a saint of whom nothing more was known than his name.

See *AA.SS.*, May, 3, and *Bibl.SS.*, 3, 324-6. The story was popular in the Middle Ages.

St Carthach, *Bishop and Abbot* (637)

Carthach (Carthage), the founder of the monasteries of Rahan (Offaly) and the more famous Lismore (Waterford), was born in or near Castle Maine (Kerry) of wealthy parents. As a boy he helped to tend the livestock; once he was so attracted by the chants of a passing procession that he decided to become a monk. The bishop, also called Carthach, gave him the pet name Mo-Chuta, by which he is also known, and ordained him a priest. In about 590 he made a small foundation of monks at Kiltulagh, near his home in Kerry, but was driven out by clerical opposition and spent a year at Comgall's monastery of Bangor. This was in about 594. He then visited other monasteries and founded Rahan, five miles west of Tullamore (Ossory) in about 595. Here the interesting archaeological remains with Eastern influences seem to belong to a slightly later time. His monastery prospered exceedingly, and he wrote a Rule for it in Irish, which survives in a later manuscript. This is an important memorial and not only regulates the austere lives of the monks but also contains general recommendations for kings, bishops, and priests.

It is likely that Carthach was a bishop by this time and ruled his border monastery and its neighbourhood. But once again, after forty years, he was expelled, probably by the kings of the northern Ui Neill. Whatever the reason, he and his large community, together with the patients of the leper hospital he had founded, made their way southward to Lismore, whose church he probably owned already, in about 636. By now an old man and rather disturbed by the noise of necessary building, he lived for a year or more as a hermit at nearby Inch, situated on the river Blackwater, as Lismore is, on the site of the present-day Lismore Castle.

When he felt near his death, he was carried to the monastery and died near a cross, which survived him and was called "the cross of migration." Carthach was buried close to the present entrance to Lismore Castle. His monastery and the leper hospital (which cared for various skin diseases) both flourished in the Middle Ages. It is believed that the crozier found in Lismore Castle in 1814 was his; at the same time a book called *The Book of Lismore* was discovered. It is a fifteenth-century manuscript book of prayers copied from other, older books, especially that of Monasterboice. The Rule mentioned above describes itself as "the way to the kingdom of the Prince—noble is its virtue, love of God with the whole soul, with heart and deed." Bishops, whom all must obey, should themselves be obedient to Christ. They must be always just, attentive to preaching, gracious and kind. Abbots should love the souls of all like their own, and increase good by "continual preaching of the Gospel to instruct all, and offering of the body of the great God on the altar."

Carthach is regarded as the founder of the see of Lismore (united to Waterford in 1363). Lismore's great monastery and school established its reputation as a holy city, a place of both pilgrimage and learning.

Latin Lives in *AA.SS.*, May, 3, pp. 375-87, and in C. Plummer, *V.S.H.*, 1, pp. 170-99. Irish Life in *Bethada Naem nErenn*, 1, pp. 291-9, with Eng. trans. in vol. 2. The Rule is in *Irish Ecclesiastical Record* 26 (1910), pp. 495-517. See Fr Carthage, O.C.R., *The Story of St Carthage* (1937).

St Erembert (*c*. 615-72)

Recent research has clarified the life of this saint. He was born at Villiolicourt (Seine-et-Oise) to a wealthy family and served at the courts of Clotaire II and Clotaire III (657-73), through whom he was appointed bishop of Toulouse. But in 661, owing to political difficulties, he had to abandon his see. So he retired to his birthplace and established a small monastery and church dedicated to S. Sernin (Saturninus, 30 Nov.), the apostle and patron of Toulouse. He became a monk at Fontanelle (founded by, and often known as, S. Wandrille), making profession to St Lambert (14 Apr.), abbot from 668 to 678. After Erembert's death the estate of Villiolicourt was given to Fontanelle, whose priory it became. His body was translated to Fontanelle in 704. One of the miracles claimed for Erembert is the sudden extinction of fire at his command, when he had emerged from his church of S. Sernin with pastoral staff after a long period of prayer. There are three feasts in his honour: 14 May (his date of death), 30 April (for the translation in 704), and 1 July (for another translation at Fontenelle in 1027).

See J. Laporte, "Vie de S. Erembert," *L'Abbaye Saint Wandrille de Fontenelle* 5 (1955), pp. 8-12; E. Delaruelle in *D.H.G.E.* 15, 694-7; *Bibl.SS.*, 4, 1311-2.

St Hallvard of Oslo, *Martyr* (1043)

The patron saint of Norway's capital, Oslo, was the son of a Norwegian noble landowner of Husaby. Like many of his contemporaries he was engaged in trading (and perhaps raiding), mainly in the Baltic Sea. One day he was crossing the Drannenfiord (now part of the Oslo fiord) by boat, when a pregnant woman called out to him to save her in his boat from her enemies, who were in pursuit. As she was in great distress, he agreed. Three men then accused her of theft, which she denied. Hallvard said he was ready to give them the value of what she was supposed to have stolen. This, however, was not enough for her pursuers: one of them drew his bow and killed both of them with arrows. They then fixed a stone to Hallvard's neck; but his body floated, and this drew attention to what had happened. Hallvard, a young and energetic man, was venerated as a martyr for defending an innocent victim, in which he was regarded (like John the Baptist and Alphege) as a martyr for justice. His body was taken to nearby Oslo for burial, and a stone church was built over his tomb in the late eleventh or early twelfth century. Little detail is known about Oslo's principal patron, but his cult is both early and lasting.

AA.SS., May, 3, p. 401; *Bibl.SS.*, 5, 894; S. Undset, *Saga of Saints* (1934), pp. 149-62.

Bd Giles of Portugal (*c.* 1187-1265)

Giles (Aegidius) was the third son of Rodrigues de Vagliatos, governor of Coimbra during the reign of Sancho the Great. Giles was "destined for the Church" and studied at Coimbra University. Although the king gave him a canonry and other benefices, he was more interested in experimental science than in theology. He chose therefore to study in Paris but for some reason changed his mind and went to Toledo instead. There he studied physics and alchemy and dabbled in necromancy and black magic. After seven years he returned to Paris and practised there successfully as a doctor. This was supposedly due to a dream or vision in which a ghost warned him to amend his life. He later burned his books of magic, destroyed his phials, and set out for his native Portugal.

Again he chose a roundabout route, as he arrived at Valencia (in eastern Spain), where he was kindly received by the Dominicans. Here he sought absolution, amended his life, and became a Dominican friar. Soon after his profession he was sent to Santarem (Ribatejo, Portugal); later he was assigned to Paris, where he became friendly with Humbert of the Romans, a future master general of his Order. After an exemplary life, he was chosen as provincial of Portugal, but he soon resigned the post owing to ill health and old age. His last years were spent at Santarem, where he experienced ecstasies and was endowed with the gift of prophecy.

His cult was approved in 1748. A legendary accretion to his Life claims that at Toledo he sold his soul to the devil, but that seven years after he became a friar Our Lady, in a vision, gave him back the deadly document, which enabled him to overcome all anxiety on this score. Giles was venerated for solid virtue and not because of implausible legends of this kind with their obvious resemblance to the story of Dr Faustus.

See *AA.SS.*, May, 3, pp. 400-36; J. Procter, *Lives of Dominican Saints* (1900), pp. 130-3; *Bibl. SS.*, 4, 964-5.

St Michael Garicoïts, *Founder* (1797-1863)

The oldest son of Arnold and Gratianne Garicoïts, Michael worked on the land from an early age. His home was in the village of Ibarra, in the Lower Pyrenees. He was hired out to a farmer to be a shepherd boy like many of his own age in that district, but he wanted to be a priest. His parents refused because they were too poor, but his grandmother devised a way for him to study while doing part-time work for the Church as well. This was partly in the bishop's kitchen, partly as odd-job man for the clergy. First he went to the college of S. Palais, then to Bayonne, and then, in 1819, to the diocesan seminary at Dax. Now his part-time work was teaching in a preparatory school. He was ordained priest in 1823, a fitting reward for his own hard work and for his parents' commitment to helping the exiled faithful clergy in the time of the French Revolution.

His first appointment was as curate at Cambo (Pyrénées-Atlantiques). Here he won the respect of freethinkers but also encouraged his somewhat Jansenistic flock to practise frequent Communion and the devotion to the Sacred Heart. Next he was appointed to the seminary of Bétharram, first as lecturer (1825) and then as superior (1831). However, the bishop decided to merge this seminary with the one at Bayonne, and Michael found himself redundant in 1834.

From this unpromising situation he decided to train priests in and through community life to do mission work. Jesuit advice and help came to him through Fr Le Blanc at Toulouse. This priest helped him to write Constitutions, closely modelled on those of the Society of Jesus. Life vows and a far-flung missionary apostolate were integral elements of the plan for the new Congregation. But then a new bishop stepped in and required him to confine himself to the diocese and work under the bishop's orders. Only in 1852 (fourteen years after its foundation) was the community allowed to choose its superior. During the early years Michael had been encouraged by St Elizabeth Bichier des Ages (26 Aug.), the foundress of the Daughters of the Cross, who had made foundations in the Basque country from her native Poitiers. In several ways the two Congregations were similar. However, Michael's Congregation of the Sacred Heart of Bétharram was approved by the Holy See according to the founder's original ideals only in 1877, fourteen years after Michael's death. Michael and Elizabeth were both canonized in 1947.

Biographical summary in *A.A.S.*, 15 (1932), pp. 263-9; Lives in French by B. Bourdenne (1921) and A. Bordachar (1926), and D. Buzy (1947); in English by C. Otis-Cox (1935) and P. E. Collier (1938): *Bibl.SS.*, 9, 460-2.

St Mary Mazzarello (1837-81)

The birthplace of the foundress of the Salesian Sisters was Mornese (Piedmont), not far from Genoa. Mary (Maria Domenica) was the eldest daughter of a hard-headed peasant and his wife. They moved to a house up the hill away from the village; there Mary and her brothers and sisters worked long hours in the fields and vineyards. This made her tough and strong, enabling her to walk frequently to the church for Mass and to join actively in the work of a Marian sodality started by the parish priest, Don Pestarino, who was inspired by the example of St John Bosco (31 Jan.), then working in Turin. This was in 1855, but in 1860 a typhoid epidemic broke out and the sodalists were asked to nurse its victims. Mary did so, but caught the fever and nearly died.

Weakened as a consequence of this, she took up dressmaking and with her friend Petronilla started a business which gave employment to local girls. This was the beginning of the Salesian Sisters, who aimed at doing for girls what Don Bosco did for boys, combining piety with work and education in a very natural and joyful way. Maria was chosen as superior; eleven Sisters took their vows in 1872 and lived in a building originally designed for a boys' school. Six years later six of the Sisters went to help the Salesian Fathers on a mission to Argentina, while in 1879 the mother-house was reconstituted at Nizza Monferrato in a former Capuchin friary.

In spite of her limited education Mary was successful in government. The Congregation expanded rapidly in Italy, France, and South America, always conspicuous for natural gentleness and happiness as well as hard work in education and training. Encouragement, not repression, was her policy. In 1881 she saw off some of her nuns to South America from Marseilles. She was seriously ill for six weeks, returned to Nizza Monferrato, and asked Don Bosco if she would recover. He gave her to understand that she would not but encouraged her to "lead, even in death." On 27 April she was anointed and asked the priest: "Now you have given me my passport, I can go any time, can't I?" A few days later she died, aged only forty-four. Her body is enshrined side by side with that of St John Bosco in Turin. She was canonized in 1951. Nowadays her Congregation has 1,400 houses in fifty-four countries.

See her Life by H. L. Hughes (1933) and Italian ones by F. Maccono (1947) and G. Favini (1951); articles in *N.C.E.*, 9, 523, and *Bibl.SS.*, 8, 1062-3.

St Leopold Mandic (1866–1942)

Born at Castelnuovo (a small port at the southern tip of Dalmatia), the twelfth child of Croat parents, Leopold was always small (four feet five inches in height when fully adult) and physically weak. At the age of sixteen he joined the Capuchin Franciscans at Udine, about fifty miles north-east of Venice (to whose province their houses in Croatia belonged). His status was that of a student who hoped to join the Order. In spite of his poor health and the customary Capuchin austerities, he made his profession in 1885 and was ordained priest in Venice in 1890.

He had long desired to be a missionary in eastern Europe, but he was not allowed to realize his desire. Instead, he was sent to various friaries in the Venetian province, including some in his native Dalmatia. In 1906 he was assigned to Padua, where, except for a year spent in a prison camp in the First World War for his refusal to renounce his Croat nationality, he was to spend the rest of his life. Instead of being a missionary abroad he was a spiritual director in Italy, spending many hours every week for forty years in the confessional. There, like the Curé d'Ars before him (4 Aug.), he gave himself in total compassion as one who recalled and personified the love and forgiveness of God. His human weakness, underlined by stomach pains and by chronic arthritis, which gave him gnarled hands and a permanent stoop, not to mention a long-standing tendency to stammer, actually emphasized the spiritual strength of a man whom many might have despised for his fragility.

He celebrated the golden jubilee of his ordination to the priesthood, but his health declined rapidly after that. After his death at Padua on 30 July 1942 a cult arose and flourished. He was beatified by Pope Paul VI in 1976 and canonized by Pope John Paul II in 1983. His life and death may be seen as a reminder of the importance of the sacrament of penance as an occasion of finding God's pardon and peace.

Leopold over and over again insisted on the importance of faith. He also reminded others of the importance of Our Lady of Sorrows: "The Virgin, our mother, who at the foot of the cross suffered as much as is possible for a human creature, understands our troubles and consoles us." In reference to his unfulfilled desire to be a missionary, he said, "I am like a bird in a cage, but my heart is beyond the seas." Perhaps only those who have experienced long hours in the confessional can fully understand the comparison to a cage.

See *St Leopold Mandic O.F.M. Cap.*, by a Capuchin of Greyfriars, Oxford (pamphlet).

R.M.
St Maximus, martyr in Asia (third century)
St Isidore, martyr on the island of Chios (third century)
SS Justa and Heredina, martyrs (*c.* 300)
St Isaac of Nitria, monk (*c.* 400)
St Aprunculus, bishop of Langres (488)
St Gall, bishop at Clarmont (551)

15

SS Torquatus and Companions, *Martyrs* (Third Century)

These reputed early evangelists of Spain were all bishops and were seven in number. They were not, as was previously believed, sent by SS Peter and Paul but belong to a later period, as do several founders of French bishoprics. Torquatus evangelized Guadix (Granada); the other six were founders of other sees in southern Spain and are commemorated on their respective days. This feast, based on the Mozarabic Breviary, has been retained in the new draft Roman Martyrology.

St Rheticius, *Bishop* (Fourth Century)

Bishop of Autun in the early fourth century, Rheticius is believed to have taught the rudiments of the Christian faith to the emperor Constantine. He was present also at the Lateran synod of 313 under Pope Miltiades, which upheld the lawful bishop of Carthage, Cecilian, against the agitations of Donatus and his followers. All this took place only a year after Constantine's famous victory at the Milvian Bridge and a year before the election of St Silvester (31 Dec.) as pope. This pope summoned the First Council of Arles (314), which confirmed the earlier decision. Rheticius figured prominently in the calendar of Autun (Burgundy).

Jerome, *De viris illustribus* (*P.L.*, 23, 689); Augustine, *Contra Pelagium* (*P.L.*, 44, 644).

St Rupert of Bingen (Ninth Century)

A native of Bingen (near Mainz, in Rhein-Hessen), Rupert, who was of ducal family, consecrated himself and his mother to God when they were on pilgrimage to Rome. Afterward he returned home and built several churches before settling at Bingen with his mother to lead the life of hermits. He is said to have died at the age of only twenty. The calendars of Mainz and Limburg witness to his feast; his cult was further propagated by St Hildegard (17 Sept.).

St Vitesindus of Córdoba, *Martyr* (855)

It often happens that accounts of martyrdom concentrate on the steadfastness and consistency of the martyrs, often portrayed, too, as models of Christian living before their death. In reality Christian martyrs came from many levels of commitment, and sometimes the decision to accept martyrdom was comparatively sudden and unexpected. Vitesindus was one who had apparently abandoned Christianity for Islam in the predominantly Muslim society of early medieval southern

Spain. He still, however, practised his faith in secret in the time of persecution under Mahomet I (852-87). But then, for some reason, he changed his mind; he confessed his Christian faith, was condemned to death, and was executed. The precise date of his death is unknown. Even the fact of his martyrdom might have been forgotten had it not been recorded by Eulogius in his *Memorial of the Saints*. This work was published only in 1574. At Córdoba and elsewhere his feast has for long been kept, as it is today, on 15 May.

See *AA.SS.*, May, 3, p. 509; *Bibl.SS.*, 12, 1416-7.

St Isaiah of Rostov, *Abbot and Bishop* (1090)

Born at Kiev (Ukraine), Isaiah became a monk in the famous Monastery of the Caves during the lifetimes of its founders, Antony and Theodosius. Both capable and devout, he was chosen to be abbot of the monastery of St Demetrius (also in Kiev) in 1062. In 1077 he was chosen bishop of Rostov, an ancient city north of Moscow (not to be confused with Rostov on the Don, which was founded in the eighteenth century). This area still needed vigorous evangelization and consolidation, so he devoted his energies both to converting the heathen and to strengthening the faith of those already baptized. Tireless in works of mercy of all kinds, he preached very effectively. His word was said to be confirmed by miracles. His cult as a saint began at his death, and in 1160 his relics were enshrined in Rostov cathedral.

Bibl.SS., 7, 944-5.

St Isidore the Farmer (*c.* 1080-1130)

Isidore, also called the husbandman, is an example of an almost unknown saint who attained considerable posthumous fame, ending as patron saint of Madrid after being formally canonized in 1622 at the same ceremony as SS Ignatius Loyola (31 July), Francis Xavier (3 Dec.), Teresa of Avila (15 Oct.), and Philip Neri (26 May). The known details of his life show a humble peasant who worked for the same employer for most of his life and who married an ordinary peasant girl named Maria de la Cabeza, also subsequently venerated as a saint (8 Sept.). Isidore was born in or near Madrid and worked on the estate of Torrelaguna (outside the town), owned by Juan de Vergas. The couple had a son, but he died young; after this, it is claimed, they lived in perfect continence. Isidore was notably devout. He would visit a church on his way to work in the early morning, would pray during ploughing for long hours, and used to visit local shrines on pilgrimage when possible.

His biography was written about 150 years after his death, probably by a Franciscan, which perhaps accounts for the legendary stories about birds being fed corn seed by Isidore pouring out half of his grain on the ground for them. Not only were they saved from starvation in a hard winter but the sack was still full when opened later, and the seed yielded twice the usual amount of corn. Another time he is said to have arrived late for a Confraternity dinner because of long prayer, accompanied by a crowd of poor men for whom the food was mysteriously multiplied. Other stories claim that angels were seen helping Isidore in his work.

Isidore died in 1130, several years before his wife. In 1170 his body was translated to a beautiful shrine, this process being the equivalent in those days to canonization. Miracles were claimed through his intercession, and he was credited (like St James) with showing in a vision a secret path to King Alphonsus of Castile, by which he was able to defeat the Moors in battle. In about 1615 King Philip III of Spain was mortally ill until the shrine of Isidore was carried from Madrid to the sick king's room, when he completely recovered. This led to the king petitioning successfully for Isidore's canonization. The saint's body survives entire, either incorrupt or mummified, in the church of St Andrew, Madrid.

Contemporary interest in lay saints such as Homobonus of Cremona (13 Nov.) and Godric and Walstan from Finchale and Bawburgh (21 and 30 May, below) underlines their existence and their cults from medieval times. Thus the lay saints of the present time are by no means without precursors, of whom Isidore is but one.

See *AA.SS.*, May, 3, pp. 512-50; *Bibl.SS.*, 7, 953-7.

Bd Andrew Abellon (1375-1450)

Andrew was born at Saint-Maximin (Provence) and became a Dominican there in the famous church of St Mary Magdalen, which claimed to possess an important relic of her head. He was an artist as well as a friar, like the more famous Fra Angelico. Later he became prior and was distinguished not only for ruling his own house but also for restoring regular discipline in other priories. These he ruled by patience and example rather than by high-handed decrees. He was also outstanding as a missioner. His cult was confirmed by the Holy See in 1902. Some of his paintings survive in Dominican churches in the south of France.

See Life by H. Cormier (1903) and *Bibl.SS.*, 1, 67-8.

R.M.

SS Peter, Andrew, Paul, and Denis, martyrs of the Hellespont (third century)

SS Heraclius and Paul, martyrs (third century)

SS Cassius and Victorinus, martyrs (third century)

St Eutychius, martyr of Ferentino (*c.* 300)

St Simplicius, martyr of Sardinia (*c.* 300)

SS Bachtiesus, Isaac, and Symeon, martyrs of Persia (fourth century)

St Achilleus, bishop in Thessaly (fourth century)

St Ellerius, abbot in Tuscany (558)

St Nicholas the Mystic, bishop at Constantinople (925)

16

St Alexander of Caesarea, *Bishop and Martyr* (*c.* 250)

One of the many saints of this name, today's Alexander was bishop of Cappadocia until he came to Jerusalem, where the bishop and people pressed him to become their coadjutor bishop, to help and eventually succeed the aged current bishop, Narcissus. This seems to be the first recorded example of the transfer and coadjutorship of a bishop. Thanks to Eusebius we have some information about Alexander, whose fine library at Jerusalem was used by this first historian of the Christian Church.

Alexander was a convert from paganism and had studied at Alexandria under Pantenus and Clement before being chosen as bishop of Cappadocia. His transfer to Jerusalem was ratified by the bishops of Palestine in 212. He was described by Origen as excelling all other prelates in his kindness and in the attractiveness of his sermons. The help he gave Origen, whom he encouraged to teach as a layman and subsequently ordained, however, incurred the criticism of Demetrius, bishop of Alexandria. Another of Alexander's achievements was the founding of a school of catechesis.

In extreme old age he was seized in the persecution under Decius. He made a second public confession of faith—he had made the first during the persecution by Severus (202-3) many years earlier in Cappadocia—and this time was condemned to death by being thrown to the wild beasts at Caesarea. They, however, refused to attack him, we are told, and he was sent back to prison where he died in chains. Like others who sufferd a similar fate, he was venerated as a martyr by both Eastern and Western churches.

Eusebius, *H.E.*, 6, pp. 255-61; *Bibl.SS.*, 1, 783-4.

St Possidius, *Bishop* (*c.* 440)

Possidius is possibly best known as the biographer of the great St Augustine (28 Aug.). For most of his life he was the colleague and friend of the saint, and from 397 he was bishop of Calama, a diocese in Numidia (North Africa). All that is known of his early life is that he was a native of proconsular Africa and studied under Augustine at Hippo.

As bishop, Possidius ruled a diocese greatly disturbed by Donatism as well as by persistent paganism. Donatism was a form of schismatic rigorism that refused to recognize the validity of sacraments conferred by so-called *traditores* (traitors). It had been in existence for about one hundred years and had rival churches, bishops, and liturgy. Its extremists also took to violence and attempted, unsuccessfully, to assassinate Possidius. His importance in combating this schism was recognized by Pope Innocent II at the Council of Mileve (416).

When the barbarian Vandals crossed the sea from Spain to Africa, they soon conquered all Mauretania, Numidia, and proconsular Africa except the strong fortresses of Carthage, Citra, and Hippo. Calama was destroyed and with it Possidius' religious foundation based on Augustine's, so Possidius took refuge at Hippo. Not long after this Augustine died, with the Vandals at the gates. Their leader, the Arian Genseric, drove out Possidius and two other bishops.

Possidius was alive in 437, by which date he had written his Life of Augustine, but died not long after this, possibly at Mirandola (near Mantua in north-eastern Italy). He was a "straightforward and pertinacious disciple," who presented the complex personality of Augustine in terms of the tranquil life he had created for others. His portrait indeed tells us much of the everyday life of Augustine in old age: the daily poverty, the punishment of his companions at table with the loss of wine if they swore, the daily meals with silver spoons but poor crockery. The clothes and furniture were modest but decent and not slovenly. He was hospitable but frugal; the clerics of his household lived the common life. Sometimes Augustine melted down plate to redeem captives. In describing such matters, Posidius shows something of himself as well as of Augustine. His biography has been greatly appreciated (within its limitations) for centuries.

AA.SS., May, 4, pp. 27-34, for contemporary record of Possidius; see also *Bibl.SS.*, 10, 1055-6, and P. Brown, *Augustine of Hippo* (1967), esp. pp. 409-10.

St Brendan of Clonfert, *Abbot* (*c.* 486-575)

Born near Tralee and educated by Erc, bishop of Kerry, Brendan became a monk and later abbot. His principal area of activity was western Ireland, and the main abbeys he founded were Clonfert (*c.* 559), Annadown, Inishadroun, and Ardfert. His fame as their founder is confirmed by the place-name of Mount Brandon in the Dingle peninsula, the most westerly point of Europe. He is said also to have founded abbeys in Scotland and Wales and to have visited St Malo in Brittany. His cult was certainly strong in all these Celtic countries.

What gave his cult even greater diffusion was the famous romance called *The Navigation of St Brendan*. This delightful story, written in ninth-century Germany by an exiled Irish monk, tells of a sea voyage with a group of monks to an island of promise in the Atlantic Ocean. This quest for a happy other world retains some features from early apocryphal Christian writings and others from Irish folklore. Still attractively readable today, it tells of various adventures on the way. Judas Iscariot appears as an example of the damned, while a Hibernicized Paul the First Hermit is an example of the saved. Numbers are symbolical, and the journeys marvellously coincide with the feasts of the liturgical year, as laid down by a bird: "On this journey four seasons have been determined for you; that is, the day of the

Lord's Supper is to be celebrated with the holy man, Easter on the island, which is really the back of a sea monster, and from Easter to Pentecost with us on Paradise Island, and Christmas on the Island of Ailbe up to Mary's feast on Candlemas. At the end of the seventh year you will reach the land you are seeking, and you will be be there forty days and then be borne back to your homeland." Wherever the monks go, the birds join in the psalms. They meet whales, icebergs, and volcanoes.

Some of the details may be based in reality, as Irish monks did in fact travel to the Faroes and to Iceland, but the dialogue and much else seem to be based on the charming imagination of the narrator. Some idea of the extent of diffusion of this text can be inferred from the fact that 116 medieval manuscripts of it survive, both in Latin and most Continental vernaculars.

The text of the *Navigation* is most easily available in J. F. Webb and D. H. Farmer, *The Age of Bede* (1988). Extracts in E. C. Sellner, *Wisdom of the Celtic Saints* (1993), pp. 58–66. See also T. Severin, *The Brendan Voyage* (1978), and *O.D.S.*, p. 69, for further refs.

St Carantoc, *Bishop* (Sixth–Seventh Century)

This saint, like several other Celtic ones, had a cult in Ireland, Wales, Cornwall, and Brittany. To Carantoc is also attributed the building of an ancient monastic church at Carhampton in Somerset. The new draft Roman Martyrology says that he was born in Ireland and became abbot and bishop of Cardigan in Wales. Here and in the other three Celtic areas mentioned, several churches were dedicated to him. The Cornish village of Crantock is named after him, and records of his church there go back to the thirteenth century. In Brittany a parish called Caranted reflects his patronage and possibly his work as founder, while in Wales he is called Carannog.

All that can be safely asserted about him is that he was a monk and bishop who founded several churches and monasteries at about the time of the Anglo-Saxon invasions, when notable Celtic migrations beween the countries mentioned above were also taking place. The most lively details about him are to be found in the Cornish sources. William Worcestre mentions his chapel near Padstow, where he was invoked for destroying worms "when people drink the water of a well there." The seventeenth-century antiquary Roscarrock mentions a church with seven churchyards dedicated to him, whose parishioners used to come each year bringing relics, which were placed on special stones like altars. The one constant element is the date of his feast, which ensures that the cults are of one and the same saint, in spite of some disparities in his name.

See A. W. Wade-Evans, *Vitae Sanctorum Brittanicorum et Genealogiae* (1944), pp. 142–50; G. H. Doble, *The Saints of Cornwall*, 4 (1965), pp. 31–52; J. A. Robinson, "St Carantoc in Somerset," in *Downside Review* 46 (1929), pp. 234–43.

Forty-Four Martyrs of Palestine (614)

There are several groups of martyrs of Palestine listed in the pre-1970 Roman Martyrology. Those venerated today, retained in the latest draft, are the forty-four monks of the monastery of St Sabas (5 Dec.), who were massacred in the reign of the emperor Heraclius. They were victims in the war against the Persian Chosroes II (591-628), who inflicted great disaster on the Byzantine Empire, conquering Syria, Palestine, and Egypt in the course of his wars. He had also previously captured the Holy Cross, which Heraclius eventually recovered.

The monastery of St Sabas was justly famous. Sabas was one of the most notable monastic founders of the sixth century; his monastery, which survives today, is siutated in a gorge of the river Cedron, ten miles south-east of Jerusalem in the desert that leads to the Dead Sea. It has produced many saints in the course of its long history, among them St John Damascene (27 Mar.), St John the Silent (13 May, above), and, by no means the least, the forty-four martyrs venerated today. In their heroic witness they may be compared to the groups of monks martyred in the Viking invasions of the ninth century, or in the Spanish Civil War of the twentieth.

St Simon Stock (1265)

Very little is known of Simon's early life. It is likely that he became a hermit in England and joined the early Carmelites in the Holy Land, when their way of life was eremitical. Owing to Saracen hostility, they left the Holy Land for Europe, where they established houses in their own countries. Simon was elected general of the Order at a general chapter held at Aylesford (Kent) in 1247. His tenure of office was a period in which Carmelite houses were established in university towns and elsewhere (Paris, Bologna, Oxford, Cambridge, as well as in East Anglia and London); at the same time they became a mendicant Order, preaching and teaching, like the Dominicans and Franciscans. This revision was approved by the papacy in 1247 and 1252. So Simon was important in the development of the Carmelite Order as we know it today, and his connection with Aylesford is certain. Two antiphons to Our Lady used in the Carmelite liturgy are also attributed to him.

Much less certain but probably better publicized is the saint's connection with the Brown Scapular devotion. This stems from a supposed Marian vision and promise, for which there is no contemporary evidence. According to the story, known in the fifteenth century, Mary appeared to Simon and promised that whoever wore the Brown Scapular of Our Lady of Mount Carmel would be saved. There has been much controversy both about the history and the content of this supposed private revelation.

Simon died in Bordeaux and was buried there. His cult began in the Carmelite Order and was approved by the Holy See in 1564, just three hundred years after his death, for the Order and several dioceses. His relics were brought back to Aylesford in 1951. This restored Carmelite friary, of considerable beauty and historical interest, has become a retreat and conference centre of some importance.

See articles by B. Zimmerman, O.C.D., and H. Thurston, S.J., in *The Month* for June, July, and October 1927; (for a more conservative view) B. M. Ziberta, O.C.D., *De visione S. Simonis Stock* (1950); *Bibl.SS.*, 11, 1188-91.

St Andrew Bobola, *Martyr* (1591-1657)

Andrew was born into a Polish family of the lesser nobility in the Palatinate of Sandomierz. He studied at the Jesuit school at Vilna (now Vilnius, capital of Lithuania, then in Poland) and entered the novitiate there in 1611. Ordained priest in 1622, he was pastor of the church at Nieswiez, connected with the Jesuit school there. After a short but effective apostolate he returned to St Casimir's church at Vilna, where his preaching was outstanding and his charge of sodalities fruitful. It was from this band of the devout that he chose assistants in his visits to prisoners and the poor. Later they became catechists and heroically nursed the sick during the plagues of 1624 and 1629. In 1630 he was sent to Bobruisk, again as pastor; there he built a church for the local Catholics, who, because of the shortage of priests, had conformed to the Orthodox Church and faith. From 1643 to 1649, however, his health was bad and his known activities few.

Meanwhile, hostility to Catholics in general and to Jesuits in particular increased. Although the agreement reached in the Union of Brest-Litovsk (1569) provided for the peaceful coexistence of the churches of Rome and of Russia, some of the Orthodox, supported by Cossack brigands, wanted to annul it and to remove Catholics and their churches from this territory. The Cossack leader, Bogdan Chmielnicki, powerful and fanatical, did all he could to force out the Catholics. By 1655, he had taken over much of White Russia. In the same year Andrew was back in Vilna when it was sacked by Russian troops at war with Poland. By this time Poland had become the scene of a bitter and bloody conflict. The Jesuits were driven from their churches and colleges and took refuge in the swampy district of Podlesia. There Prince Radziwill invited them to his residence at Pinsk, where Andrew went to encourage the persecuted Poles to continue in their faith and their attachment to Rome. His success was acknowledged by all, and some tried to sabotage his efforts by organizing gangs of children to throw mud and stones at him and to try to shout him down.

Pinsk was captured in 1657. After massacring Jews and Catholics at Janow, the Cossacks captured Andrew at nearby Peredil. (All these places are east of Warsaw and south of Vilna.) Andrew's sufferings make his martyrdom one of the most horrific in history; they were verified by medical examination of his body. First, to make him abjure Catholicism, the Cossacks whipped him and then tied him to horses, which dragged him back to Janov. Then they stretched him out on a butcher's table, tore the skin off his body, and cut holes in the palms of his hands. Then they jabbed an awl into his chest and finally killed him with a sword. The thought behind all this seems to have been that he should be butchered like a pig.

Soon after this, some Poles arrived, too late to save him, but at least they were able to place his body in the local church and then bury him at Pinsk. In 1808 the body was transferred to Polotsk (Byelorussia), and in 1922 the Bolsheviks took the relics to a Moscow museum. These had been examined in 1730 and found to be incorrupt. In 1923 two American Jesuits requested the saint's body in the name of Pius XI. It was taken to Rome to be re-examined, and the details of his tortures could still be discerned. Andrew was beatified in 1853 and canonized in 1938. His body was returned to Poland and is now in the Jesuit church in Warsaw. He is venerated as apostle of Lithuania and patron of Poland.

There are Lives by L. Rocci (1924), H. Beylard (1938), and J. Mareschini (Eng. trans. by L. J. Gallagher and P. V. Donovan, 1939); articles by H. Thurston, S.J., in *Studies*, Sept. 1938, pp. 381-93, and L. J. Gallagher in *The Month*, Feb. 1924; see also *Bibl.SS.*, 1, 1153-5.

R.M.
St Peregrine, bishop of Auxerre (fourth/fifth century)
SS Felix and Gennadius, martyrs in Africa (?)
SS Abdas and Companions, martyrs in Persia (375)
St Fidolus, priest in Gaul (540)
St Honoratus, bishop in Gaul (*c.* 600)
St Germerius, bishop of Toulouse (late seventh century)
St Ubald, abbot of Fermo (*c.* 1210)

ST BRENDAN OF CLONFERT (pp. 87-8)
Sea monsters.

17

St Paschal Baylon (1540-92)

The Eucharistic Congresses of the Catholic Church, devoted as they are to propagating the understanding and veneration of the Holy Eucharist through elaborate and splendid celebrations, have as their patron a Spanish Franciscan lay brother of peasant stock who was little known in his lifetime.

Fortunately we can learn much about Paschal from the contemporary Life written by his religious superior Fr Ximenes. Paschal (Pascal) was born at Torre Hermosa on the borders of Castile and Aragon on Whitsunday 1540 of a shepherd family. His education was rudimentary, and he is said to have taught himself to read while looking after the flocks of his own family and others. Devout as well as scrupulous, he was assiduous in prayer but also concerned to make good the damage done to others' vineyards through the incursions of his sheep.

When he was twenty-one, he joined the Loreto convent (200 miles away) of the reformed Franciscans of St Peter of Alcántara (d. 1562; 19 Oct.). This austere version of Franciscan life was known for its extreme poverty allied with assiduous prayer. It was highly esteemed, with its founder, by St Teresa of Avila (15 Oct.). Pascal's charity toward the sick and the poor was both exemplary and good humoured. He refused to tell visitors that the superior was "not at home" when he was really there; he would only say "he is engaged." When Pascal was refectorian, he once shut himself in the refectory and performed an elaborate dance in honour of Our Lady, whose statue was placed over the door. Fortunately for posterity, another brother saw him through the buttery hatch. His biographer testified that "in no single case do I remember to have noted even the least fault in him, though I lived with him in several of our houses and was his companion on two long journeys." The long hours spent in prayer, kneeling before the Blessed Sacrament without support, sometimes late at night and before dawn, were characteristic practices from quite early in his religious life; so too was his devotion in serving Masses.

In contrast to this admirable cloistered life was an episode during the religious wars, which shows him in a different but no less worthy light. He was sent to France carrying letters to the minister general of the Observant Franciscans. How or why he was chosen is not known, nor do those who sent him seem to have been very well informed about the dangers. Paschal travelled as far as Orleans without apparently knowing any French and delivered his letters in spite of repeated attacks by Huguenots. Once he was stoned, and his shoulder was badly injured, causing him pain for the rest of his life. However, he returned safely to resume the hidden and unspectacular life which had been his before, continuing, like several other Franciscan lay brothers, his help to the poor and the sick who came to the friary for help.

He died in the friary at Villareal, also on Whitsunday, at the age of only fifty-two. Cures were reported even before he was buried. He was beatified in 1618 (before Peter of Alcántara). Curious knockings *(golpes)* were also reported at his tomb and regarded as portents of some kind. They are said to have continued for two hundred years. Paschal was canonized in 1690. His assiduity in prayer and Eucharistic devotion earned him the patronage later of the Eucharistic Congresses. During the Spanish Civil War his grave was devastated and his relics burned.

AA.SS., May, 4, pp. 48-131; Lives by V. Facchinetti (1922) and A. Groeteken (1929); see also *Bibl.SS.*, 10, 358-64.

Bd Peter Lieou, *Martyr* (1834)

This martyr, also called Ouen Yen, was a Chinese catechist who was strangled for the name of Christ. Before he died he encouraged his sons in prison. He was one of a group of martyrs of China, both European and Eastern, who were killed in the nineteenth century. They were beatified in 1900.

See "Martyrs of China," 17 Feb.

Bd Antonia Mesina, *Martyr* (1919-35)

Like St Mary Goretti (5 July), Antonia is venerated as a martyr of chastity. The life stories of the two girls are remarkably similar. In spite of her name, Antonia's short life was spent entirely in Sardinia, not Sicily. She was a member of a large family of eleven children, born to parents who were conventionally poor but honest. From the age of twelve her whole life was spent in her home, the fields and the church. Her childhood was exemplary, not only with weekly Communion and family rosary but also with helping her mother with the care of young twins.

At the age of sixteen, by which time she had been involved with a Catholic Action group, she was one day collecting wood for the family needs with a companion named Annette. A young man of twenty jumped on her from behind. Antonia resisted him several times and her opposition was deliberate and complete. While Annette had fled to raise the alarm, the man, named Giovanni-Ignacio Catgiu, repeatedly assaulted her and finally killed her with stones. Antonia sustained seventy-four wounds and died in an attitude of self-defence, her hands grasping her dress around her knees.

Catgiu tried to hide the incriminating evidence, but two days later he confessed. He was condemned to death and was executed in 1937, having repented of his crime, and received the last sacraments. Antonia's family prayed for the young man and expressed no hatred or desire for vengeance. The virtuous life of Antonia was declared by witnesses as was her commitment to a crusade of purity in her parish. She was beatified by Pope John Paul II in 1987, just over fifty years after her death.

See T. Lelièvre, *Nouveaux Saints et Bienheureux de 1985 à 1988* (1989), pp. 142-5; *Bibl.SS*, Suppl. 1, 918; M. di Pietra, *Antonia Mesina* (1943); P. Fortunato, *Antonia Mesina, uccisa come santa Maria Goretti* (1974).

R.M.

St Restituta, martyr at Carthage (304)

SS Solochon and Companions, martyrs (fourth century)

St Adrio, martyr of Alexandria (fourth century)

St Victor, martyr of Rome (fourth century)

ST ERIC OF SWEDEN (pp.97-8)
Three gold crowns and blue and silver
waves, on red field.

18

St John I, *Pope and Martyr* (526)

A Tuscan by birth, John had joined the clergy of Rome as a young man; by the time he was chosen as pope in 523, he was archdeacon, but elderly and infirm. He was a friend of Boethius, the retired civil servant who had written *The Consolation of Philosophy* and other works. His policy as pope was to enhance the reunion between East and West accomplished by his predecessor Hormisdas. This had succeeded a state of turmoil following the Council of Chalcedon (451) and the Acacian Schism (484-519) and had resulted in the Easterns' acceptance of the Formula of Hormisdas being signed by the patriarch of Constantinople and all bishops and abbots then present. This acknowledged not only the teaching of Chalcedon but also the unique position of Rome as the apostolic see in which the Catholic faith had always been preserved in its purity.

When John became pope, Italy was ruled by the Arian ruler Theodoric the Goth, hitherto tolerant of his Catholic subjects. But he had been enraged by the persecution of Arians in the Eastern empire and summoned John to Ravenna to lead a delegation of ecclesiastics to Constantinople in order to bring it to an end. The emperor Justin I (518-27), who had initiated this persecution of Arians (including Goths), warmly welcomed John in 526. John was acclaimed by the crowd at the twelfth milestone, was given a throne in the cathedral higher than the patriarch's, sang Mass in the Latin rite, and placed the usual Easter crown on the emperor's head. Justin agreed to all of Theodoric's demands except that of allowing Arians who had conformed under pressure to revert to heretical practices. When John returned to Ravenna, Theodoric, morbidly suspicious and already responsible for the execution of Boethius, was furious with Pope John and obliged him to wait in Ravenna, now deprived of Theodoric's trust and protection. Some say that he died of shock, shattered by the appalling fate that awaited him. Others claim that he was imprisoned and then died from the ill treatment he received. His body was translated to Rome for burial in the nave of St Peter's on 27 May 526. His contemporary epitaph proclaimed him "a victim for Christ." He lived and died in a conflict between two powerful secular rulers whom he could not simultaneously satisfy. His story is one in a long list of victims of ruthless kings bent on enforcing religious conformity in matters beyond their legitimate jurisdiction. A more peaceful achievement of John's pontificate was the introduction, on the advice of Dionysius Exiguus, of the Alexandrian system of Easter computation. This had been under dispute before, but John's acceptance of it was decisive in its general use by the Church in the West.

See L. Duchesne, *Liber Pontificalis*, 1 (1886), pp. 257-8; J. Richards, *The Popes and the Papacy in the Early Middle Ages* (1979), pp. 109-20; *O.D.P.*, pp. 52-55; *N.C.E.*, 7, p. 1006.

St Potamon, *Bishop and Martyr* (*c.* 340)

Potamon or Potamion, bishop of Heraclea (Egypt), suffered twice in his lifetime for fidelity to the Christian faith. The first time was in the persecution of Maximinus Daia in 310, when his bold confession before the pagans was punished by torture which resulted in permanent lameness and the loss of one eye. Fifteen years later these sufferings made him conspicuous at the Council of Nicaea, in which he took a prominent part. In 335 he was with Athanasius (2 May) at the Council of Tyre, where he vigorously defended him. A few years later in the reign of the Arian emperor Constantius, Philagrius, the prefect of Egypt, and Gregory, the usurper of the see of Alexandria, together persecuted or banished the orthodox. Potamon was a prominent target because of his fidelity to Athanasius; he was beaten with clubs and left for dead. Although he partially recovered through the care bestowed on him by the believers, he died soon afterward from the injuries received.

See *AA.SS.*, May, 4, p. 166, for the contemporary witness of SS Athanasius and Epiphanius; also *Bibl.SS.*, 10, 1060.

SS Theodotus and Companions, *Martyrs* (Fourth Century)

The Acts of these martyrs, in the short and the long recensions, are considered by the Bollandist H. Delehaye to be nothing more than a pious romance based on a story by Herodotus and falsely attributed to one Nilus, supposedly a companion and eyewitness of the saints. The story is placed in Ancyra (Turkey) and plausibly relates how Theodotus, an innkeeper, acquired the relics of St Valens, rescued from a river, when he met a party of Christians who sat down to a picnic lunch with their priest Fronto. The latter was given his ring by Theodotus as a pledge that he would provide relics for a chapel to be built there. Soon after, a feast was held to Artemis and Athene, whose statues were bathed in a pond with the priestesses who looked after them. Seven Christian girls were stripped, carried to the pond, and drowned with stones round their necks, as they refused to become priestesses. Theodotus recovered their relics but was betrayed and decapitated. Meanwhile Fronto came to Ancyra with his ass to sell wine. He plied the soldiers reputed to guard Theodotus' body with so much wine that they became drunk, then laid the body on the back of his ass and sent it off in the dark. It returned to Malus, as he had anticipated, and the chapel was built to house his relics, with his ring replaced on Theodotus' finger. This story was for long regarded as authentic but nowadays even the existence of these martyrs is questioned.

See the relevant texts in P. F. de'Cavalieri, *Studi e Testi*, 6 (1901), and 33 (1920); comments by H. Delehaye in *Anal. Boll.* 22 (1903), pp. 320-8, and 23 (1904), pp. 478-9; *Bibl. SS.*, 12, 309-12. The feast was found in some Byzantine calendars but reached the *R.M.* only under Baronius (sixteenth century).

St Eric of Sweden, *King and Martyr* (1160)

Eric IX, king of Sweden from 1150, took a prominent part in the consolidation of Christianity in his own country and in its spread to Finland. In this latter enterprise he was strongly supported by the Englishman St Henry of Finland (19 Jan.). At Old Uppsala Eric completed the building of the cathedral. This is a comparatively small but deeply impressive building, surrounded (as at Jelling, Denmark) by the mounds which contain the remains of earlier pagan kings. Old Uppsala indeed was the political and religious centre of the Svea kingdom. Eric's cathedral replaced a pagan temple on the same site, it is generally claimed. Another achievement of Eric's reign was the collecting and codifying of old laws. Like his predecessors, he was a warlike king; and a coalition of Danes, Finns, and discontented Swedes led ultimately to his violent death at Uppsala, where the present cathedral was built in his memory. In religious matters he was largely guided by St Henry, who was consecrated bishop of Uppsala by the English papal legate Nicholas Breakspear, who subsequently became Pope Adrian IV (1154-9).

We know few details about the reign of Eric but more about his death. From 1152 onward he had waged war against the Finns, who had made a series of raids into Sweden. This punitive expedition led to their being offered peace if they would accept Christianity. This policy resembled that of Charlemagne toward the pagan Saxons. The Finns refused and were utterly defeated in battle. Henry remained for some years in Finland, where he was killed in 1156. A few years later, Eric was faced by a hostile force of Danes under Prince Magnus of Denmark and rebel Swedes, supposedly discontented by his vigorous support of the Church in its plans for building churches and assuring support for them through the payment of tithes, as elsewhere in Europe.

On the feast of the Ascension, 1160, he went to Mass in the church on the site of the present cathedral of Uppsala. One of his men told him that there were enemies outside the town who should be met with weapons. He answered that he preferred to listen in peace to the celebration of this great feast. After Mass he left the church, armed himself, and went with his few followers to meet a large force outside. He was at once attacked by many Danish soldiers and fell from his horse to the ground. There he was repeatedly wounded, tortured, and ridiculed. Eventually they cut off his head. He was buried at first in the old church at Old Uppsala, which he had helped to build.

Various miracles were claimed very soon either in connection with his body or with the spring which appeared close to the present cathedral. His relics, in a shrine which resembled a small gothic church, were translated on 24 January 1273 from the old to the new cathedral. This shrine was melted down at the Reformation, but its contents were kept intact. In 1580 they were once again enshrined by King John III. Made from thirty-four kilograms of silver and then gilded, this third shrine can still be seen in Uppsala cathedral. It contains much of the king's skeleton with sword wounds as well as the crown of St Eric, made of gilded copper decorated with red, green, and blue stones. It is the oldest surviving royal crown in Sweden.

Another extant memorial to Eric is the series of fifteenth-century mural paintings in this cathedral. Prominent in his story is his English bishop, Henry. These memorials to one of the most notable medieval kings of Sweden are also notable and welcome reminders of the cult and pilgrimage to St Eric in the days when Sweden was a Catholic country. Although it would seem that he was never formally canonized by the Holy See, his cult was widespread and at least tacitly approved. As both king of his people and a vigorous champion of the Church, he may be compared to England's royal saints like Oswald of Northumbria (5 Aug.) and Edmund of East Anglia (20 Nov.). Eric's banner was frequently carried in battle, and he was regarded as Sweden's principal patron up to the Reformation.

See *H.S.S.C.*, 6, 133-8; *Bibl. SS.*, 4, 1322-6; B.S. Safstrom, *Uppsala Cathedral* (1986); R. Folz, *Les Saints rois du Moyen Age en Occident* (1984); A. Jönsson, "St Eric of Sweden—the Drunken Saint?" in *Anal. Boll.* 109 (1991), pp. 331-46.

Bd William of Toulouse (1369)

William became an Austin Friar at Toulouse when very young. After his ordination he was sent to the University of Paris (then at the height of its reputation) for higher studies. He became famous as a preacher and spiritual director. Another aspect of his life includes his visions of evil spirits and his skill in exorcism.

A few of his sayings are worth recording here. He regarded his religious profession as explicit consecration to the Holy Trinity: obedience to the Father; poverty to the Son, who became poor; and chastity to the Holy Spirit, "spouse" of Mary and other devout souls. Another time a rich lady asked him to pray for her dead relatives. He answered: "Eternal rest give to them O Lord . . . may they rest in peace." The lady was disappointed and expected more prayers for her offering of a bag of gold. But when William wrote the prayer and put it in a scale with the gold, the prayer outweighed the gold. William's cult was for long unofficial, arising as it did in what became France's second city amid plenty of other local cults, but it was confirmed by the Holy See in 1893. The conventual church and monastic buildings of the Austin Friars survive today as the Musée des Augustins, largely devoted to medieval architecture, sculpture, and painting.

Life by Nicholas Bertrand (*c.* 1510) in *AA.SS.*, May, 4, 196-202, and a longer one by N. Mattioli (1894) supplement the decree which confirmed the cult. See also *Bibl. SS.*, 7, 486-7.

St Felix of Cantalice (1515-87)

Born at Cantalice (Apulia) of a devout peasant family, he often looked after the animals for his father; from the age of twelve he was hired out as shepherd and later ploughman. In this occupation he suffered an accident which was nearly fatal. The bullocks panicked at a sudden appearance, knocked him down, and trampled on him, drawing the plough over his body. This experience decided him to become a Capuchin lay brother at Città Ducale. His novitiate was at Anticoli, and in 1548 he was sent to Rome, where for most of the rest of his life he acted as questor, begging each day for food and alms to enable the friars to subsist. Nearly forty years in this task brought him insults, discomfort, and fatigue. His superiors allowed him to give away some of these alms to the poor and the sick of secular society, whom he personally cared for and consoled.

The very difficult times at Rome when he lived there under a succession of Renaissance and reforming popes needed people of outstanding holiness, and such were not lacking. Felix was known personally to both St Philip Neri (26 May) and St Charles Borromeo (4 Nov.). The former became his personal friend, while the latter consulted him about the Rule for his Oblates. Felix protested his illiteracy, but on hearing the Rule read aloud made suggestions about modifying some regulations which he considered too strict. To himself, however, he was extremely severe, going barefoot in all weathers, fasting on bread and water, and wearing instruments of penance. When serving Mass, he was sometimes so absorbed in ecstatic prayer that he failed to make the responses. Known to the children of Rome as "Brother Deo gratias" because of his frequent habit of saying "Thanks be to God," he continued his rounds, at his own request, until he died after a vision of Our Lady on 18 May 1587. He was canonized in 1712 after a large number of miracles were recorded after his death. His life in many details resembles those of other Franciscan lay brothers such as Ignatius of Laconi (11 May) and Francis of Camporosso (20 Sept.). All three remind us that people of humble origin and limited education can indeed become saints.

M. da Alatri prints many eyewitness accounts of this saint in *Mon. Hist. O.F.M. Capuccinorum* (1964); see also A. Kerr, *A Son of St Francis* (1900) and *Bibl.SS.*, 5, 538-40.

Bd Blandina Merten (1883-1918)

Born at Duppenweiler (Germany) the ninth child of a devout family, Blandina devoted her life to religion by joining the teaching Ursuline Order at an early age. There she distinguished herself by total devotion to the children under her care in the context of an almost invisible apostolate of example and suffering. This last, severe and prolonged, reduced her life as a nun to only eleven years, and her natural life to only thirty-five. She died toward the end of World War I and was beatified in 1987. Scripture, the Eucharist, and prayer formed the deepest centre of her life. "Whoever loves God," she would say, "does not need to achieve exceptionally elevated actions; it is enough to love." During her life she achieved nothing extraordinary, but she accomplished her daily round of duty exceptionally well.

R.M.

St Epaphroditus, companion of St Paul the Apostle (first century)

St Felix, martyr in Dalmatia (third century)

St Dioscorus, martyr in Egypt (fourth century)

19

ST DUNSTAN OF CANTERBURY, *Abbot and Bishop* (909-88)

Dunstan's main achievements were that he restored Benedictine monastic life in England, at Glastonbury and elsewhere, and that he became a most notable archbishop of Canterbury, of considerable political as well as ecclesiastical importance. Five medieval biographies survive, as does a famous classbook of his from Glastonbury with a self-portrait of Dunstan at the feet of Christ.

He was born at Baltonsborough (Somerset) of a noble family connected by marriage with the kings of Wessex. He was educated at Glastonbury, then apparently a Celtic centre of clerics voluntarily "exiled for Christ." In spite of the patronage of his uncle Athelm, archbishop of Canterbury, he was expelled from the court of King Athelstan owing to accusations of being a magician and studying the poems and fables of the pagans. These were indirect tributes to his learning, and it is probable that at this court he heard from foreign marriage embassies of the revival of Benedictine monasticism in Burgundy and Lorraine. After some uncertainty about his future through contemplating marriage, he was ordained priest by the bishop of Winchester and probably took private monastic vows, as at this time there were no surviving Benedictine monasteries of men in England. He then returned to Glastonbury, living as a hermit and improving his skills as musician, metalworker, and embroiderer. In 939 Edmund became king of Wessex. He recalled Dunstan to favour and after a narrow escape from death while hunting near Cheddar from his local palace, he gave Glastonbury to Dunstan, appointing him abbot in 940. Continuous monastic life flourished at Glastonbury for just 600 years, after Dunstan had attracted disciples, brought in the Rule of St Benedict, and added new buildings to this monastery of great antiquity.

During this time of young and short-lived Wessex kings, Dunstan again experienced varied fortunes. Under Edred (946-55) part of the royal treasure was housed at Glastonbury, and Dunstan was rewarded with a legacy of £200 for the people of Somerset and Devon. Under Edwy, however, he was exiled to Ghent, supposedly after reproving the king for bad behaviour at his coronation feast. In exile Dunstan experienced the reformed monasteries' life and observance. King Edgar, though, soon recalled him, and in 957 Dunstan became bishop of Worcester. He was promoted to London two years later and in 960 became archbishop of Canterbury. This marked the beginning of a fruitful collaboration between a mature archbishop and a king then only sixteen in matters of both Church and State. Meanwhile Dunstan's friend and collaborator St Ethelwold (1 Aug.) had refounded Abingdon and would become bishop of Winchester (the then capital of Wessex) in

963, and St Oswald of Worcester (29 Feb.) revived Westbury-on-Trym and became a bishop also. Dunstan, however, was personally responsible for reviving Malmesbury, Bath, Athelney, Muchelney, and Westminster before or after his consecration. Distinguishing features of this monasticism were the close dependence on the royal family for protection and support, notably against the power of local lay lords; additional customary prayers with others for the royal family; and the flourishing of book production, illumination, and other crafts. In addition, the frequent promotion of bishops from the monasteries was due to their high standards of both learning and integrity.

Dunstan's influence spread far beyond monastic and court circles. He was a zealous diocesan bishop who insisted on the observance of marriage laws as well as those of fasting and abstinence. He often acted as judge and inspired some of Edgar's laws, in which together they commanded the payment of tithes, Peterpence and other church taxes, and enjoined on all priests the practice of some handicraft. He also built and repaired churches, preached and taught frequently, and administered justice. The high point of this reign was the coronation of Edgar at Bath Abbey in 973, an "imperial" consecration largely devised by Dunstan and still the basis of the coronation ceremony of English kings and queens. This had been long delayed, possibly for Edgar's scandalous conduct (see under Wulfhilda, 9 Sept.). This was followed by a meeting at Chester when all the subordinate rulers of Britain rowed the king in a boat on the river Dee. Unfortunately Edgar died only two years later.

Political disorder followed with the assassination of St Edward the Martyr (18 Mar.) in 978 at the age of sixteen and the accession to the throne of the child Ethelred, later called the Unready. Dunstan presided at the translation of Edward's relics in 980 to Shaftesbury (the nunnery founded by King Alfred), but his later years were saddened by the political situation. He continued at Canterbury until his death in 988, by which time some monks were in his household and quite possibly made Canterbury cathedral monastic. Both now and earlier his biographers attributed to him visions, prophecies, and miracles. These, as well as his obvious achievements, contributed to the early development of his cult. Already in 999 he was recognized as "the chief of all the saints who rest at Christchurch." His feast is recorded in several pre-Conquest calendars.

At Canterbury under Lanfranc there was a brief interruption in his cult, but like those of other Anglo-Saxon saints it went from strength to strength, soon afterward becoming nationwide. In the pontificate of St Anselm (21 Apr.) Dunstan's feast was celebrated with an octave; at Canterbury altars of Dunstan and Alphege (19 Apr.) flanked the high altar. Canterbury rightly claimed to have his body, but this was disputed by Glastonbury. Only in 1508 was the Canterbury tomb opened and the relics verified. Dunstan left no written works of any note that are certainly authentic, but he did contribute to Abbo's Life of St Edmund (20 Nov.) by providing material which came from the king's standard-bearer. Goldsmiths, jewellers, and locksmiths are the object of his special patronage, and at Canterbury a subsidiary feast was held on 21 October to commemorate his ordination.

Ancient lives and other material in W. Stubbs, *Memorials of St Dunstan* (R.S., 1874); most modern study in N. Ramsay and others (eds.), *St Dunstan: His Life, Times and Cult* (1992); see also T. Symons (ed.), *The Regularis Concordia* (1953); R. W. Hunt, *St Dunstan's Classbook from Glastonbury* (1963); D. Parsons (ed.), *Tenth-Century Studies* (1975); *O.D.S.*, pp. 137-9; F. M. Stenton, *Anglo-Saxon England* (1971), pp. 427-51.

St Urban I, *Pope* (230)

There has been much legendary account of this pope. In reality he was a Roman by birth and was pope for eight years. His pontificate fell in the reign of Alexander Severus, during which there was no persecution. However, the Roman see was much divided by the Schism of Hippolytus, though we do not know about the relations between them. He was buried in the cemetery of Callistus, where a grave-slab bearing his name in capitals has been found. He was not a martyr, was not connected with St Cecilia (22 Nov.) and her companions (two of whom he is supposed to have baptized) but who died over sixty years after him, but he was a real historical character, mentioned by Eusebius and the *Liber Pontificalis*. The author of the Acts of St Cecilia doubtless borrowed his name to give her greater distinction. The new Roman Martyrology says he ruled the Roman see for eight years and correctly locates his burial place, unlike its predecessor.

See *O.D.P.*, pp. 15-16.

SS Calocerus and Parthenius, *Martyrs* (304)

These two brothers were eunuchs in the household of Tryphonia, wife of the emperor Decius, according to their Acts, which also describe them as Armenians whose patron had left them in charge of his daughter Anatolia when he died. They were also fervent Christians who preferred the risk of martyrdom to offering sacrifice to the gods. They were summoned before Decius to answer both the charge of being Christians and that of dissipating Anatolia's heritage, possibly by almsgiving. After making a bold confession of their faith, they were condemned to be burned. They were then beaten on the head until they died. Anatolia buried them in the cemetery of Callistus.

Little is known of these martyrs beyond their names and cult; see *AA.SS.*, May, 4, pp. 300-3, and *Anal. Boll.* 16 (1897), pp. 240-1, and 46 (1928), pp. 50-5. *Bibl.SS.*, 3, 699-700.

St Peter Celestine, *Pope* (1210-96)

It is often asked if the pope, successor of St Peter and universal pastor, can or should resign his office. Peter Celestine is the only pope in history, it would seem, who has ever done so. Not only that, but he was formally canonized as well. How and why did this happen?

Born at Isernia (Molise) not far from Cassino, the eleventh child of a peasant family, Peter became a Benedictine at S. Maria di Faifula but in about 1231 embraced the life of a hermit. After being ordained priest in Rome, he lived for several years in a cave on Mount Morrone. Here his solitude was interrupted several times by others who wanted to join his way of life. Eventually he accepted disciples, who were later incorporated into the Benedictine Orders under the title of Celestines. Like the Camaldolese, they aimed at combining eremitical life with the Rule of St Benedict. After about forty years in this solitary life, Peter travelled in 1274 to the Council of Lyons and obtained from Gregory X a privilege confirming his Congregation's Benedictine status and its ownership of properties. This last point is significant, as his Congregation was said to have had strong links with the Franciscan Spirituals, who rejected such ownership. He held the first general chapter at Maiella, which published disciplinary and liturgical directives. In 1276 he became abbot of Faifula and prior of Maiella, the former of which was placed under royal protection by Charles I of Anjou, king of Sicily. Peter's fame had spread far and wide, but he retired in 1293 from the government of the Congregation and settled in a small cave back in Monte Morrone to pursue his life as a hermit once more.

Meanwhile a papal election was being held in Rome. For over two years the twelve cardinals, divided by personal and family interests, had been unable to elect. The deadlock continued until Peter, whose Congregation now numbered twenty monasteries, sent them a message threatening divine punishment if they continued to endanger the Church by further delay. In response to this plea, the cardinals elected Peter as pope at the age of eighty-five.

This was not the first time in history that an octogenarian had been elected pope, but this time it was a disastrous choice. The holy and unworldly abbot rode on a donkey to Aquila, accompanied by the kings of Hungary and Naples. Immense and enthusiastic crowds arrived hoping to see the beginning of a new era—that of the Holy Spirit—prophesied by the eccentric Joachim of Fiore. Peter was out of his depth in the world of papal government. The immense power in his hands was manipulated by the king of Naples, who persuaded him to live in Naples instead of Rome and to create thirteen new cardinals in the interests of Naples and of France. Peter's simplicity, his ignorance of canon law and even of advanced Latin, his desire to please all and to offend none, led to a number of unsuitable appointments and even to the allocation of the same benefices to different people. Completely unworldly, he gave away treasure for which he had no use, as well as positions of influence in a difficult world in which Christian rulers were sometimes at war with each other while all looked for support to the pope, who had important rights of intervention and arbitration.

When Advent came, Peter wanted to retire again to solitude within the palace, leaving the government of the Church to three cardinals. Advisers rightly warned that this might lead to the arrival of three rival popes. Miserable at the disorder he had caused, he consulted the able and forceful canonist, the cardinal Gaetani, about the possibility and legality of his resigning his office. Gaetani replied that it was indeed permissible and sometimes advisable to resign. In spite of the clamour from various interested parties (some of whom still looked for spiritual renewal), he read aloud his declaration of his abdication due to his age, incapacity, and lack of knowledge. He asked pardon for his mistakes and exhorted the cardinals to choose a worthy successor.

Peter retired to a monastery; the cardinals elected Gaetani as his successor, who took the name of Boniface VIII. Peter tried to leave Italy across the Adriatic Sea, but Boniface's political enemies tried to use Peter as a figurehead in claiming that Boniface's election was invalid. Boniface, ever a political realist, captured Peter and sent him in honourable captivity with a few monks to Fumone, near Anagni. His own comment was, "I wanted nothing in this world but a cell, and a cell they have given me." He died on 19 May 1296 and was buried first at Ferentino and then (1317) at Aquila in the church of S. Maria di Colmagio, where he had been consecrated bishop and crowned as pope. This translation coincided with his canonization by Clement VI in 1313. This was not unconnected with the king of France, Philip the Fair, and his notorious hostility to Boniface VIII.

Some early Lives of Peter Celestine survive. These help us to understand a hermit and founder of a religious Congregation, utterly unworldly and politically naive, who was drawn into the tangle of ecclesiastical and civil politics through holding supreme office, which he had never desired. He also had the humility and the courage to abdicate from an office for which he was quite unsuitable, thereby creating a precedent for others to do the same. His feast from 1688 to 1969 was in the universal Calendar but is now for local veneration only. It is interesting to note that in medieval England only two hermits seem to have been promoted to bishoprics. One was St Cuthbert (20 Mar.), the other St Hugh of Lincoln (17 Nov.). Both were notably successful bishops.

See *AA.SS.*, May, 4, pp. 419-536, supplemented by the work of more recent Bollandists in *Anal. Boll.* 9 (1890), pp. 147-98; 10 (1891), pp. 386-92; 16 (1897), pp. 365-487; 18 (1899), pp. 34-42. See also the excellent study by H. K. Mann, *The Lives of the Popes in the Middle Ages*, 17, pp. 247-341, and more summary notice in *O.D.P.*, pp. 206-8. There is also a perceptive novel by J. Ayscough, *San Celestino* (1935). *Bibl.SS.*, 3, 1100-9.

St Ivo of Brittany (*c.* 1235-1303)

Also called Ivo Hélory and Yves of Kermartin, Ivo was a lawyer who became a parish priest in middle age. After his death and canonization he came to be invoked as patron saint of both lawyers and judges.

He was born at Kermartin, near Tréguier (Brittany), where his father was lord of the manor. He studied canon law and theology at Paris for ten years and civil law for three more at Orleans. On his return to Brittany in 1262 he was appointed "official," or judge of the church courts, in the diocese of Rennes, but soon the bishop of Tréguier reclaimed him for the same office. Here he won a reputation for complete impartiality and incorruptibility, with special care for poor litigants. He would also often try to persuade litigants to settle out of court, thus avoiding expensive or unnecessary lawsuits. This gave rise to a Latin verse, translated as "St

Ivo was a Breton, a lawyer not a robber; astonishing in people's eyes." Surviving contemporary sources also tell of his gift for reconciliation, of his willingness to plead for poor litigants in other courts, and of his visits to them in prison.

In 1284 he was ordained priest and given the parish of Tredrez. In 1287 he resigned his legal offices and devoted himself to his parish. After a few years he was promoted to Lovannec. Here he built a hospital and looked after the sick; he also took personal care of vagrants. Even more important was his care for the spiritual needs of his people. He would preach in three languages (Latin, French, and Breton), and he enjoyed a high reputation as an impartial arbitrator in all kinds of disputes. His personal life had been austere since student days, with fasting and abstinence for which he was well known; later he would give away his corn after the harvest to the poor. In 1303 he was taken ill in Lent and died on the eve of the Ascension after saying Mass and preaching with great effort and needing physical support. He was canonized in 1347.

See *AA.SS.*, May, 4, pp. 538-614, and A. de la Borderie, *Monuments originaux de l'Histoire de S. Yves* (1887); A. Masseron, *S. Yves d'après les témoins de sa vie* (1952); *Bibl.SS.*, 7, 998-1002.

Bd Peter Wright, *Martyr* (1651)

Born of a Catholic family at Slipton in Northamptonshire, Peter went into service when young with a Protestant family. Like many others in a similar situation he conformed but returned to the Catholic Church in Liège under Jesuit direction. He entered the Society of Jesus there and was sent after ordination on a mission to English troops in Flanders. He was so successful that Sir Henry Gage made him his constant companion until his death in the Civil War under Charles I in 1644. His next patron was the marquis of Winchester, in whose house he was arrested in February 1650. He was condemned as a priest, mainly on the evidence of an apostate. He was executed at Winchester, where his behaviour on the scaffold led to several conversions; his friends were allowed to take his body away for burial. He is a rare example of a martyr under the Commonwealth.

See *M.M.P.*, pp. 499-504, and H. Foley, *Records of the English Province of the S.J.*, pp. 506-66.

St Crispin of Viterbo (1678-1750)

Pietro Fioretti was born of a poor family of Viterbo (about fifty miles north of Rome) and was apprenticed to an uncle, from whom he learned his trade of making shoes. At the age of about twenty-five he joined the Capuchin community there, choosing Crispin as his name after the saintly patron of his trade. His novitiate was spent at Paranzana, where he seemed too small and delicate to survive the austere regime. These objections were overruled and he was professed. He dug the garden and acted as cook and sometimes infirmarian with some success.

He was moved to several friaries such as Rome, Albano, and Bracciano. When assigned to Orvieto, he was appointed questor, entrusted with begging alms from the faithful. Here he was so loved by the people that when someone else was appointed in his place, the housewives refused to receive him. The guardian of the starving community was obliged to re-appoint Crispin to the charge. Crispin's last years were spent in Rome. He was famous for prophecies, wise sayings, and the multiplication of food. He was also reputed to have taught the basics of the Faith to the mountain peasants in the course of his work. He died at the age of eighty-two in 1750, was beatified in 1806, and was canonized in 1982.

See *Bibl.SS.*, 4, 311-3; there are Lives in Italian by P. di Campello (1923) and in French by P. de Langogne (1901); also I. da Alatri, *Il prediletto di Maria* (1933).

R.M.
St Colluthi, martyr in Egypt (fourth century)
St Patrick, bishop and martyr in Bithynia (fourth century)
St Hadulph, bishop of Arras in Gaul (728)
Bd Humiliana, Franciscan tertiary at Florence, (1246)
Bd Augustine Novelli, Austin canon at Siena (1309)
BB John and Peter, of Granada (1397)
Bd John of St Dominic, Dominican and martyr in Japan (1619)— see "Martyrs of Japan," 5 Feb.
St Theophilus, Franciscan friar in Tuscany

ST DUNSTAN OF CANTERBURY (pp. 100-2)
Gold covered cup, on blue field, for his
patronage of goldsmiths.

20

ST BERNARDINO OF SIENA (1380-1444)

Bernardino, a famous and well-loved preacher, also revived the Franciscan Observants to whom he belonged and was a notable theologian and canonist. He preached the devotion to the Holy Name of Jesus, recalled by a plaque with IHS written on it.

He was born at Massa Marittima in the Republic of Siena, where his father was the governor. At the age of six he was orphaned and brought up by his aunt. He was educated in grammar and rhetoric and took his degree in law. During a severe outbreak of plague in 1400 he and some other companions took over the local hospital because most of the regular staff had died. When the epidemic was over, Bernardino nursed his bedridden aunt until her death.

He became a Franciscan at Siena in 1402 but spent his novitiate at nearby Colombaio. Ordained priest in 1404 at the age of only twenty-four, he then completed his studies at Fiesole in ascetical and mystical theology and in the writings of the great Doctors of the Church as well as the Franciscan writers such as St Francis (4 Oct.) and St Bonaventure (14 July). From the first he imbibed a lifelong devotion to poverty, from the second a conviction of the importance of study in the life of the friar. His small but impressive cell may still be seen at Fiesole.

In 1417 he began his preaching in Milan and Lombardy. Later he preached in many other parts of Italy (excluding the kingdom of Naples), travelling always on foot. Practice enabled him to strengthen his voice until it was resonant enough to carry not only in churches but also from open-air pulpits, some of which survive to this day. His preaching was based on the person of Christ, but he also gave due attention to the abuses current in his day: gambling, usury, witchcraft, superstition. Against these he preached the need for penance and voluntary poverty. Like other friars of his time he used anecdotes, mimicry, acting, and denunciation. He could move audiences to laughter and to tears; he accomplished conversions, the restoration of property, and the amendment of life. It may be that his very success led to the denunciations for superstition and false doctrine made against him in 1426, 1431, and as late as in 1438. These all foundered on his orthodoxy, upright intentions, and holiness of life.

From 1430 onward he wrote his theological works. Some of these survive in his own handwriting, most in Latin but some in Italian. His theological tracts cover the principal doctrinal and moral truths of Christianity as well as the main outlines of ascetical and mystical theology and treatises on the Blessed Virgin, which emphasize her role in the mediation of grace. During these years he was offered the bishoprics of Siena, Ferrara, and Urbino, but he refused them all.

From 1438 to 1442 he was vicar general of the Franciscan Observants. Both his holiness and his preaching helped to cause a massive tenfold increase in their numbers. Under him this reform moved away from eremitical isolation into a more complete involvement through teaching and preaching. He insisted on theology to combat the "holy rusticity" promulgated by some of the friars, setting up schools at Perugia and Monteripido, well realizing that ignorance was as dangerous as riches for the friars, especially when they acted as confessors and directors.

He resigned his charge in 1442 but resumed his preaching, travelling now on a donkey instead of on foot. By this time his repute was such that he is often reckoned the most influential religious of his time in Italy. In 1444 he preached a course of fifty sermons on consecutive days in his native town of Massa Marittima. He then set out for Naples, preaching on his way, but he died at Aquila on 20 May. Here he was buried, and miracles were reported very soon. In 1450 he was canonized by Pope Nicholas V. In 1474 his relics were translated by St James of the Marches (28 Nov.), one of his most faithful disciples, who with St John Capistrano (23 Oct.) and others continued his work in the Church in the next generation. Pope Pius II called him "an excellent master of theology and Doctor of Canon Law" and one who applied the pure teaching of scripture and the Fathers to the Church of his own time. The feast of the Holy Name, which he had propagated, was extended to the Universal Church by Pope Innocent XIII (1721-4). Important in his influence in clerical circles, especially within his own Order, his wider teaching of the need for moderation in the pursuit of wealth, and the need for the ethics of commerce to be in accord with justice and charity, has lost none of its relevance over the centuries.

His iconography is abundant. Fine portraits by Pietro di Giovanni and Benedetto Bonfigli survive in the art gallery of Siena and the National Gallery of Umbria respectively, while Sano di Pietro's painting of his open-air preaching can be seen in the chapter house of Siena cathedral. Other representations by Gozzoli, Giotto, and della Robbia are also notable, but perhaps the most striking painting of him is by El Greco (in the Museo del Greco in Toledo). This depicts him as much taller but quite as emaciated as the Tuscan portraits, with three baroque mitres at his feet to represent the three bishoprics he refused.

His works in nine volumes have been republished at Quarrachi (1950-65). His Lives are in *AA.SS.*, May, 5, pp. 257*-318*, supplemented by modern Bollandists in *Anal.Boll.* 21 (1902), pp. 53-80, and 53 (1935), pp. 308-58. Modern biographies by A. G. Ferrers Howell (1913), L. McLean (1946), and V. Elmer (1953), as well as I. Origo, *The World of San Bernardino* (1963). Italian biography by G. Cantini (1945) and numerous studies on his writings, mainly in Italian and published in Rome (1944-59); *Bibl.SS.*, 2, 1294-1321.

St Thalalaeus, *Martyr* (*c.* 284)

This martyr suffered at Aegae in Cilicia, in the persecution under the emperor Numerian. A doctor by profession, he is one of those invoked by the Greeks as the "moneyless" or disinterested saints. The more famous Cosmas and Damian (26 Sept.) are also in this category. Thalalaeus is said to have come from Lebanon and to have been the son of a Roman general. After escaping to an olive grove during the persecution, he was captured and conveyed to Aegae, where he was thrown into the sea. He is said to have swum ashore and then to have been beheaded. Other martyrs have been associated in his cult, either officials charged with his execution or else sympathetic bystanders.

H. Delehaye, *Origines du culte des Martyrs* (1933), p. 165, defends both the fact of his martyrdom and the cult; see also *AA.SS.*, May, 5, pp. 178*-93*, and *Bibl.SS.*, 12, 109-11.

St Austregisilus, *Bishop* (624)

This saint, also called Outril, was bishop of Bourges for the last twelve years of his life. He was the son of an impoverished nobleman of this town and served at the court of King Guntramnus at Chalon-sur-Saône. A serious accusation by another member of the court led to an ordeal by battle by which Outril could clear himself. Just before the fight his accuser was thrown from his horse and died. This confirmed Outril in his intention of serving God in the Church. He was ordained priest and appointed abbot of Saint-Nizier at Lyons. Reputed both for wisdom and healings, he was appointed bishop. Among his disciples was St Amandus, the future apostle of Flanders (6 Feb.), who as a young man lived in a cell near Bourges cathedral under this bishop's direction. Outril's recorded words on marriage were, "If I had a good wife, I would be afraid of losing her; if a bad one, I would be better with none." These words were spoken to the king when he decided to become a priest. He is patron saint of Bourges.

Life in *M.G.H., Scriptores Merov.*, 4, pp. 188-208; see also *Bibl.SS.*, 2, 630.

St Ethelbert of East Anglia (794)

Little is known of the life of this young king of East Anglia, but his veneration as the murdered representative of an ancient people looking for independence from the tyrannical Offa of Mercia took the form of a martyr cult. His life and death explain the anomaly of Hereford cathedral being dedicated to a prince of East Anglia, as cults at this time were very local. It seems likely, but not certain, that the first Life of him, written by Osbert of Clare in eleventh-century Westminster, depends on oral tradition at Hereford, supplementing the bare mention of his death in the *Anglo-Saxon Chronicle*.

As a young prince of only fifteen, he had the temerity to request in marriage the daughter of Offa, then the most powerful king in England, who had already subjected four smaller kingdoms to his own rule. Initially Offa seemed quite agreeable and invited him to Sutton Walls near Hereford to discuss the project. For some reason (possibly his wife Cynethryth), Offa changed his mind and Ethelbert was killed there. His body was dumped in the river Lugg, while his head (subsequently venerated at Westminster) was kicked around. Following a vision, the body was re-buried in a Hereford church. His cult flourished there and in East Anglia; centuries later he was depicted as one of the English martyrs by Circongnani at the English College, Rome. There are about twelve ancient church dedications to him in East Anglia. As with some other royal saints of Anglo-Saxon England such as Kenelm (17 July) and Edward (18 Mar.), a violent death, even at the hands of Christians, seems to have led to an extension of the concept of martyrdom. There are similar examples in Scandinavia. Gerald of Wales also wrote a Life of Ethelbert.

See M. R. James, "Two Lives of St Ethelbert, King and Martyr," in *E.H.R.* 32 (1917); E. M. Jancey, *St Ethelbert, Patron Saint of Hereford Cathedral* (1994); E. C. Brooks, *The Life of St Ethelbert, King and Martyr* (1995). See also R. M. Wilson, *The Lost Literature of Medieval England* (1952), pp. 106-8; A. T. Bannister, *The Cathedral Church of Hereford* (1925), pp. 109-14.

Bd Columba of Rieti (1467-1501)

This interesting Dominican tertiary received acclaim in her lifetime as a wise counsellor and healer from the city of Perugia, where she was given a public funeral, attended by most of the city.

She was born at Rieti of a family who lived by the cloth trade. When in her teens, she was reputed to have experienced visions and even a visit to Palestine while in a cataleptic trance. She cut off her hair to repel suitors and became a Dominican tertiary at nineteen. She visited a murderer in prison and brought him to repentance; shortly before his execution was due, he was reprieved. She was also credited with healings and the ability to live with very little food. Early one morning she left home for an unknown destination. She was arrested at Foligno through mistaken identity and her relatives were brought in. With them she next moved to Perugia, about sixty miles north of Rieti, then one of the most turbulent cities in Italy.

She received a warm welcome, lodged with fellow tertiaries, and was favoured by the wealthy and influential Baglioni family. Some Dominicans and Franciscans were, however, rather reserved about her subsistence on berries and ecstasies. One of them, subsequently her confessor and biographer, recommended caution and a waiting period of ten years before any acknowledgment of her as a saint. The townspeople, however, had no such reserve and provided her with a convent, where with a few companions she took vows in 1490. In an outbreak of plague the magistrates followed her advice of instituting penitential processions. Many sick people were healed by her touch, but she caught the plague herself, attributing her subsequent recovery to her favourite, St Catherine of Siena (30 Apr.). In the bitter quarrels inside the city she acted as peacemaker, and once she warned them correctly about imminent attacks from outside it, which were consequently repelled. When Pope Alexander VI visited Perugia, he was impressed, although she later gave warnings, which were never published. Lucrecia Borgia, however, was snubbed by Columba and became her bitter enemy. Subsequent persecution and accusations of magic were believed to be due to her influence. Columba endured much physical pain also, and her deathbed advice to the Perugia rulers was to practise charity and do justice to the poor. She died at the age of only thirty-four, on the feast of the Ascension in 1501. Her cult was confirmed in 1627.

Life by her confessor, Fr Sebastian degli Angeli, in *AA.SS.*, May, 5, pp. 319-98; see also *Bibl.SS.*, 4, 101-3. Modern biography by G. Amori (1932).

R.M.

St Aurea of Ostia, martyr (second century)

St Baudelius of Nîmes, martyr (third century)

St Hilary, bishop of Toulouse (*c.* 400)

St Anastasius, bishop of Brescia (seventh century)

St Theodore, bishop of Pavia (*c.* 774)

Bd Guido of Gherardesca, hermit (twelfth century)

St Protasius Chong, martyr in Korea (1839)—see "Martyrs of Korea," 20 Sept.

ST GODRIC OF FINCHALE
Geoffrey of Coldingham tells of wild animals stealing his
fruit and vegetables, and how he reproved them.

21

ST GODRIC OF FINCHALE (*c.* 1070–1170)

Peddler, pilgrim, sailor, captain, bailiff, then hermit for fifty years or more: Godric was all of these and a writer of music and verse as well. He is a rare example of a medieval man of humble origin of whom we have personal contemporary record.

He was born at Walpole (Norfolk) of an Anglo-Saxon peasant family. Instead of working on the land, he became a peddler, working in Lincolnshire (where his family had moved) from 1085 to 1089. He then made his first pilgrimage to Rome. Soon afterward he went to sea, trading in Scotland, Flanders and Denmark. He made good financially, buying a quarter share in one ship and a half share in another, of which he became the captain. In 1101 he made a pilgrimage to Jerusalem, presumably by boat. It is possible but unproved that he was the Godric, "an English pirate," who took Baldwin I to Jaffa in 1102. He was sufficiently affluent to return from the Holy Land via Compostela. Not long afterward, he went again to Rome and to Saint-Gilles in Provence. These journeys were followed by a third pilgrimage to Rome accompanied by his aged mother, who must have been nearly as tough as he was.

He now decided to renounce the world and sold all his goods. He made his first attempt at hermit life in a forest near Carlisle; then he joined another hermit at Wulsingham (near Durham) until the latter died in 1108. A few months later he made another penitential pilgrimage to Jerusalem. He visited the Holy Places, joined other hermits in the desert of St John the Baptist, and worked in the famous hospital of Jerusalem for several months. Again he seemed uncertain what to do, even resuming his old trade of peddler to occupy a deserted hermitage near Whitby. A year later he came to Durham, was sexton in the church of St Giles, and went to school with the choirboys at St Mary-le-Bow. Now over forty years old, he finally settled at Finchale on the river Wear, first at "St Godric's Garth" and then on the site now occupied by Finchale Priory. There the site of his chapel can still be seen, incorporated though it is in the present church.

Now began the deliberately chosen life of the traditional hermit. At first undirected, he lived on roots and berries; later he grew vegetables, milled barley for bread, and cut down trees for a wooden hut. Later a small stone church was built, joined to his cell by a wattle and daub cloister. Although his biographer, Reginald of Durham, stressed the element of devout pilgrimage in his seafaring life, Godric accused himself of fraud and impurity in his earlier years—sins for which he made expiation by his extremely austere penitential regime. Solitary and usually uneventful, his life was not without danger. Once he was nearly drowned when the

Wear overflowed its banks; another time (1138) he was beaten severely by Scottish soldiers, who believed he had hidden treasure. A great change came in his life when Roger, prior of Durham, gave him a rule of life, provided an indispensable token for visitors who wished to see him, and offered him confraternity with the Durham monks. But Cistercians also esteemed and visited him, such as St Aelred of Rievaulx (12 Jan.) and St Robert of Newminster (7 June).

A contemporary pen-portrait of Godric described him as "strong and agile, and in spite of his small stature his appearance was very venerable. . . . He had a broad forehead, sparkling grey eyes, and bushy eyebrows which almost met. His face was oval, his nose long, his beard thick." Another called him a good listener, always serious, and sympathetic to those in trouble. This last point has led some writers to emphasize that medieval hermits came to be accepted as village counsellors. This often became their lot, but we must realize that it was not the purpose of their life. Eremitical life is spent in great solitude and is made up of long prayers of the liturgy alternating with silent contemplation of God and the divine mysteries, the whole carried on in penitential austerity. This hidden life at Finchale was indeed modified by visits, but the incidents connected with them must not blind us to the unchanging severity of the régime. Diabolical manifestations (or poltergeist phenomena) were not lacking, nor was acute physical suffering, especially in his last years. In all he spent nearly sixty years at Finchale. Near the end of these he encouraged messengers from St Thomas of Canterbury (29 Dec.) and even received a letter of encouragement from Pope Alexander III, which survives.

A subsidiary activity that contributed to his fame was his writing of verse (the first in Middle English) set to music, close in style to Gregorian chant. There is one hymn to the Blessed Virgin, another to St Nicholas, and a third, sung by his sister Burchwen, who stayed a little while at Finchale before becoming a Sister in the hospital at Durham. These are all short and simple and have been transcribed and recorded in our own day. They survive in a fourteenth-century manuscript in the British Library.

After Godric's last, long illness, in which he became bedridden and was nursed by Durham monks, he died on 21 May 1170. Finchale became a cell of Durham and his tomb a place of pilgrimage. Records of the miracles claimed there include an unusually high proportion of women healed. This may be explained by the Durham monks making St Cuthbert's tomb inaccessible to women because of his supposed (but untrue) aversion to them. The Finchale shrine grew and prospered, but Godric, like many early saints, was never formally canonized. His cult at Durham and Finchale as well as among the Cistercians was well established. He deserves to be better known, and three contemporary writers provide varied but substantially accurate information about him.

Life by Reginald of Durham (ed. J. Stevenson, Surtees Society, 1838) and a shorter one by Geoffrey of Coldingham in *AA.SS.*, May, 5, pp. 70-85; William of Newburgh, *Historia* (R.S.), 1, pp. 149-50. See also V. M. Tudor in *Benedict's Disciples* (ed. D. H. Farmer, 2d ed. 1995), pp. 195-211, and F. Rice, *The Hermit of Finchale* (1994). Record of his songs in "Medieval English Lyrics" by ARGO, RE 443 (1965).

St Paternus of Vannes (Fifth Century)

The identity and feast day of this saint are uncertain. The new Roman Martyrology for today identifies him as bishop of Vannes (Brittany), who was consecrated bishop of this town by St Perpetuus of Tours. Paternus of Avranches (usual feast 15 or 16 Apr.) must not be confused with Paternus of Vannes nor with a Welsh saint of the same name. The consecration of today's Paternus at a council of bishops of the province of Tours in 467 is a welcome datum in a period of very little documentation. It seems that he was the first bishop of this Gallo-Roman city before it was affected by substantial immigrations from Britain and Ireland. Paternus founded a monastery at Vannes and possibly died in exile, but this last point is not certain. The Viking raids led, as in other examples, to the movement of his relics. In 933 they were translated to Dools and in 946 to Issoudun; later (in 1000) they were taken to a safer place in the same town. There were recognitions of the relics in 1186, 1223, and 1513, but they were destroyed in 1793. However some fragments of his skull are still preserved in the abbey of St Paternus at Vannes. This ancient cult of a saint of Brittany, dating back further than many such, was confirmed by Pope Paul VI in 1964.

See *Bibl.SS.*, 10, 385-90, and for the two saints of this name, P. Grosjean in *Anal.Boll.* 67 (1949), pp. 384-400.

St Theobald of Vienne, *Bishop* (1001)

Theobald (Thibaut) was born at Toluon (Isère). He was orphaned at an early age and decided to become a priest. He was consecrated bishop in 957. His name appears in official documents from 970 to 999. He was a proponent of the reform movement in the Church of his time, in which he was particularly associated with St Odilo of Cluny (1 Jan.). Theobald's legislation concerned forbidding clerical liaisons with women, insisting on the need to take viaticum to the sick and to replace the sacred species every seven days. After his death on 21 May 1001 his relics were translated to Saint Cluf. His cult was formally approved in 1903.

AA.SS., May, 5, pp. 47-8; *Bibl.SS.*, 12, 200-1.

Bd Charles de Mazenod, *Bishop and Founder* (1782-1861)

Charles de Mazenod was both bishop of Marseilles and founder of the Oblates of Mary Immaculate. This began as a diocesan Congregation, but it soon developed into an important power for good in the then missionary world, being especially successful in Canada and the United States of America.

Such a notable outcome must have seemed extremely unlikely to a contemporary observer. Charles was born at Aix-en-Provence not many years before the French Revolution; he died before the First Vatican Council. His life was thus passed in a period of crisis for the Church. Charles was a man of his time, not of ours. Like many loyal Catholics of his time, he was in favour of the papacy retaining temporal power, but his Ultramontanism was of a moderate kind. As a child he and his family had gone into exile in Italy during the worst excesses of the French Revolution; as a young man he had heard of Napoleon's imprisonment of Pope Pius VII at Savona and Fontainebleau.

In spite of the many difficulties, he entered the seminary in 1808 and was ordained in 1811. Inspired by missionary ideals, in 1816 he founded the Missionary Society of Provence, which in 1826 was renamed the Congregation of Oblate Missionaries of Mary Immaculate, for the attainment of better standards among the clergy and consequently among the laity. Not a separate Order, the Oblates remained diocesan priests in the manner of the later Oblates of St Charles (Borromeo), founded by Cardinal Manning in England. Meanwhile Mazenod's zeal was noticed and approved. His uncle was bishop of Marseilles, and Charles was appointed his coadjutor and later became his successor in 1837.

His external appearance and his nepotistic appointment may have recalled the lifestyle of bishops of the *ancien régime*, but his zeal and efficiency in tackling the problems of a large port, whose population rapidly doubled, need to be stressed. He set up new parishes and built new churches for the expanding population, some of it immigrant. He reformed the administration of the diocese but also took part in controversies of national importance. Meanwhile his Oblates prospered exceedingly. From 1826 they had extended their scope to the foreign missions. They were active in South Africa, Ceylon, and South America, not to mention European countries such as England. Initially they worked through institutions such as seminaries, which they directed from early times; but later, especially in North America, they took on the care of parishes as well. Some idea of their importance in Canada and the U.S.A. can be grasped from the fact that nearly all the bishops of western Canada were of their Institute, while in the U.S.A. the province founded in the mid-nineteenth century developed into four regional provinces, with a fifth one for French-speaking immigrants. Charles died on 21 May 1861 and was beatified in 1975.

See *N.C.E.*, 9, pp. 522-3; *Bibl.SS.*, *9, 251-5*. Lives by R. Boudens (1951) and J. Leflon (3 vols., 1957-65).

R.M.
St Timothy, deacon and martyr (second-third century)
St Polyeuctus, martyr (second-third century)
The Pentecost Martyrs of Alexandria (357-8)
St Hospicius, hermit of Nice (*c.* 580)
St Mancius, martyr of Portugal (sixth century)

22

St Quiteria, *Martyr* (Fifth Century)

Many churches in south-western France and northern Spain are dedicated to this saint. This is one sign among others of the extent to which these two areas formed one cultural whole in the early Christian centuries. Several apostles (such as Saturninus of Toulouse, 29 Nov.) worked on both sides of the Pyrenees, and it must not be forgotten that some centuries later most of southern Spain was ruled by Moors; this tended to increase these trans-Pyrenean links. The centre of the cult of Quiteria is her fine ancient tomb at Aire in Gascony (Landes), situated on the river Adour about halfway between Auch (capital of Gers) and the Atlantic coast at Bayonne. It is also on a north-south road across the Pyrenees.

Her name appears in the Roman Martyrology, while ancient dedications strengthen the evidence for her cult. Gregory of Tours also mentioned her. She is venerated as a virgin and martyr, but details about her life are legendary. She was supposed to be the daughter of a prince of Galicia, who fled from home because her father wished her to marry and abjure Christianity. This she refused to do and took refuge at Aire. Emissaries of her father pursued her and she was beheaded. Because she is invoked popularly against the bite of mad dogs, she is portrayed with a dog on a lead. There is also a cult of Quiteria in Portugal, which has a different legend to explain her.

Ancient Lives are printed by A. Desert in *Revue de Gascogne* 48 (1907), pp. 463-9; see also A. Breuils, *Les légendes de Sainte Quitterie* (1892); *Bibl.SS.*, 10, 1334-5; Gregory of Tours, *De gloria confessorum*, in *M.G.H., Scriptores rer. merov.*, 2, p. 747.

St Julia, *Martyr* (Sixth Century)

Patron saint of Corsica and of Leghorn, which claim her relics, she was put to death by Saracen invaders at or near Cape Corso, the most northerly tip of this island and almost opposite Leghorn. Her seventh-century legend, stimulated no doubt by the wish to know more details about one who was "just a name," made her a Carthaginian lady sold as a slave to one Eusebius, a pagan merchant of Syria. He went ashore at Cape Corso to a pagan festival, while she stayed behind. The ruler of the island regarded her absence as an insult, but failed to convince Eusebius that four other female slaves would be a fair exchange. The governor, when Eusebius was drunk, did his best to induce her to sacrifice. But she steadfastly refused and was ultimately crucified after being beaten and having her hair torn out. Her relics were translated to Brescia in 763 and are now in the seminary there. Details of the legend with anachronistic elements do not inspire confidence, but the presence of this saint in the so-called martyrology of Jerome affords a strong presumption for her historical existence. Interesting twelfth-century sculptures survive in the Christian Museum at Brescia. These depict her both holding a cross and being crucified.

AA.SS., May, 5, pp. 168–72; *Bibl.SS.*, 6, 1164–8.

St John of Parma, *Abbot* (990)

John was born at Parma in northern Italy (Emilia Romagna) and became a canon of the cathedral. He was a zealous pilgrim, reputed to have been six times to Jerusalem and to have become a monk there. Later he was abbot of St John's in Parma from 983 to 990. Under his rule it adopted the Cluniac observance of St Majolus of Cluny (11 May), whose contemporary and helper he was. His life reminds us of the expansion of Cluny outside France in the tenth century. Patron of the city of Parma at least since 1534, he was venerated in the Benedictine Congregation of St Justina of Padua, to which his abbey belonged in the sixteenth century, following translation of his relics in 1588 and 1661. His feast is celebrated on 22 May in the diocese and the abbey of Parma.

Bibl.SS., 8, 864–6.

St Humility of Florence (1226–1310)

In turn wife, mother, nun, recluse, and foundress of the Vallombrosian nuns, her life was extraordinary for its variety and achievements. She was born of a noble and wealthy family and was named Rosana. At the age of fifteen her family obliged her to marry a local nobleman called Ugoletto. They had two sons, but both died in infancy. They were an ill-matched couple, and for nine years Rosana, earnest and devout, tried hard to amend her husband's frivolity and infidelity. His serious, almost fatal, illness led him to accept a life of continence, as she desired. They then both joined the monastery of St Perpetua, outside Faenza, near Bologna—she as a choir nun and he as a lay brother.

Now twenty-four and called Humility, she sought further solitude and austerity, first in a Poor Clare convent and then in a cell attached to the church of St Apollinaris, where she was enclosed by the abbot of St Crispin, a Vallombrosian monastery. She subsisted on bread, water, and vegetables. Meanwhile her husband had moved to St Crispin's, where he died three years later without (it would seem) their meeting again.

After she had been a recluse for twelve years, the Vallombrosian abbot general and the local bishop persuaded her to emerge and to found a convent for women. This was at Malta, outside the walls of Faenza, where she became the first abbess of Santa Maria Novella alla Malta. She then founded a second nunnery of St John at Florence, of which she also became abbess, dying there at the age of eighty on 22 May 1310. Her incorrupt body was exhumed in 1311 and translated to Varlungo, near Florence, in 1534. She is reputed to have composed some treatises, one of them on the angels, with whom she claimed to live in constant communion. Her immemorial cult was confirmed in 1721, and she was nominated patron of Faenza in 1942.

See *AA.SS.*, May, 5, pp. 203-22; Life by M. E. Pietromarchi (1935); works edited by T. Sala (1884); *Bibl.SS.*, 12, 818-22. See also A. Simonetti, *I Sermoni di Umiltà da Faenza. Studio e edizione* (*Biblioteca di Medioevo latino*, 14, 1995). There is a fine picture of her with twelve scenes from her life in the Uffizi Gallery, Florence (fourteenth century). In 1966, the seventh centenary of the foundation of Faenza monastery, commemorative studies were published.

St Hemming of Abo, *Bishop* (1290-66)

Hemming was born at Balinge (north of Uppsala, Sweden), and he studied at both Uppsala and Paris. His main subjects were theology and canon law. In 1329 he became a canon of Abo cathedral (in modern Helsinki, Finland), and in 1338 he was elected bishop. Although a zealous diocesan bishop, he had to spend much time travelling. He had border disputes with Uppsala (from which some parts of Finland had been evangelized), and in 1347 he accompanied St Bridget of Sweden (23 July) to France. Hemming supported her twin aims of ending war between England and France and of persuading Pope Clement VI to return from Avignon to Rome.

Acts survive of Hemming's diocesan synod of 1352. Its decrees include the celebration of feasts of Our Lady, of the Holy Cross, of the apostles and St Michael and of SS Laurence, Henry, Eric, and Olaf (the last two are the kings and patrons of Sweden and Norway). There were also instructions about the custody of the Blessed Sacrament and about the administration of church property, and it was mandated that no fees were to be taken from the poor for dispensations or for funerals.

Hemming died on 22 May 1266 and was buried at Abo cathedral. Miracles were recorded at his tomb by the canons. In 1514 the Holy See authorized the translation of his relics and their enshrinement in a reliquary. A fine altar frontal survives from the church of Urdiala (Finland), which depicts Hemming with St Bridget. An angel holds the mitre over Hemming's head, which is believed to denote that he was especially chosen by God for his office.

Bibl.SS., 7, 584-6.

St Rita of Cascia (1377-1457)

A medieval widow who became an Augustinian nun and mystic is now a popular saint, especially in Italy, where she is especially invoked (not unlike St Jude, 27 Oct.) as patron of desperate cases.

She was born into a peasant family in Roccaporena (Umbria), an unexpectedly late arrival and so quite possibly overprotected. Although she wished to be a nun, her parents decided that she should marry but made an unfortunate choice. Her husband proved to be notoriously violent and was repeatedly unfaithful to her.

She endured much from him for eighteen years, and their two sons were deeply influenced by him. One day he was brought home dead from multiple wounds sustained in a vendetta. The sons wished to avenge him, but they died too soon to achieve this. With no more family ties and (according to one account) her husband's late repentance to mitigate her sorrows, she was now free to pursue her original choice of becoming a nun. This she achieved in about 1407, at S. Maria Maddalena at Cascia. Nevertheless, in spite of innumerable precedents of widows becoming nuns, the Augustinian authorities three times refused to give her the habit because she was not a virgin. Only in 1413 did they relent.

As a nun, Rita excelled both in obedience and in mortification. This sometimes took unexpected turns, and the extraordinary elements in her earlier life were more than matched by her religious exploits. By constant meditation on the passion of Christ for the sake of sinners' repentance, she experienced a wound in her forehead, as if made by a crown of thorns, which lasted for some years and would not heal. There seems to be no record of other stigmata, but there is evidence—fortunately—of her devoted care of sick nuns and her counselling skills for lay visitors to the convent. The wound in her forehead healed when she successfully applied for permission to visit Rome for the Jubilee of 1450.

Rita died of tuberculosis on 22 May 1457; her incorrupt body was translated to an ornate tomb, which survives to this day. The local bishop's written approbation of her cult also survives, as does an authentic portrait. Early records of miraculous cures led to her beatification in 1626 and her canonization in 1900.

In 1946 a new basilica was built at Cascia with a hospital, school, and orphanage. Her cult flourishes today in Latin countries, the United States, and Ireland. In modern Italy she is widely invoked as a patron of difficult cases, particularly those connected with marriage. Roses are blessed on her feast in memory of her request for roses and figs on her death-bed, which were found out of season in her old garden. Bees which reappear on and after her feast and a vine reputed to survive from her lifetime are in evidence at Cascia today. All in all, the life of this saint, recorded well after her death, presents some unsolved problems, as does the surprisingly persistent cult in our own day.

AA.SS., May, 5, pp. 224-34; Life by G. Bruni (1941); others in English by R. Connolly (1903) and M. J. Corcoran (1919); see also *N.C.E.*, 12, 541, and *Bibl.SS.*, 11, 212-27; *O.D.S.*, pp. 417-8; L. Scaraffia, *La sancta degli impossibili. Vicende e significati della devozione a S. Rita* (1990).

Bd John Forest, *Martyr* (1538)

At the age of seventeen John Forest joined the Franciscan Observants, recently renewed by St Bernardino of Siena (20 May), at their community in Greenwich. After nine years he was sent to Oxford to study theology. Although comparatively young, he was greatly esteemed for his learning and wisdom. When the court was in residence at Greenwich, he acted as confessor to Queen Catherine of Aragon. His Order opposed the divorce plans of Henry VIII, who threatened to suppress it.

This threat was executed after the papal decision that the marriage was valid and could not be annulled (1534).

John seems to have spent the next four years in captivity of varying strictness. He was brought to trial for allegedly denouncing the Oath of Supremacy to Lord Mordaunt and others. He initially gave consent to some articles, but when they were presented in writing, he repudiated them as equivalent to apostasy. Then condemned to the stake, he was again offered pardon if he would recant. This he clearly refused, declaring that burning, hanging, and dismemberment would not make him abandon his profession of loyalty and obedience to the Bishop of Rome. He was then burned at the stake and with him a statue of the Welsh saint Derfel Gadarn (5 Apr.). This, it had been predicted, would one day "set a Forest on fire."

See J. H. Pollen, *Lives of the English Martyrs* (ed. B. Camm), 1 (1904), pp. 276-326; Fr Thaddaeus, *Life of Bd. John Forest.*

R.M.

SS Castus and Aemilius, martyrs (*c.* 250)

St Basiliscus, bishop and martyr (fourth century)

SS Agrippa and Companions, martyrs (fourth century)

St Ausonius, bishop of Angouleme (fourth-fifth century)

St Lupus, bishop of Limoges, (637)

St Atto, Vallombrosian monk and bishop (1153)

St Michael Ho Dinh Hy (1857) and St Laurence Ngon (1862), Martyrs in Tonkin—
    see "Martyrs of Vietnam (Tonkin)," 2 Feb.

23

SS Montanus, Lucius, and Companions, *Martyrs* (259)

These Carthaginian martyrs all suffered in the same persecution under Valerian as St Cyprian (16 Sept.). Their contemporary Acts are generally accepted as genuine and inspire confidence. They provide a direct link with those who suffered for Christ in third-century Africa.

The procurator Solon had been the object of an insurrection in Carthage; but instead of searching out the guilty, he arrested eight Christians, most of them Cyprian's clergy and all of them his disciples. Immediately after their arrest the governor's servants told them that they would be burned alive. The future martyrs prayed efficaciously to be delivered from this punishment, and instead they were consigned to "a very dark and incommodious prison . . . but we were not dismayed at the filthiness of the place, for our faith and joy in the Holy Spirit reconciled us to our sufferings, though these were such as cannot readily be described." Meanwhile Renus had a vision of several prisoners going out, each preceded by a lighted lamp. These were the future martyrs, following the lamp representing Christ.

The next day the governor sent for them to be examined. "It was a triumph for us to be conducted as a spectacle through the market-place and the streets with our chains rattling." The governor interrogated them; their answers were modest and firm. They were sent back to prison, but without any food or drink for several days. Other visions followed. At length the priest Lucian contrived to have food brought them by a subdeacon and a catechumen. This "never-failing food" might well have been the Eucharist. Equally striking is the claim to share the spirit of charity: "We have all one and the same spirit which unites and cements us together in prayer, in mutual intercourse and in all our actions. These are the bonds of affection which put the devil to flight, which are most pleasing to God . . . these are the ties which link hearts together and which make men the children of God. . . . It is impossible for us to attain the inheritance of heavenly glory unless we keep that union and peace with our brothers which our heavenly Father has established among us." These are the words of the martyrs; the rest of the story was written by other people present, as recommended by Flavian, one of these martyrs.

After being imprisoned for several months in harsh conditions and suffering extreme hunger and thirst, they made a glorious confession. Each walked to the place of execution and exhorted the people. One of them, named Montanus, denounced the pride and obstinacy of heretics, telling them that they could recognize the true Church by the multitude of its martyrs. He exhorted those who had lapsed to complete their penance and exhorted the group of virgins to preserve their purity and honour the bishops. He then prayed aloud that Flavian, who had been reprieved at the people's request, might follow them on the third day. He cut his blindfold handkerchief into two, leaving half for Flavian and asking that they might share the same tomb. He was then executed by the sword. Flavian followed him a few days later, after consoling his mother and suffering the rack. He told his fellow-Christians that St Cyprian had told him in a vision that "the body feels no pain when the soul gives herself entirely to God." At his place of execution he prayed for the peace and unity of the Church and the unity of the brethren. Binding his eyes with the halved handkerchief of Montanus and kneeling in prayer, he received the last stroke. These martyrs were formerly venerated on 24 February.

See *A.C.M.*, pp. xxiv-vi, 214-39. Also H. Delehaye, *Les Passions des Martyrs...* (1921), pp. 72-8. These Acts in some ways resemble those of SS Perpetua and Felicitas (possibly their model); it has also been suggested that they are the work of Cyprian's biographer, Pontius. *Bibl.SS.*, 9, 572-4.

St Desiderius of Vienne, *Bishop and Martyr* (607)

Nothing is known about the early life of Desiderius (or Didier). He lived in the turbulent times of the Merovingians and he enforced clerical discipline, suppressed simony, and denounced the immorality of the court. He thus incurred the enmity of the notorious Queen Brunhild, who induced a council to exile Didier on false charges. He returned after four years. Desiderius is also known as one of several bishops to whom St Gregory the Great (3 Sept.) sent letters to safeguard the journey of St Augustine (26 May) and his companions to England. Attempts were made to discredit Didier in the eyes of the pope because of his taste for classical literature, but Gregory completely exonerated him. Desiderius for his part denounced Theodoric, king of Burgundy, for his scandalous life. On his way home the bishop was attacked by three hired men, who killed him at the place now called Saint-Didier-sur-Chalaronne.

The account of his death can be found in *Anal.Boll.* 9 (1890), pp. 250-62, and in *M.G.H.*, *Scriptores rer. merov.*, 3, pp. 620-48.

St Leontius of Rostov, *Bishop and Martyr* (1077)

A Greek from Constantinople, Leontius became a monk at the famous Monastery of the Caves in Kiev (Ukraine). He was the first monk of this house to become a bishop when he was appointed to Rostov (Yaroslavsk, north-east of Moscow) in 1051. Although persecuted by the pagans, he was nonetheless their successful apostle. Reputed to have had a gift of miracles, he did not escape death at their hands; however, this was from the ill-treatment he received rather than by formal sentence of death. Two laymen, SS Boris and Gleb (d. 1015; 24 July), seem to be the first martyrs of Russia to be venerated as such, but Leontius is called the "hieromartyr," that is, the first martyr who was also a priest. His incorrupt body was translated to the crypt in Rostov cathedral; his cult was approved in 1190 and 1547.

Bibl.SS., 7, 319-20.

St Euphrosyne of Polotsk (1173)

This saint has a rare distinction, that of being the only single woman saint to be venerated by the Russians; the other eleven holy women venerated were all married. She was the daughter of Prince Svyatoslav of Polotsk (Byelorussia). She became a nun when very young and became a solitary at the church of the Holy Wisdom. Her staple occupation was copying books, which she sold for subsistence and almsgiving. She also travelled, both to found a nunnery at Seltse and to visit Byzantium, where she was a given an icon by the patriarch Michael III. Later she ventured even farther afield on pilgrimage to the Holy Land, where she was received by the king and the Latin patriarch of Jerusalem, Amaury. Euphrosyne visited the monastery of Mar Saba, between Jerusalem and the Dead Sea. She died in Jerusalem and her body was brought back to Kiev for burial. She is venerated by Ruthenians and Lithuanians as well as by Russians.

St William of Rochester (1201)

Also called William of Perth from his birthplace, this Scotsman was a baker by trade. He was converted as a young man, heard Mass daily, and gave alms generously. One day he found a baby left at the church door. He paid for the child to be nursed and later adopted him as his son, calling him David the foundling. With the approval of his parish priest, William left on pilgrimage to the Holy Land, taking with him his adopted son. They reached Rochester and spent a few days there before leaving for Canterbury. For unknown reasons David led William into a wood, where he treacherously killed him and fled. The corpse was discovered by a madwoman who used to wander about half-naked. She made a garland of honeysuckle and put it on William's head. A few days later she returned and put the garland on her own head, which cured her of her madness immediately. When she told the people of Rochester what had happened, they brought the murdered pilgrim into Rochester and gave him honourable burial. His tomb was visited by pilgrims, including royalty; in 1256 Lawrence of St Martin, bishop of Rochester, went to Rome to petition for his canonization. This does not seem to have been achieved, but the unofficial cult continued and was the occasion of substantial offerings being made at the shrine. In recent times a hospital (on the site of his death), a church, a road, and a school have all been named after William.

See *N.L.A.* (ed. M. Gorlach, 1994), p. 176; W. St John Hope, *The Cathedral and Monastery of St Andrew at Rochester* (1900); T. E. Bridgett in *The Month* (1891), pp. 501-8.

St John Baptist Rossi (1698-1764)

Born at Voltaggio near Genoa, one of four children of respectable parents, he was educated from the age of ten by a Genoese nobleman and his wife. Through Capuchin relatives, he was invited to Rome and entered the Roman College at the age of only thirteen. He studied too hard, was indiscreet in mortification, and suffered a breakdown due to epilepsy.

He recovered well and was ordained priest in 1721. He loved to visit hospitals and a night refuge for the destitute founded by Pope Celestine III. Here he worked for forty years, consoling and teaching the inmates. He also frequently visited the hospital of the Trinità dei Pellegrini. In addition, he helped cattle drovers who sold their animals in the market at the Roman Forum. Homeless women and girls, beggars, and prostitutes were cared for in his refuge of St Aloysius.

For some years he was too diffident to hear confessions but discovered his gift for direction after a convalescence. In 1731 he became assistant priest at St Mary in Cosmedin. Penitents of all classes flocked to his confessional to such an extent that he was dispensed in part from the obligation of saying the divine office. He succeeded his cousin as a canon but devoted the salary to charity and to providing an organ and an organist for his church. He himself lived in an attic in extreme poverty. Pope Benedict XIV entrusted him with courses of instruction for prison officials and other civil servants, including the public hangman. He enjoyed considerable renown as a preacher, notably in houses of religious.

He suffered a stroke in 1763 and died the next year at the age of sixty-six. He left so little money that the Trinità paid for his funeral. But this was led by an archbishop followed by 260 priests and accompanied by the papal choir. Supernatural gifts and miraculous cures followed his death. His cause was begun in 1781, and he was canonized in 1881. On 23 May 1965 his relics were translated into the new Roman parish church dedicated to him.

Lives in French by F. Cormier (1901) and in Italian by E. Mougeot (1881), trans. into English by Lady Herbert (1906); *Bibl.SS.*, 6, 959-63; *N.C.E.*, 12, pp. 680-1; M. Escobar, *Le dimote romane dei santi* (1964), pp. 256-311.

R.M.
St Ephebus, bishop in Campania (fourth century)
St Eutychius, abbot (487)
St Honoratus, abbot at Subiaco (late sixth century)
St Syagrius, bishop of Nice (787)
St Michael, bishop in Phrygia (826)

24

SS Donatian and Rogatian, *Martyrs* (*c.* 304)

These two martyrs of Nantes (Brittany), certainly datable to the persecutions in Roman times, are still venerated there under their popular name of "Les Enfants Nantais." Some of their reputed relics are kept there in a church dedicated to these two brothers.

Their story is told in their Acts in this way: The younger brother, Donatian, belonged to a Romano-Gallic family of some standing and was a Christian. He was charged with professing Christianity and with impeding others, notably his brother, from worshipping the gods. He made a bold confession and was imprisoned. Rogatian, who desired baptism and was constant in his belief, soon joined him in captivity. Owing to the absence of the bishop, he had not been baptized. The brothers spent a night together in prayer before being brought before the prefect. He condemned them to be racked and eventually killed by the sword. Rogatian is regarded as a classic example of "baptism by blood." Their feast occurs in ancient martyrologies.

AA.SS., May, 5, pp. 279-81, completed by *Anal.Boll.* 8 (1889), pp. 163-4. For a modern treatment, see J. B. Russon, *La passion des Enfants nantais* (1945).

St Vincent of Lérins (*c.* 450)

Vincent was a monk in the island monastery of Lérins near Cannes, now called Saint-Honorat. He was the author of an important theological work, the *Commonitorium,* or reminder—a letter of instruction, which has proved controversial. Its main element is a series of rules for distinguishing Christian truth from falsehood but it also deals with the relation between scripture and tradition and how true tradition (in the theological sense) can be discerned. This is necessary for interpreting the Bible, whose variable interpretation requires a standard outside it, that is, the living tradition of the Church.

Vincent called himself a stranger and a pilgrim who had fled from the service of this world and its vanities to enter the service of Christ in the seclusion of the cloister. His book of forty-two chapters, abridged because the second part was lost and the first rewritten, provides the famous criterion in the recognition of Christian doctrine that it has been held "everywhere, always, and by all." It must be admitted, however, that the criterion is not easy to apply in practice and seems to need modification in view of Newman's treatise on the development of doctrine. It is interesting to note that it does not appear to have been quoted either in the

teaching of Vatican II or in the new *Catechism of the Catholic Church*. The importance given to it by Catholic-reformation theologians such as St Robert Bellarmine
(17 Sept.) does not seem to have been maintained at the present time. There is
reason to suppose that Vincent, in reacting against some elements of Augustine's
later works, adopted semi-Pelagian positions when there was still latitude to do so.
Some passages of the *Commonitorium* are remarkably similar to the clauses of the
Athanasian Creed. This has led some writers to ascribe this Creed to Vincent.

Gennadius, *De viris illustribus*, is the principal source, reproduced in *AA.SS.*, May, 5, pp.
284-96; Eng. trans. of the *Commonitorium* by T. H. Bindley (*Early Church Classics*, 1914);
see also J. Madoz on the concept of tradition in St Vincent in *Analecta Gregoriana* (1933).
N.C.E., 14, pp. 681-2; *Bibl.SS.*, 12, 1142-6.

St Simeon Stylites the Younger (521-92)

A number of Stylite saints' lives have been recorded in the Eastern Church but
none in the West. The most famous was Simeon Stylites the Elder (390-459; 1
Sept.), probably the first of all. He was followed by Daniel the Stylite (409-93; 11
Dec.), who inherited Simeon's cloak as well as his way of life. Today's Simeon was
born about 517 at Antioch and lived on top of a pillar for some forty-five years in or
near Antioch, like his namesake.

The exaggerations of some Eastern hagiographers, especially in describing austerities, make it very difficult to accept all their statements at face value. Nevertheless, it seems just credible that this Simeon chose the extraordinary condition of
hermit life on a pillar from the age of twenty; that he was ordained priest at the age
of thirty-three (the bishop climbing a ladder to lay hands on him); that crowds
came to seek his advice or to be cured by a miracle; that he sometimes knew the
secrets of hearts, prophesied, and gathered disciples around him.

Writings attributed to him include one urging the emperor to punish the Sa-
maritans for attacking their Christian neighbours and another (claimed by St John
Damascene, 14 Dec.) in favour of the veneration of images. Simeon's diet was fruit
and vegetables; like other practitioners of this extraordinary way of life, he moved
from one pillar to another and was apparently approved of by the bishops. Contemporaries questioned the way of life of the Stylites but recognized their power
for good—their personal humility and charity, their skill in persuading others to
become Christians, their occasional interventions for good in the political world.
Icons of the Stylites had a household use in assuring visitors of the protection and
patronage of a "holy man of antiquity." However curious or even bizarre their way
of life seems, the Stylites gave permanent witness to the need for prayer and
penance in an age of licentiousness and luxury. Their arresting and permanent
régime made people stop and think, and helped at least some to amendment of life.

H.S.S.C., 3, pp. 290-1 adopts a more traditional account of the detailed chronology of this
saint's life than the above account, including Simeon's choice of the Stylite life from the age
of seven. For a more general conspectus, see H. Delehaye, *Les Saints Stylites* (1923),
especially pp. 238-71. *Bibl.SS.*, 11, 1141-57. *AA.SS.*, May, 5, pp. 300-90.

St David of Scotland (1085-1153)

The youngest son of King Malcolm Canmore and his wife, St Margaret of Scotland (16 Nov.), David lost both his parents when aged only eight, but his subsequent life showed him a worthy son of them both. He was educated for some years at the court of Henry I of England, who had married David's sister Matilda. On the accession to the throne of Scotland of his brother Alexander in 1107, David became prince of Cumbria (including Lothian) and married another Matilda, this one the daughter of Waldef, or Waltheof, the Anglo-Saxon patriot earl of Northampton and Huntingdon. David thus became an English earl. He became king of Scotland in 1124.

England's northern border was not yet fixed, but he was regarded in England as a basically friendly neighbour. During the civil war in Stephen's turbulent reign (1135-53), David took the side of the empress Matilda against him. He captured several border castles in 1135. The following year he claimed the earldom of Northumberland and invaded the north of England in 1138. He was defeated in the Battle of the Standard (at Northallerton) in this year but obtained Northumberland and Cumbria as the price of peace. He then devoted himself with renewed commitment to the good of his kingdom.

His achievements were notable in every way. He instituted a feudal system of land tenure, and he introduced Anglo-Norman colonists and judicial systems. He fostered the growth of towns such as Edinburgh, Berwick, and Perth, where trade flourished. He reorganized the church in Scotland through closer contact with Rome, partly through papal legates. He founded five bishoprics, including Aberdeen, and numerous monasteries and churches. These comprised both Cistercian and Augustinian houses (at Melrose, Kinloss, Holyrood, and elsewhere). He also increased the endowments for the Benedictines of Dunfermline, founded by his mother and destined to be his burial place and the centre of his cult.

The eloquent panegyric of him by St Aelred of Rievaulx (12 Jan.), who had been master of his household before becoming a monk and was a devoted friend after doing so, survives. This eulogy tells of his reluctance to become king, his justice in administration, and his accessibility to all. More personal elements include his conversations about buildings, gardens, and orchards. His chastity was exemplary. He sometimes said the divine office, frequented the sacraments of penance and the Eucharist, and gave alms in person. In these last respects he closely resembled his mother. The one criticism of him was his use of barbarous troops from Galloway in the invasion of England in 1138. These left an appalling memory for their atrocities in the north. On his death-bed he prayed many psalms and then asked the bystanders: "Allow me to think about the things of God, so that my soul may be strengthened. . . . When I stand before God's judgment-seat, none of you shall answer for me, none of you protect me, none of you deliver me from his hand." He died on 24 May 1153 (the same year as St Bernard and Prince Eustace). He did not live to see Matilda's son Henry II succeed to the English throne, but he did see him recognized as King Stephen's heir.

The cult of David started at Dunfermline, and soon his translation was authorized. Some of his successors criticized him for lavish endowment of the Church, but his cult continued until the Reformation, and his feast was inserted by Archbishop Laud into the calendar of the Scottish prayer book. Like his mother, St Margaret, he has sometimes been criticized for being too Anglophile, but all in all he is one of the more impressive king-saints of the Middle Ages. His influence in Scotland in political as well as religious matters was deep and lasting.

Aelred's panegyric is in *P.L.*, 195, 701-38, with other material; for a modern view see G. W. S. Barrow, *David of Scotland: The Balance of New and Old* (1984), and his "Scottish Rulers and the Religious Orders 1070-1153" in *T.R.H.S.*, 5th Series, 3 (1953), 77-100; *M.O.*, 239-49.

Bd John of Prado, *Martyr* (1631)

Born of a noble Spanish family at Morgobejo (León), he was educated at Salamanca University and became an Observant Franciscan in 1584. After his ordination he desired strongly to serve in the foreign missions to the pagans. At this time missionaries were already at work in many parts of the world, but the place of John's work was ultimately to be Morocco. He was sent first, however, to preach in his own country and to serve as novice-master and later guardian in several places. In spite of his holiness and humility he became the victim of a false accusation and was removed from the post of guardian. "The only thing that grieves me," he said, "is the discredit it may bring upon our Order and the scandal it may cause to the weak." His innocence was completely vindicated later, and in 1610 he was appointed minister of the new province of San Diego.

Three years later the plague killed all the Franciscans who were working in the difficult mission in Islamic Morocco. The first Franciscans to work there had done so in the thirteenth century. John's term of office was just over, and he asked to be sent to help. Pope Urban VIII then named him apostolic missionary with special powers. With two companions he started to minister to the Christian slaves. In spite of being ordered to leave, they continued to bring the sacraments to the Christians and to reconcile those who had apostatized. They were then arrested in Marrakesh and thrown into prison, where they had to work at grinding saltpetre for gunpowder. When they were brought into the sultan's presence, they boldly explained their Christian beliefs, so they were scourged and returned to prison. In a second public examination, John addressed some apostates who were also present, largely ignoring the sultan. Thereupon Muley-al-Walid struck John, now an old man, to the ground, and he was pierced by two arrows. He was then taken away to be burned alive. As the flames rose, he urged his executioners to follow Christ, until one of them crushed his head with a stone. He was beatified in 1728.

See F. Fernández y Romeral, *Los Franciscanos en Marruecos* (1921); H. Koehler, *L'Eglise chrétienne du Maroc* (1934), pp. 65-83; *Bibl.SS.*, 6, 870-1.

Bd Louis Moreau, *Bishop* (1824-1901)

Bishop of Saint-Hyacinthe in Canada (about fifty miles east of Montreal), Louis was known as an outstanding pastor both inside and outside his diocese. He was born at Betancour in French Canada, educated at the local seminary, and ordained priest in 1846. His consecration as bishop followed in 1876, and for twenty-five years he was conspicuous for boldly identifying and overcoming obstacles in his large diocese. The education of the young, the care of the sick, the organization of mutual aid, setting up new parishes and forming the priests to serve in them, all occupied his zealous attention. He loved visiting parishes and schools. He well realized the value of nuns, whom he sought to help in the many tasks appropriate to his place and time. Unlike some bishops he was very close to his priests, whom he cared for by stimulating their intellectual as well as their spiritual life. He was a clear and persuasive speaker, both in public and in private.

He was recognized outside his diocese as a clear thinker about the problems of his time who with firmness and moderation defended basic principles and essential values. He was also remarkable, in a land of divided race and religion, for his work for unity among all Christians. All in all, he was one of the most impressive of French Canadian bishops in the nineteenth century. He died on 24 May 1901 and was beatified in 1987.

See *N.C.E.*, 9, pp. 1142-3.

R.M.

St Zoëllus, martyr in Lycaonia (second-third century)

St John Psychaitas, imprisoned and exiled in the Iconoclast persecution (*c.* 820)

Bd Philip Suzanni, Austin friar of Piacenza (306)

SS Augustine Yi, Agatha Kim, and Companions, martyrs in Korea (1839)—see "Martyrs of Korea," 20 Sept.

ST BEDE THE VENERABLE (over page)
Gold pitcher with light from heaven as silver
rays from gold sun, on blue field.

25

ST BEDE THE VENERABLE, *Doctor* (673-735)

An outstanding monk and scholar of his own time, Bede was deservedly declared a Doctor of the Church by Pope Leo XIII in 1899, the only Englishman ever to gain this distinction. He was a versatile scholar in scripture, chronology, history, and hagiography. His spiritual life was based on the monastic liturgy, which he sang daily in the church and from which he quoted the Ascension antiphon *O rex gloriae* on his death-bed.

He tells us something about himself at the end of his most widely read work, *The Ecclesiastical History of the English People*. "I was born on the lands of this monastery, and on reaching seven years of age, I was entrusted by my family first to the most reverend abbot Benedict [St Benedict Biscop, 12 Jan.] and later to abbot Ceolfrith [25 Sept.] for my education. I have spent all the remainder of my life in this monastery and devoted myself entirely to the study of the scriptures. And while I have observed the regular discipline and sung the choir offices daily in church, my chief delight has always been in study, teaching and writing. I was ordained deacon in my nineteenth year and priest in my thirtieth . . . until my fifty-ninth year I have worked, both for my own benefit and that of my brethren, to compile short extracts from the works of the venerable Fathers on Holy Scripture and to comment on their meaning and interpretation." He then added a list of his many works up to that date (731) and added a final prayer: "I pray you, noble Jesu, that as you have graciously granted me joyfully to imbibe the words of your knowledge, so you will also of your bounty grant me to come at length to yourself, the fount of all wisdom, and to dwell in your presence for ever."

Thus outlining his ideals in a simple and articulate style, Bede was making use of the resources provided by the two saints just mentioned, whose achievements he described in his Lives of the Abbots of Wearmouth and Jarrow. Benedict Biscop went several times to Rome through France and brought back for his monasteries many precious books and paintings as well as craftsmen for building and for glass-making. Archaeologists have recently unearthed impressive samples of stained glass at Jarrow. Ceolfrith's work of consolidation included the writing of no less than three complete copies of the Bible in Latin, done with great accuracy and fine penmanship. When Ceolfrith resigned the abbacy, he took one of them as a present to the pope; this survives as the *Codex Amiatinus* at Florence. Bede's own education was based firmly on the Latin Bible, and he may well have been one of the scribes employed in writing the three copies. He also taught Latin to numerous Anglo-Saxons who came to the monastery, as he had done, with no knowledge of Latin.

His own Latin style, especially as revealed in his *History*, is impressively readable, whether in the descriptive passages or in those of historical synthesis. They could only have been written by one with a considerable and enviable command of the Latin tongue. Old English, however, was his mother tongue. He loved Old English poetry, and he stressed the importance of the vernacular for communicating Christian belief to his compatriots in his famous account of the poet Caedmon.

Bede's monastic life was seemingly uneventful, filled as it was with the normal round of prayer, study, and teaching. He also preached, at least occasionally, to his community and to the people (an Easter Vigil sermon by him mentions some of his hearers as about to receive baptism). We know that he was greatly appreciated as a teacher from the account of his death and that his books of scripture commentary were in demand both in England and in Germany, as St Boniface (5 June) asked for them. Near the end of his life Bede wrote a formal letter to Egbert, bishop of York, which showed his sensitivity to pastoral issues as well. He was concerned at the lack of instruction to communities in remote settlements; he wanted there to be more bishops in Northumbria; he wanted all the people to know and sing by heart the Lord's Prayer and the Creed; and he thought that the lives of some of the laity were so blameless that they should receive Holy Communion every week or even every day. These remarkable recommendations were not realized, but his insights into the abuses of the so-called family monasteries were brought to the attention of the Council of Clovesho.

It was, nonetheless, as a writer that he most influenced the Church—in the Middle Ages by his commentaries (especially on those books of the Bible on which there were few other commentators) and in later times, including our own, by his *History* and chronology. Few people who use "A.D." dating realize Bede's importance in popularizing it, while readers of his *History* have never been so numerous as they are today. From these works can be deduced some of Bede's interests and characteristics. He was a humble man ("marvellously learned and not at all proud," in the words of his imitator and successor, William of Malmesbury); he was a keen observer as well as a sympathetic judge of character; he was musical and appreciated musicians; he also showed knowledge of cooking, carpentry, and the tides.

He was at once deeply Roman and deeply English. He had little sympathy for the Easter calculation of Iona and northern Ireland, although he greatly admired their monastic saints; he was deeply regional in his patriotism, like virtually all his contemporaries, which led him to ignore or undervalue Welsh or Mercian matters (he found it hard to forgive an "unholy alliance" of these two powers in their devastating invasion of Northumbria). In his *History* he was concerned with the Christian Church among the Anglo-Saxons, united by the Latin language and by loyalty to Rome, manifested by pilgrimage. For him the best age of the Church in Britain had been the episcopate of Theodore (d. 690), an inspired papal appointment of an older man of Greek origin and culture who promoted order in the Church through councils and appointments to new bishoprics and fostered learning to a high degree in the schools he founded or encouraged.

Bede died as he had lived. The letter describing his death, written by his disciple

Cuthbert (a future abbot of Jarrow), is as moving an account as any of the death of a saint. Bede's last illness began before Easter 735. He was cheerful and joyful, giving thanks to God until the Ascension (26 May). Each day he gave lessons to his students, and the rest of these days were spent in saying the psalms and in meditation. He was especially busy with two works: one was the translation of John's Gospel into English "for the Church's benefit," the other the rendering of some excerpts from Isidore's *Book of Cycles* for the needs of his students. On Rogation Tuesday he took a turn for the worse, but he continued his work until the procession with the relics of saints took place. After this he urged his disciple to finish writing the book. In the afternoon he had the priests of his monastery summoned so that he could distribute a few small presents and ask for their Masses and prayers on his behalf. "They were all very sad and they all wept, because he had said that they would not see his face much longer in this world." Bede himself had said: "I have lived a long time and the Holy Judge has provided well for me during my whole life. The time of my release is near; indeed my soul longs to see Christ my king in all his beauty." The boy who had written his book told him it was finished. Bede asked him to take his head in his hands and help him to sit "opposite my holy place where I used to pray." Thus on the floor of his cell, singing "Glory be to the Father and to the Son and to the holy Spirit" he breathed his last.

Bede's cult as a saint was both early and lasting. Fulda in Germany had some relics, as did York Minster. In the eleventh century Alfred Westow translated relics believed to be his from Jarrow to Durham, where they now rest in the Galilee chapel. This setting is appropriate, but it must be admitted that the chance of their being genuine is not great and certainly far less than for the relics of St Cuthbert (20 Mar.) in the same cathedral. A genuine relic of Bede is a Greek and Latin copy of the Acts of the Apostles in the Bodleian Library, Oxford. The earliest surviving manuscript of his *History* survives in St Petersburg, but its colophon is not, as has sometimes been claimed, in Bede's own hand.

In assessing Bede's achievements it is necessary to stress the immense difficulties he and his contemporaries faced. In a barbarian and largely illiterate province on the edge of the civilized world, they preserved for posterity much that was best in the classical and Christian culture of the ancient world. Bede's writings had an important practical value: to enable his contemporaries to teach the scriptures in the tradition of the Fathers to an audience in which pagan survival and half-understood Christianity were strong and the full commitment of monks and nuns comparatively rare. He spoke to both groups, sometimes to the first through the second. As a historian he aimed at and largely succeeded in writing the story of the Church in Anglo-Saxon England, as Eusebius had done for the early Church as a whole. The best epitaph ever written on him is that of St Boniface: "The candle of the Church, lit by the Holy Spirit, is extinguished." Bede and Boniface indeed are the two most impressive products of early Anglo-Saxon England: one as a monk-scholar, the other as a monk-missionary. They stand worthily in comparison to any of their contemporaries.

The works of Bede can be found in *P.L.*, 90-95; modern critical editions by D. Hurst and others in *Corpus Christianorum* (1955-); his *History* has been often printed, *e.g.* by C. Plummer (1896), B. Colgrave and R. A. B. Mynors (1970), and most accessibly in Penguin Classics (ed. L. Sherley-Price and D. H. Farmer, 1990, with his Letter to Egbert and the account of his death by Cuthbert). See also P. Hunter Blair, *The World of Bede* (1970); *Famulus Christi* (ed. G. Bonner, 1976); B. Ward, *The Venerable Bede* (1990). Bede's Lives both of St Cuthbert and of the Wearmouth-Jarrow abbots are in J. F. Webb and D. H. Farmer, *The Age of Bede*, also in Penguin Classics (1983); the Irish symposium "Bede and his World" is in *Peritia* 3 (1984), pp. 1-130.

ST GREGORY VII, *Pope* (*c.* 1021-85)

Controversial in life and after death, Gregory is regarded as the champion of the liberty of the Church against the secular power and of the holiness of the priestly vocation. One of the greatest movements of renewal in the Church's history is named "The Gregorian Reform" after him. He was not the instigator of this movement (that distinction belongs rather to Leo IX), but he was the outstanding personality in it, both before he was elected pope, when he served several comparatively short-lived popes as their secretary, and after his election, when he was in fact acclaimed the new bishop of Rome in 1073. Like other great men, he was not without faults, both in his treatment of others and in the intransigence with which he asserted the rights of his office.

He was born at Rovaco (Tuscany) and baptized Hildebrand. He was educated at Rome at S. Maria in the Aventine and in the Lateran Palace. He was first promoted by his teacher, John Gratian, who became Pope Gregory VI. But when the latter died in 1047 after being virtually deposed by the emperor, Hildebrand retired to Cluny. It has often been claimed that he became a monk at this point, but on balance this seems unlikely. If he was a monk, he had more probably become one earlier in Rome.

As pope he faced a daunting task. Not only were the age-old abuses of simony and Nicolaitism (clerical marriage and irregular unions) still rife, but the Church also had to face the consequences of these failings, such as the alienation of church property, partly through hereditary benefices and the passivity or hostility of the secular rulers. Germany was governed by a tyrannical and dissolute emperor, France by a discreditable king, Philip I. Gregory's task was to abolish, if he could, the whole system of investiture, that is, the appointment to church offices by laymen and the ruler's conferring on them the pastoral staff, the symbol of their spiritual office. Like his predecessor Leo IX, Gregory held councils both inside and outside Italy to promulgate his decrees. The second of these deposed unworthy and disobedient bishops and forbade all lay powers to invest bishops with the insignia of their office. This had for long been closely connected with the appointment of bishops in return either for money (simony) or political services. No doubt some kings (such as William I of England) had often made good appointments, but the conflict was both theoretical and practical: theoretical because ultimately about the source of spiritual jurisdiction, and practical because the other abuses mentioned had flourished under the protection given by the secular power to irregular clergy when the popes tried to discipline them.

Gregory's convictions have sometimes been misinterpreted. He saw the society of his time as a closed field in which the true disciples of Christ had to fight a decisive battle against the forces of evil that had taken over much of the Church's life. To liberate the Church, the primacy of the spiritual had to be clearly affirmed. It was no longer enough just to foster individual spiritual life and leave all the rest to the sovereign. The spiritual mission of the Church needed to be realized in and through its head, the pope, whose task was to make the kingship of Christ recognized in the whole known world. Thus would be inaugurated the ideal society, anticipating the heavenly Jerusalem. In this process good laity were better than bad clergy; they were defined in terms of their willingness actually to support the pope's leadership. To save the world, monasteries alone were not enough; also needed were militant, committed Christians who would share actively in reforming society, even by force if necessary. It was surely no accident that only ten years after Gregory's death the first Crusade began.

Two incidents in Gregory's life are especially famous. One is the dramatic personal confrontation with the emperor Henry IV at Canossa; the other is his tragic death in exile. The first was the result of long controversy, with the emperor and his followers seeing no reason to abandon their traditional control of appointments. These had, in fact, sometimes included the appointment of certain bishops of Rome. As early as 1076 the emperor at Worms had proclaimed through his bishops the deposition of Gregory VII. He, however, replied by excommunicating the emperor and releasing his subjects from their obedience to him. Henry was opposed in Germany itself and in January 1077 travelled to Canossa to ask for pardon and absolution. The dramatic character of this confrontation between the spiritual and temporal rulers, when Henry was kept waiting in the bitterly cold snow, has often been appreciated. What is less often seen is that Gregory, as the spiritual father of the emperor, had really no choice but to absolve him.

Henry, after eliminating his rival Rudolf of Swabia, revived the conflict, invaded Italy, declared Gregory again deposed, and supported the election of the antipope Clement III. He even penetrated Rome and was crowned emperor by the antipope, who had been intruded into St Peter's. The emperor besieged Rome for two years and captured it in the third. Gregory retired to the castle of St Angelo until he was rescued by Robert Guiscard, the Norman duke of Calabria. The Norman troops' excesses in "liberating" Rome infuriated its citizens, whose resentment turned on the pope who had invited them in, so Gregory retired to Monte Cassino and then to Salerno. He was deserted by several of the cardinals but made a last appeal to all who believed that "the blessed Peter is father of all Christians, their chief shepherd under Christ, that the holy Roman Church is the mother and mistress of all the churches." On his death-bed he forgave all his enemies and lifted all excommunications except those of the emperor and the antipope Guibert of Ravenna. "I have loved justice and hated iniquity, that is why I die in exile." These were his last words.

Although he died in apparent failure, Gregory's influence was enormous. He was not ambitious in a personal sense, but he did identify the cause of God and the Church with support for the papacy in its probably necessary work of reform through centralization, insofar as this could be achieved in the eleventh century. His famous *Dictatus Papae* are now acknowledged to be twenty-seven chapter heads of a canonical collection, a digest of ecclesiastical law which would support the positions he took up to resolve the problems of his time. Both dense and concise, they express the convictions of this energetic pope, who fought with all his strength for the papacy and the Church. He was also much concerned with the needs of the Church in Scandinavia, Spain, and eastern Europe. The medieval papacy owed much to his example and to his thought, but his cult as a saint attained official recognition only with beatification in 1584 and canonization in 1606. In 1728 his feast was extended to the Universal Church (to the disgust of the Gallicans), while in the nineteenth century he was seen as a precursor of the teaching of the First Vatican Council. His influence in England was unusual: on the one hand William I rejected Gregory's claim to feudal homage for his kingdom (and was right to do so); on the other hand, Gregory's insistence on the liberty of the Church and the need for reform contributed strongly to the stand of St Anselm (21 Apr.) and St Thomas of Canterbury (29 Dec.) in their prolonged conflicts with the kings of their time.

See H. X. Arquillière, *S. Grégoire VII* (1934); A. Fliche, *La Réforme Grégorienne* (3 vols, 1926); *Bibl.SS.*, 7, 294–379. E. Caspar edited Gregory's Letters in *M.G.H., Epistolae Selectae*, vol. 2 (1922), trans. E. Emerton (1932). See also H. E. J. Cowdrey, *The Cluniacs and the Gregorian Reform* (1970), and *Epistolae Vagantes* (1972); J. K. Mann, *Lives of the Popes VII* (1910); *O.D.P.*, pp. 154–6; the series *Studi Gregoriani per la storia della "Libertas Ecclesiae."*

St Denis of Milan, *Bishop* (*c.* 360)

Denis became archbishop of Milan in 351. In 355 he attended a council which had been convoked to condemn St Athanasius (2 May) in the palace of the Arian emperor Constantius. Nearly all the bishops present signed the decree through fear, but Denis, with Eusebius of Vercelli and Lucifer of Cagliari, refused to do so. They were therefore banished, Denis going to Cappadocia, where he died in 360 not long before the emperor Julian sanctioned their return. From Cappadocia St Basil (2 Jan.) sent his relics back to Milan. His letter to St Ambrose (7 Dec.) on how to authenticate the relics still exists.

For St Basil's letter see *P.G.*, 32, 712–3; *Bibl.SS.*, 4, 642.

St Zenobius of Florence, *Bishop* (*c.* 310–90)

Although many paintings of Zenobius by early Renaissance masters survive in Florence, not much is known of his life. His early date and his role as bishop made him a patron of the town. He is said to have been a member of the Geronimo family and to have been baptized by Theodore, bishop of Florence, at the age of twenty-one; this bishop subsequently ordained him priest and appointed him archdeacon. Impressed by his learning and piety, St Ambrose (7 Dec.) recommended him to Pope St Damasus (11 Dec.), who sent him on a mission to Constantinople. On Theodore's death he was appointed bishop of Florence, where he became conspicuous for sanctity and miracles. A Life of him claims that he raised five people from the dead (unlikely) including a child run over by a cart in front of the cathedral. Zenobius lived to be eighty and was buried at San Lorenzo before being translated to the Duomo.

The eleventh-century Lives are in *AA.SS.*, May, 6, pp. 49-69; see also *Bibl.SS.*, 12, 1467-70.

St Aldhelm, *Abbot and Bishop* (639-709)

Little is known for certain about the spread of Christianity in Wessex (southern England from Hampshire to Devon) during the greater part of the seventh century. Its western half is particularly thinly documented, but here Aldhelm was clearly the most notable ecclesiastical figure, while the king, Ina (688-726), left an important code of laws, endowed monasteries and ended his long reign by abdicating and going to Rome, where he died not long afterwards.

Bede's rather fragmentary account of Wessex was derived mainly from Daniel, bishop of Winchester 705-44, who corresponded with Boniface (5 June) as well as with Bede and was appointed bishop when the Wessex diocese was divided. Naturally he was less informative about Wiltshire and Dorset (as they subsequently became) than he was about Hampshire, the Isle of Wight, and even Sussex. The point to stress here is that the Church in Wessex in which Boniface, of European importance, grew up, was already well developed, perhaps more so than the Northumbrian Bede realized. Bede did however devote a chapter of his history to Aldhelm and recorded the abdications of both Cadwalla and Ine (his successor as king of Wessex) for the sake of pilgrimage to, and residence at, the sacred shrines of Rome.

Aldhelm was related to the Wessex kings and was educated first at Malmesbury where he became a monk and later at Canterbury in the school founded by St Theodore (19 Sept.) and Hadrian, abbot of the monastery there founded by Augustine (27 May). This was a lively and important clerical school, where exegesis of the literal, Antiochene kind was taught, together with rhetoric, computistics, grammar, music, and other subjects, including Greek as well as Latin. Aldhelm described the school in one of his letters and claimed that it was now superior to anything Ireland could offer, and indeed that Irish students went there in preference to the centres in their own country.

In about 675 Aldhelm returned to Malmesbury as abbot. Most scholars nowadays regard the supposed Irish founder, Maildub, as mythical, so Aldhelm is the first abbot of Malmesbury of whom anything is known. He was both a learned man and an energetic founder. He made monastic foundations at Frome and at Bradford-on-Avon, while he wrote in both Latin and Old English. His poems survived in the days of Alfred, who praised them highly. They were written to be sung to harp accompaniment: their purpose was to encourage the townspeople to come to church. Unfortunately none has survived; but their known existence, like those of Caedmon in Northumbria (described by Bede), remind us of an important and lost aid to the work of preachers. The Anglo-Saxons, a race skilled in poetry, often with pagan heroic themes, warmly welcomed Christian and biblical subjects for vernacular verse.

Aldhelm's Latin works were esteemed both by Bede and by later generations. Their style was praised but not imitated by the former. His own limpid simplicity was not matched by Aldhelm, who preferred a hermeneutic style, with a somewhat ostentatious parade of unusual and arcane words, sometimes of Greek origin. His influence is clear in the writings of the young Boniface and some eighth-century hagiographers as well as in charter and other writings of the tenth. These were the centuries when manuscripts of his works were most in demand. The principal and most famous one was a treatise *On Virginity* in both prose and verse. This was in fact a study of particular examples of virginity in both the Bible and the early history of the Christian Church. An illuminated manuscript of this work survives: it contains a picture of Aldhelm presenting this treatise to the abbess and nuns of Barking (founded by Erconwald, bishop of London 675-93, for his sister Ethelberga). They, like many readers of today, might well have found the Latin difficult and needed the Old English glosses written between the lines of this and other treatises. Other works are *Aenigmata* (riddles), inspired by Isidore and containing an element of play which came from the self-conscious mastery of a new and foreign language. Besides these, there are Latin poems that throw light on how the Wessex churches were built and decorated. These are unique and insufficiently studied. Of more general interest is his small number of letters on the Canterbury schools, on the necessary loyalty of St Wilfrid's clerics to their patron in exile, and on the controversy about the date of Easter. This was addressed to Geraint, British king of Dumnonia (west Devon and Cornwall). Here too Aldhelm shows his loyalty to Wilfrid and the Synod of Whitby: his letter, although much shorter, can be compared to that of Abbot Ceolfrith (25 Sept.) to Nectan, king of the Picts.

In 705 Aldhelm became first bishop of Sherborne. This reflected a division of the Wessex diocese into two, in accordance with the general and admirable policy of Aldhelm's old master, Theodore (d. 690). The westward expansion of Anglo-Saxon Wessex through Somerset, Dorset, and into Devon made this necessary, as the kingdom was now too large for a single bishop. Aldhelm proved an energetic bishop for the four years of life remaining to him. He built or rebuilt a small cathedral at Sherborne, as well as churches at Wareham and elsewhere in the Isle of Purbeck. The presence of British runes at Wareham reflects, like Ine's laws, a policy of assimilation of these people into Anglo-Saxon society: at least some of them were of comparatively high status and even served in the royal household. Overall these laws reflect a self-confident Christian society in which Church and State worked in harmony and the king's laws enforced ecclesiastical laws in such matters as Sunday observance, the necessity of baptism, and the collection of church dues. Wide-ranging and of great interest, they were promulgated shortly before Aldhelm was consecrated bishop and reveal clearly how advanced at this time was the kingdom of Wessex. They were subsequently used by king Alfred (871-99), under whom Wessex began to attain its permanent and dominant stature.

The life of Aldhelm, monk and writer of prose and poetry in Latin and Old English, builder and administrator, and a relative of the king, reveals considerable and little-known achievements. At least he has the distinction of a headland in Dorset being named St Aldhelm's (not St Alban's) Head. Aldhelm died at Doulting (Somerset) and was buried at Malmesbury: a series of crosses of stone (according to William of Malmesbury) once marked the stages of his body's journey back to his monastery. The same authority, writing in 1125, ascribed to him a journey to Rome and the bringing back of an altar across the Alps; in those days too a chasuble, believed to be Aldhelm's was preserved at Malmesbury.

This, rather than Sherborne, was the centre of his cult, as the monastery possessed his tomb and relics. His cult was interrupted for a time at the Norman Conquest, but it was happily restored by St Osmund of Salisbury (d. 1099; 4 Dec.), who authorized a new translation of Aldhelm's relics in 1078. This is recalled by the subsidiary feast of 3 October, whereas that of 5 May marks an earlier translation in 986, which followed after St Dunstan's restoration of Benedictine monasticism at Malmesbury.

Bede, *H.E.* 5, 7 and 18; William of Malmesbury, *Gesta pontificum* (ed. N. Hamilton, R.S., 1870), book 5; M. Lapidge has edited *Aldhelm: the Prose Works* (1979) and *Aldhelm: the Poetic Works* (1985); see also his "The hermeneutic style in tenth century Anglo-Saxon literature," in *Anglo-Saxon England* 4 (1975), pp. 67-111; H. M. Mayr-Harting, *The Coming of Christianity to Anglo-Saxon England* (1972), pp. 192-9; E. S. Duckett, *Anglo-Saxon Saints and Scholars* (1958); D Whitelock (ed.), *English Historical Documents*, 1 (1968), pp. 364-72.

St Gennadius, *Abbot and Bishop* (936)

Gennadius was one of the most notable figures of the Church in Spain of the late ninth and early tenth centuries. Following the Muslim invasions and consolidation in the south, Christians were strongest in the north, which had strong cultural links with southern France. Gennadius' life was spent entirely in northern Spain, in which he followed monastic life and also for some years exercised a noteworthy political role.

The first recorded mention of him is in 880, as a monk of Ageo. Two years later, with his abbot's approval, he led a community of twelve monks to restore the monastery of St Peter-of-the-Mountain. This had been founded three centuries earlier by St Fructuosus of Braga (16 Apr.) on one of his estates near Vierzo. The foundation prospered and Gennadius was blessed as abbot by Ranulf, bishop of Astorga. In 898 Ranulf died, and Gennadius was chosen as his successor by Alfonso II, king of Asturias.

Now he became one of the most important people in this kingdom. First came his duties as a bishop. Partly overlapping with these were the roles of counsellor, confessor, and confidant of the king, as well as collaborator in his rule, and, eventually, executor of his will. But he always remained a monk at heart with a deep love both of solitude and of monasteries. He founded two of these when bishop and restored three more.

In 920 he resigned his see. His act of renuciation has survived: "I, Gennadius, unworthy, but by God's grace bishop, have sometimes strayed from the yoke of this charge and have been impeded by the stormy pressure of this world and been prevented from pursuing the contemplative life, which I desire to live for the remaining days of my life, as a solitary in the company of hermits living here. Therefore, to sustain those who live there and to ensure that they always remember me in their prayers, I promise and donate to them these various lands." The list of properties then follows. In the terms of his will his library, which consisted of bibles, service-books, various named patristic commentaries, and monastic rules, was to be shared by the various monasteries he had founded, who used them in turn without any single monastery owning them. This must be very early evidence for a "lending library."

The place to which he retired was the desert of Monte del Silenzo (near Vierzo), for long specially dear to him. Initially he lived in a cave near Penalba for solitude and penance. He was visited here by neighbouring abbots and monks as well as by counts and other secular notables, even by the King of León. Bishop Forte (920-31) built him a house and his successor Solomon (931-51) refurbished it. Gennadius died in 936, over eighty years old, in the arms of Urban, abbot of Penalba. Bishop Solomon built his tomb in the monastery church there. Soon after his death he was venerated as a saint: dust from his cave and from his tomb were said to have special curative powers. In the sixteenth century the Duchess of Alba translated his relics eventually to Valladolid.

AA.SS., 6 May, pp. 94-100; *D.H.G.E.*, 20, 474-6; *Bibl. SS.*, 6, 130-2.

St Mary Magdalen de' Pazzi (1566-1607)

This Italian Carmelite nun, who came from one of the wealthiest families in Florence, spent her first sixteen years in preparation and the subsequent twenty-five as a mystic and ecstatic in the austere environment of a Carmelite convent. Detailed records were kept of her mystical experiences, which make her one of the best-documented saints of her kind and of her time.

She was born Caterina di Geri de' Pazzi of an ancient noble family, which had been involved in the rivalries and plots of Renaissance Florence. In spite of the reforms of St Pius V (30 Apr.) and other popes, many of the clergy were lukewarm, ignorant, or dissolute. Her interest as a child in religion was exceptional, and she experienced her first ecstasy at the age of twelve in her mother's presence. She experienced another at the age of sixteen, when she entered Carmel in spite of family opposition. Her contemporary portraits reveal a beautiful young woman at this age. Instead of a profitable marriage she chose a life of prayer, obedience, and humility. Two of her sayings reveal her outlook: "God does not germinate in sad souls; he wants a heart that is free and happy," and "You know, Lord, that my soul has desired nothing apart from you."

She passed her novitiate largely uneventfully, until in 1584 (when she was aged eighteen) a mysterious illness, with high fever and violent coughing and pains, confined her to bed. The doctors thought she was dying. She was carried into the chapel to make her profession. Immediately afterwards she experienced a violent ecstasy, which united her to the Holy Trinity and left her in tears. She described the experience in terms of giving her heart beforehand, receiving it back in the experience, and being given a supreme gift of purity like that of the Blessed Virgin. "Then Jesus, caressing me gently like a newly-wed, united me to him and hid me in his side, where I tasted sweet repose. The Lord then seemed to take away from me my will and all my desires, so that I can no longer wish or desire anything except what he wills."

This was followed by a dated series of mystical experiences. On 8 June 1584 she saw the drama of the passion of our Lord; on 10 June she exchanged her heart with that of Jesus; on 28 June she received the stigmata; and on 6 July a crown of thorns, which she felt all the rest of her life. A witness described how she was ravished in ecstasy, not only in prayer but also in any other activity. For months at a time, there was no day when she was not "rapt in God." The following year there was another series. On 15 April 1585 she had a vision of the five wounds and of the body of Jesus exuding blood and sweat; on 28 April she received a ring, the sign of her mystical marriage; and on 21 May she was told to live only on bread and water, except on Sundays, in reparation for men's sins against God. Her director, fearing illusion, told her instead to follow the normal régime of the convent, but she was physically sick when she did so. For five years she endured this affliction and was then told to reduce her sleep to five hours each night. If she tried to resist ecstasy, she was thrown to the ground.

Also in 1585, she was told that she would be completely deprived, not of grace but of the perception of grace, and that she would have to live through a long trial of spiritual dryness and desolation. She would call it "the lions' den." Doubts, blasphemies in her ears, the feeling of abandonment by God, to whom she could no longer lift her heart, were all part of this trial. She was even tempted to suicide in despair, but at last left her knife at the feet of the statue of Our Lady. In her long struggle against gluttony, impurity, distaste for God, and rebellion, she placed herself entirely in the hands of the prioress and chose only the most basic mortifications. In her care for the young nuns she recommended poverty and obedience, the elimination of self-love, and abandonment to the will of God. In 1598 she became novice-mistress, in 1604 subprioress. Soon after this appointment she fell ill and experienced three years of desolation. She died of exhaustion in 1607 while the Sisters recited the Athanasian Creed around her bed.

The sources of her spirituality were the Bible, St Augustine, and St Catherine of Siena (29 Apr.), who was a special inspiration to her through her letters and *Dialogue*. Mary Magdalen also corresponded with the Dominican nun St Catherine dei Ricci (2 Feb.), a fellow-Florentine mystic who was prioress in nearby Prato. She was inspired by the Incarnation and by the work of the Holy Spirit in the soul, which brought about total love of Jesus, especially in his passion and cross. This is the "bridge" or "ladder" by which we can recover our heavenly fatherland. The soul is united to God in the measure that it strips itself of everything and becomes a "nothing." The transforming union makes one thing out of two, while each also keeps its individual being. Like other mystics, Mary Magdalen de' Pazzi enjoyed wonderful visions and ecstasies but also underwent extraordinary sufferings. Her almost incredible life story is based firmly on abundant contemporary witness, both from her confessors and the Sisters in her convent. Of few other saints could it be said to the same extent that she made up what was wanting to the sufferings of Christ. Her cult began almost as soon as she died and is centred on her still-incorrupt body at S. Maria degl' Angeli, Florence. She was canonized in 1669.

The principal source for the above is the article in *H.S.S.C.*, 8, pp. 189-93; see also *Bibl.SS.*, 8, 1107-31. Early Lives in *AA.SS.*, May, 6, pp. 177-351; her writings ed. by F. Nardoni, 7 vols. (1960-). Modern Lives by Sr Maria Minima (1941, Eng. trans. 1958) and by A. Ancilli (1967).

St Madeleine Sophie Barat, *Foundress* (1779-1865)

Madeleine can be regarded as a striking example of the vitality of the Church in France after the Revolution. By the standards of any age her long life and her foundation of the Society of the Sacred Heart, which had grown in her lifetime to a Congregation of over 3,500 nuns in eighty-six houses. would have been remarkable. But this was achieved in a deeply divided environment in terms of both politics and religion, and on an educational foundation which would be considered repressive today.

She was born at Joigny (Yonne), less than thirty miles north-west of Auxerre and Chablis. Here her father owned a vineyard and worked also as a cooper. This part of Burgundy (the diocese of Sens) was still deeply influenced by Jansenism, almost a century after the death of St Margaret Mary Alacoque (17 Oct.), who had propagated devotion to the Sacred Heart and to Christ's love for all against Jansenist their rigorism and harshness. Madeleine's brother Louis, eleven years older than her, was her godfather at Baptism. He believed it his duty to instruct her from the age of ten onward as seminarists were educated at the time, in Latin, Greek, history, physics and mathematics, without interruption or companionship. He seems also to have blamed and punished excessively instead of praising. Whether because of or in spite of this treatment, she developed a real love of learning, coupled with strict self-discipline, both of which qualities produced abundant fruit in her life and others.' During the "Reign of Terror" in 1793, Louis was imprisoned in Paris. He returned home as a priest and resumed the charge of his sister's education. From the age of fifteen her main subjects were the Bible, the Fathers, and theology. To these were added the ascetical disciplines of penance and self-examination. She is said to have accepted all this "with cheerful resignation."

Meanwhile, after the suppression of Christian schools at the Revolution and the exile of the religious who had taught in them, many asked themselves how the

future education of the young would be achieved according to Christian principles. A Fr Varin d'Ainville, who had worked for of the restoration of the Jesuits,
was deeply concerned for the education of both boys and girls. With his emphasis
on devotion to the Sacred Heart in his Congregation of the Faith, of which he
founded a college at Amiens, he looked for someone to provide for girls what he
provided for boys. As Madeleine's director he guided her away from her initial
idea of becoming a Carmelite lay sister and encouraged her instead to become a
teaching Sister in a new foundation. With three companions she began this new
life at Amiens in 1800, teaching in a school and making her profession in 1802. This
house at Amiens became the first convent of the new Society. Soon a second
school, for the poor, was opened. Their commitment to the education of both rich
and poor was most appropriate in post-revolutionary France. Meanwhile postu-
lants came and went, and the first superior also departed. At the age of twenty-
three Madeleine was appointed in her place, and although this could not then be
foreseen, she was to remain as superior for sixty-three years. Her nuns shared high
spiritual ideals "to offer themselves to their spouse in many ways and to instruct
the young according to the exemplar of Christ and to propagate his worship, his
love and his glory."

In 1804 Madeleine took over a semi-derelict convent at Grenoble and with it
some members of a Visitation community (founded by St Francis of Sales, d. 1622;
24 Jan.). One of these was St Philippine Duchesne (18 Nov.), who subsequently
brought this Society into the United States. After Grenoble came Poitiers, where
an abbey of Cistercian Feuillants was offered to her and where she set up the
novitiate. In 1806 she was elected superior-general.

Like several other founders and foundresses, Madeleine suffered from discord
in her Congregation. During her absence a local superior, aided and abetted by the
Amiens chaplain, made a determined attempt to alter the Constitutions without
consultation and ultimately to depose the foundress. This opposition persisted for
several years but collapsed in 1815, when the original Constitutions of Fr Varin
were accepted by all. Now there followed a period of both consolidation and
expansion. The Congregation spread widely in France, as well as in Italy, England, Belgium, and the U.S.A. This required her presence at Louisiana in 1817.
Meanwhile Paris had become the principal house and here all the local superiors
convened to draw up a common syllabus for all the schools. General principles,
based on the Jesuits' *Ratio Studiorum*, were agreed, and room was left for adaptation to meet the changing needs of the times. The Paris boarding-schools had been
so successful that there had arisen a strong demand for them to be replicated
elsewhere. Madeleine's Congregation, providing for the education of both rich
a.nd poor by a vigorous, well- trained body of teachers, was new and unconnected
with any Order under the *ancien régime*. On the other hand they also represented
traditional spiritual ideals, which they communicated to a post-revolutionary society without accepting the reactionary attitudes of the families they helped.

In 1826 the Society of the Sacred Heart received formal, papal approbation. The
1830 revolution necessitated the removal of the novitiate to Montet in Switzer-

land, but in 1839 another attempt was made to alter the Constitutions, which Madeleine eventually overcame with patient persistence.

The rest of her life was spent in both travel and writing. Many letters and spiritual conferences survive. These reveal a quasi-monastic spirituality with a strong emphasis on prayer and the interior life. The glorification of Jesus, total fidelity to him in the mysteries of the Incarnation, the Eucharist, and the Sacred Heart, rather than the activities of the Congregation, were the fundamental purpose of both the foundress and the members. The biblical and theological elements through the writings of Ignatius, Teresa of Avila and the author of *The Imitation of Christ* were strong from first to last. Madeleine was regarded as the living exemplar of these ideals, wherever she went and whatever she did.

Her extensive travels on behalf of her Society took her to Rome three times and once at least to Switzerland, Austria, and England. She said herself that she was "always on the road"(frequently in France), often busy with writing letters, with administration and with seeing visitors. She wrote to one of her nuns that "too much work is a danger for an imperfect soul, but for one who loves our Lord, it is an abundant harvest." Her happiest and most fruitful years, it is claimed, were when she lived in the novitiate houses of Grenoble, Poitiers, Montet, and Conflans. She died in the last of these after accepting a vicaress in 1864. Her nuns have always been conspicuous for their constant commitment to the children under their care, while not a few of them have followed their foundress in attaining intellectual achievements of considerable value. Madeleine was beatified in 1908 and canonized in 1925. Her incorrupt body rests at Jette in Belgium.

Her circular letters and conferences were first printed privately in two volumes, then in four. From these a *Recueil de pensées et de maximes* was published in 1870 (rp. 1925). There were two nineteenth-century biographies, by L. Baumard (1876) and A. Cahier (1884) and several more recent ones, such as those by G. de Grandmaison (1909, 1925), A. Brou (1925), and J. de Charry (1965). In English there are Lives by M. Mona Han (1925), C. E. Maguire (1960) and M. Williams (1965). The history of the Society of the Sacred Heart in general was treated by G. Bernoville (1951) and F. Charmot (1953), while L. Call an wrote *The Society of the Sacred Heart in America* (1937).

R.M.

SS Pasicrates and Valentio, martyrs (*c.* 302)

St Canion, bishop and martyr (third-fourth century)

St Leo, abbot (seventh century)

St Gerius, hermit and pilgrim (1326)

Bd James Philip Bertoni, Servite friar (1483)

St Peter Doan Van Van, catechist in Tonkin (1865)—see "Martyrs of Vietnam (Tonkin)," 2 Feb.

St Denis Ssebuggwawo, martyr in Uganda (1886)—see "Martyrs of Uganda," 3 June.

26

ST PHILIP NERI, *Founder* (1515-95)

Philip must be one of the most attractive saints of his or of any other time. His natural gifts of perspicacity, sensitivity, and common-sense realism were crowned by his constant joy, based above all on his perpetual realization of God's presence. Called "the apostle of Rome," he exemplified Christian holiness in a difficult environment caused both by the neo-paganism of some aspects of the Renaissance and by the reaction by church authorities, seen in the Holy Office and the Index. Through those critical times Philip lived by the love of God, humanizing religion, spreading joy and confidence, and combining solitude and silence with a deep love for his brothers of the Oratory and for all who came into contact with them.

He was not Roman, but Florentine by birth. His father was a notary with a taste for alchemy; his mother bore four children but died when Philip was only five years old. His baptism took place in the famous cathedral baptistery, and his first religious instruction was at the Dominican church of San Marco, made famous by Fra Angelico's numerous paintings. He and his father sympathized with the cause of Savonarola, and Philip had a lifelong esteem for the Dominicans. At San Marco he saw the portrait, the cell, and the bible of Savonarola, whose programme for reform included a return to the scriptures. There also he took part in the religious processions and the singing of popular hymns to counteract the parades and amusements of the time. When the Medicis returned to Florence in 1532, Philip left and never came back. His father was in financial difficulties and had previously opposed the Medicis.

Philip travelled south to live with an uncle, a merchant of San Germano, between Rome and Naples. From there he frequently visited Monte Cassino, where he learned to love the liturgy and the Desert Fathers, stability, and community life. At this time he also felt a great desire for solitude, satisfied in part by visits to a mountain chapel, where he may well have had some sort of mystical experience. He stayed at San Germano for about a year and then left for Rome, knowing that the life of a merchant was not for him. This was in 1533.

At this time Rome was in a critical state. When Charles V's mercenaries sacked the city in 1527, they left a trail of desecrated churches, with a vast number of works of art and manuscripts destroyed. Until 1534 the pope was Clement VII, of the Medici family, but he was succeeded by Paul III, whose pontificate almost exactly coincided with Philip's life as a layman in Rome. Philip took lodgings near the Pantheon with a customs agent from Florence, to whose two sons he was tutor. His régime was one of extreme simplicity: a minimum of furniture in his bedroom and a diet of bread, olives, wine, and water. He also began serious studies of philosophy and theology from the works of St Thomas Aquinas. This was an eremitical period in his life, with nights spent in prayer in one or other of the Seven

Churches. It ended with his selling his books to concentrate on prayer and solitude. He also frequented the catacombs, where in 1544 he had a mystical experience with physical consequences that affected him for the rest of his life. His first biographer described it in these terms: "He suddenly felt himself divinely filled with the power of the Spirit with such force that his heart began to palpitate within his body and to be inflamed with such love that, his nature being unaccustomed to such palpitations, he indicated that he was completely unable to bear it." In his later years Philip confided that he saw a ball of fire enter his mouth and then felt his breast expand over his heart. He threw himself on the ground and cried: "Enough, Lord, enough! I cannot take any more." He long experienced an interior physical heat and violent trembling caused by the beating of his heart. Philip always did his best to hide these phenomena and was extremely reticent about anything extraordinary. Another physical phenomenon was a swelling over his heart the size of a man's fist: the autopsy revealed some broken ribs, which enabled the heart to expand and contract. This seemed to be something supernatural. It enabled him to live a long life, even with such a strange malady.

In 1551 he was ordained priest. His experience of God led him more and more toward his fellow men. Reform was in the air. SS Ignatius of Loyola (31 July) and Francis Xavier (3 Dec.) were among his friends. So too were many of the patients at the hospital of San Giacomo, where he served the sick, and St Camillus of Lellis (14 July) sought his guidance. The other institution, of more permanent influence, in Philip's life was that of San Girolamo. This was an association of secular priests who provided free food and board for their inmates, but with no salary. The freedom of this régime suited Philip well. He said Mass at the end of the morning, spent plenty of time in the confessional, preached, and practised the Forty Hours Devotion. Conversion and submission to Christ were at the heart of his spirituality, as they were for the contemporary reformed Orders such as the Jesuits and the Theatines. Confession was seen as the means of helping people toward Christ, and this apsotolate occupied many hours and continued to the last day of his life. Here, he believed, the love and mercy of Christ could change people's lives from the laxity and unbelief then common in Renaissance Rome. In this encounter with souls it was above all Philip's abounding kindness that attracted people, but stories of his clairvoyance also should not be discounted. Those directed by him became a group who would go to Vespers or visit one or other of the Seven Churches together. From such beginnings the Oratory developed.

Philip had early decided not to join an established religious Order. Characteristically, he sought to find his special way pragmatically: "Lord, as you know and as you will, so do with me." There had been various precursors to the idea of an Oratory, but Philip's formula was the most successful and has stood the test of time. The meetings always started with reading and speaking about a book, either of scripture or the mystics. The book thus became the "instrument of the Spirit." After reading, the group passed to prayer and then either to a short pilgrimage to the churches or else to music. During the excesses of the Roman carnival Philip did not give "hell-fire" sermons but rather took his group, initially about thirty strong and later to be counted in hundreds, on visits to the ancient basilicas of Rome. The Oratory itself was never limited to an élite but attracted people from many walks of life: artisans and shoemakers, scholars and artists, doctors and noblemen. All were attracted to the joyful holiness of Philip, but some were disconcerted by his practical jokes. He expected all, however wealthy and well dressed, to serve in the hospitals and to beg for and with the poor. His own almsgiving was generous, secret, and only subsequently known.

With the accession of Paul IV, a vigorous but autocratic reforming pope, Philip was called before the cardinal vicar of Rome, acting for the Holy Office. Philip was suspended from hearing confessions for a fortnight and was accused of ambition and pride, as well as introducing novelties. The visit of a mysterious friar told them that after their next Forty Hours Devotion the persecution would be lifted. So indeed it was; but in 1567 under St Pius V (30 Apr.) it was revived, this time by secret machinations. Even the closing down of the Oratory had been decided, but it was saved by St Charles Borromeo (4 Nov.). The gossip, suspicion, and envy experienced by Philip caused him deep suffering, but his patience and humility ensured his perfect correctness.

After these difficult times, a new spirit filled the air under Gregory XIII (1572-85). Morals improved, the power of wealth seemed broken, education through the founding of national colleges for the clergy brought Tridentine reforms into several countries, and it was no accident that this pope approved both the Oratory of St Philip and the Carmelite reforms of St Teresa (15 Oct.). The approval of the Oratory came in 1575, by which time the Oratorians had a modest church of their own, which they rebuilt as the Chiesa Nuova with the help of donations from rich and poor, and 8,000 crowns from the pope. The church, though incomplete, was used from 1577. The new building of transepts and choir required the demolition of the Oratorians' own house, but Cardinal Cesi found them a derelict convent nearby. Immense crowds came to their church, and Philip moved into the new house, occupying an attic in as much solitude as was compatible with receiving many visitors. At one time would-be recruits were so numerous that some had to be refused, but Philip's ideals and practice had proved so attractive that other Oratories were founded elsewhere in Italy, notably in Bologna and Naples. There were some juridical difficulties in the latter foundation, which sought to develop in some ways like other religious Orders. Never one for multiplying regulations, Philip would even say, "If you want to be obeyed, don't make commandments." The informality of his régime was constant.

He never set out to reform the Church or the Curia, yet his influence was a powerful force in this necessary achievement. Cardinal Newman described Philip's apostolate in terms of being kept at home not to evangelize but to recover. "The confessional was the seat and seal of his peculiar apostolate. As St Francis Xavier baptized his tens of thousands, Philip was every day and almost every hour for forty-five years restoring, teaching, encouraging and guiding penitents along the narrow way of salvation." The return to apostolic life that he inspired led to his being called the second apostle of Rome. The daily use of the word of God, not only read but preached, with the frequent use of the sacraments achieved the renewal desired by many. This he had in common with Savonarola, but Philip was more compassionate, more patient, and his attitude of reverent submission to ecclesiastical authority contrasted with the fiery diatribes of the famous Dominican. This summary of Philip's method is the work of a contemporary: "With the word of God he miraculously enkindled in many men a holy love of Christ. He had nothing else in mind but to put them on fire with the desire for prayer, for frequentation of the sacraments and for works of charity."

The spirit of a saint is notoriously elusive, and that of Philip is best understood in his maxims. Here are a few: "It is easier to guide cheerful persons in the spiritual life than the melancholy"; or again, "One should not wish to become a saint in four days, but step by step." He also knew the importance of fresh air and sound diet for those who seemed out of sorts. More generally, he would say, "Be good if you can"; "the man who does not pray is like a dumb animal"; and touching his forehead, "Sanctity lies within the space of three fingers." Over and over again Philip's shrewd humour disarmed criticism.

The last years of his long life were spent in the same tireless activity but the same quest for solitude as well. He frequently experienced ecstacy during Mass. He continued his Roman walks and seemed to like nothing better than to be taken for a crazy eccentric. His death was foreseen by him and prepared with care. His last day was filled with celebrating the Eucharist and hearing confessions, and he died in the early morning of 26 May 1595. His popular acclamation as a saint was immediate, and he was formally canonized in 1622. At his death the Oratory numbered seven houses, all in Italy, but now it has spread to many countries, in the New as well as the Old World. Among its most famous members are the Italian scholar Baronius, the French spiritual writer Bérulle, and John Henry Newman, one of Philip's most eloquent followers. In recent years the founding of an Oratory in Oxford after more than a century of planning has fulfilled one of his cherished plans.

This notice is based principally on P. Turks, *Philip Neri: the Fire of Joy* (trans. D. Utrecht, 1995) and on *H.S.S.C.*, 8, pp. 216-23. L. Ponnelle and L. Bordet, *St Philip Neri and the Roman Society of his Times* (trans. R. F. Kerr, 1932), is still a standard work. Other recent biographies include M. Trevor, *Apostle of Rome* (1966), and L. Bouyer, *St Philip Neri: A Portrait* (trans. M. Day, 1995). J. H. Newman's "The Mission of St Philip Neri" is in *Sermons Preached on Various Occasions* (1904 and 1968).

St Eleutherius, *Pope* (d. 189)

Eleutherius was the thirteenth bishop of Rome. He was a Greek from Nicopolis in western Greece and reigned for fifteen years. Previously he had been a deacon to Pope Anicetus (d. 166). Lucius, king of Edessa (Mesopotamia), sent inquiries to him about Christianity and was later converted. The *Liber Pontificalis* or its sources confused this Lucius with the British king of the same name. This led Bede and other writers to suppose, wrongly, that a British king had become a Christian in the second century. In 188 St Irenaeus (28 June) wrote a letter telling of the persecution and martyrdoms of this town, which was used by Eusebius in his *History*. It also described Montanism (an apocalyptic sect tinged with "enthusiasm" and using prophetesses), but we have no records to judge the pope's reaction. Eleutherius' reign seems to have marked a period of peace in Rome; the first mention of him as a martyr comes in the ninth-century martyrology of Ado. The claim that he was martyred is tacitly abandoned in today's entry in the new Roman Martyrology.

See *O.D.P.*, pp.11-12; Eusebius *H.E.*, 4, 22; 5, 3-4.

Bd Andrew Franchi (1401)

A member of the noble family of Franchi Boccagni of Pistoia, Tuscany (near Florence), Andrew became a Domincan friar in Florence when a young man. He was famous for preaching and for sound administration and was three times appointed prior. In 1378 he was promoted to be bishop of Pistoia. He not only built churches and relieved the poor, but also in his new state still observed the same Rule he had followed as a friar. In the critical years that followed the Black Death he restored the priories of his Order and encouraged the groups of penitents who prayed for peace and the mercy of God. In 1400 he resigned his office and returned to his priory, where he prepared for death. This took place on 26 May 1401. His cult was confirmed by Benedict XV in 1921 for the Dominican Order and the diocese of Pistoia.

See *A.A.S.*, 14 (1922), pp. 16-19; Life in Italian by F. Taurisano (1922); *Bibl. SS.*, 5, 1245-8.

St Mary Ann of Quito (1618-45)

Quito was in Peru when Mariana Paredes y Flores was born of a noble Spanish family. Her parents died when she was very young, and she was brought up by her sister and her brother-in-law. She was allowed to make her First Communion when only seven and at twelve wanted to go and convert the Japanese to Christianity. Attempts to enable her to join a convent were frustrated, and she decided to live as a solitary in her brother-in-law's house, under Jesuit direction.

The following years are described by her biographers as a time of extraordinary penance and austerity, which seem today to be either incredible or misguided. They may, however, be due to hagiographers' tendency to exaggeration or to "go one better" than the Lives of other saints. (It should not be forgotten that St Rose of Lima [23 Aug.] had died in 1617 at the age of only thirty-one, just before Mariana was born. Rose's life also was one of penance and solitude.) Mariana, we are told, lived a régime based on the barest physical necessities, received many spiritual favours, and had gifts of healing and prophecy. In 1645 Quito was devastated by an earthquake and epidemic, and Mariana publicly offered her life in the church as a victim for the sins of the people. The earthquake ceased; the epidemic abated; but Mariana suffered a combination of illnesses that caused her death at the age of only thirty-one on 26 May 1645. At some stage in her life she had become a Franciscan tertiary and was known as the "Lily of Quito." She was beatified in 1854 and canonized in 1950.

See *Bibl. SS.*, 8, 1033–5; *N.C.E.*, 10, 999–1000.

Bd Peter Sanz and Companions, *Martyrs* (1747-8)

These five martyrs were all Spanish Dominicans who left their own country for the dangers of the foreign missions in China. Peter, who came from Asco (Catalonia), was sent to Fu-kien in 1714. Here he worked with considerable success and was appointed bishop of Mauricastro with the actual rule as vicar apostolic of Fu-kien, implying the supervision of the whole mission. Persecution flared up and subsided, but in 1746 it was renewed after a man of Fogan denounced Peter for breaking the laws and winning thousands of people to Catholicism. Three of the Dominicans (Peter, Royo, and Alcober) were imprisoned, then chained and removed to Foochow. Here their patience under torture and mistreatment won the admiration of many. After a year in appalling conditions Peter was beheaded. His last words were, "Be of good courage; must we not rejoice that we are to die for the law of our God?" The other four Dominicans, one of whom, Francis Serrano, was appointed coadjutor bishop, were all executed in prison in 1748. They were beatified together in 1893.

See *Bibl. SS.*, 11, 643–6; M. J. Savignol, *Les Martyrs Dominicains de la Chine au XVIIIe siècle* (1894). See also "Martyrs of China," 17 Feb.

R.M.

St Simetrius, martyr (second century)

St Felicissima, martyr of Umbria (third-fourth century)

St Zacharias, bishop of Vienne (fourth century)

St Godo of Troyes, abbot (seventh century)

St Berengarius, monk in Narbonne (1093)

Bd Francis Patrizi, Servite friar (1154)

St Joseph Chang Songjib, martyr at Seoul, Korea (1839)—see "Martyrs of Korea," 26 Sept.

SS John Doan Trinh Hoan and Matthew Nguyen Van Phuong, martyrs in Tonkin (1861)—see "Martyrs of Vietnam (Tonkin)," 2 Feb.

St Andrew Kaggwa, martyr in Uganda (1866)—see "Martyrs of Uganda," 3 June.

27

ST AUGUSTINE OF CANTERBURY, *Abbot and Bishop* (*c.* 604)

Pope St Gregory the Great (3 Sept.) initiated the conversion of the Anglo-Saxons, and Augustine was the pioneer who began to execute it. Like the conversion of other nations, this was an immense task that exceeded the capacity of any one man. Augustine set out for England in 596 but died less than ten years later. His achievement was to initiate the conversion process in the south-east of England in the then most important of the seven Anglo-Saxon kingdoms, whose ruler he baptized and in whose principal town of Canterbury he built a small cathedral and a monastery. He also founded the dioceses of Rochester and London and built several churches in Kent. The calendar date of his death is known (26 May) but not the year in which he died. The principal sources for all we know of him are the Letters of Gregory and the *History* of Bede.

Augustine was Italian by birth and a pupil of Felix, bishop of Messana. He became a monk, and later prior, of the monastery of St Andrew on the Celian Hill at Rome. In 596 he was sent by Gregory, by then pope, as the leader of the party of monks, to bring the Christian faith to the Anglo-Saxons. The king of Kent, Ethelbert, already had a Christian wife, Bertha. One reason for the enterprise was the failure of neighbouring Christians (that is, the Welsh) to undertake their conversion. This had been revealed to Gregory in previous correspondence. The author of the earliest Life of Gregory, a monk of Whitby (who wrote about 710 but used older traditions) tells of how Gregory, before he was pope, was impressed by the sight of Anglo-Saxon slaves for sale in the Roman Forum, which inspired the famous "not Angles but angels" remark.

It seems likely that Gregory would have liked to lead such a mission himself, but after becoming Bishop of Rome had to delegate it to others. The motivation, at least in part, for this unusual move was that in Gregory's view the times were so evil and so full of disasters that there might not be much time left in which to bring the gospel to all nations. This bold and dangerous initiative was nearly spoilt before it began. The party set off from Rome, but when they reached Provence, some of them wished to give up because it was too uncertain, dangerous and arduous. Gregory refused to cancel the venture and wrote a famous letter telling them to trust in God and in Augustine, now promoted to be their abbot. They had already been provided with letters of introduction, thanks to which their route can be traced. This included Lérins, Marseilles, Aix-en-Provence, Arles, Vienne, Lyons, Autun, and Tours. From there they probably went northward by land, crossing the Channel from Boulogne or Quentavic. On the way they acquired some Frankish clergy to act as interpreters. When they reached Kent, the party numbered about forty—perhaps thirty monks and ten Franks—and by now (it seems certain from Gregory's letters) Augustine had already been consecrated bishop by the bishops in the Reims area. They landed in Thanet (traditionally at Pegwell Bay). They met Ethelbert, saying they were bearers of good news, namely the promise of eternal joy in heaven in an eternal kingdom with the true and living God. The king told them to remain on the isle of Thanet and ordered that they should be provided with everything necessary until he decided their future. He then came to meet them there in the open air (for fear of spells) and sat down with his retainers to hear their preaching. He gave them a dwelling in Canterbury with appropriate "provisions" (or the land on which to produce them) and freedom to preach.

After this good beginning, Bede tells us, they lived the apostolic life of the early Church, busy with prayers, vigils, and fasts. The first church for their liturgy was that dedicated to St Martin (a Frankish saint), while its structure was believed to be Roman. The turning point for any Christian mission to a barbarian race was the conversion of the king. He would not easily venture on a change of religion without the support of his principal noblemen. Time must have been necessary to ensure this support. At some unknown date between 597 and 601 Ethelbert became a Christian. The roles of Bertha (his wife) and of her bishop-chaplain, Liuthard, are unknown. The former was gently reproved by Gregory for not doing more, while the latter may have been old or infirm. Bede's narrative, interrupted by his addition of the questions of Augustine and the answers of Gregory (now recognized as substantially authentic), covers several years' apostolate and tells of the sending of more monks from Rome, of plans for expansion, and of the re-use of pagan structures for Christian worship. Inevitably, the problems were enormous.

To help resolve them, Augustine wrote to Gregory for guidance. The pope answered that revenues should customarily be divided into four: one part for the bishop and his household, one for the clergy, one for the poor, and one for the repair of churches. The bishop should live with his clergy in one household. Those in minor orders were free to marry and then receive stipends from outside but would still live a regular life and attend to chanting the psalms. Details of the liturgy Augustine had found in Gaul could be re-used at Canterbury. Those who rob churches should be punished in love, but the Church should not gain any financial advantage. The churches of England and Gaul have no authority over each other. Varied moral guidance followed. Elsewhere Gregory provided for the future of the Church in England by sending the *pallium* to Augustine, providing for a northern province based in York with twelve suffragans under an archbishop, just as there would be twelve suffragans under Augustine in the south. Gregory, using old records of Roman Britain, assumed that the southern metropolitan see would be at London, but from the earliest times Augustine set his see in Canterbury, the main town of England's most powerful ruler. This arrangement was continued after his death.

It now seems agreed that many of Augustine's arrangements were based on contemporary Roman thinking. He established a monastery of SS Peter and Paul outside the walls (this was called St Augustine's after his death); he dedicated the cathedral as Christ Church (the earliest dedication of Rome's oldest cathedral, later called St John Lateran); and he set up a "suburban" see at Rochester. This was based on those at Rome, but as the Canterbury establishment was so small, there was but one of these compared to Rome's seven. Roman martyrs were also chosen as patrons of early Kentish churches, such as Pancras (12 May) and the Four Crowned Martyrs (8 Nov.), whose relics might well have been sent to England with the reinforcements of 601.

Details about Augustine's apostolate are hard to find. Christianity had been a predominantly urban religion, and in Kent (apart from Reculver, Canterbury and Rochester) there are few surviving traces of buildings. Gregory's general instructions to monks expected them to stay in their monasteries and leave evangelization to the diocesan clergy, but in sending about thirty monks to England Gregory with his habitual wisdom must have realized that a pioneering venture must have some flexibility. We should not readily accept assertions made in the eleventh and twelfth centuries that the cathedral had always been staffed by monks. On the contrary, the monastery (built within a stone's throw of the cathedral) underlines the need for two centres, not one, from the beginning. So far as we know, the monks of Augustine were not formally Benedictines but monks of the Roman "basilican" type, devoted primarily to the liturgy and possibly a school rather than to itinerant preaching to a small and scattered rural peasantry. In Canterbury itself it seems likely that (in accordance with Roman practice) the monks from St Augustine's would have joined the cathedral clergy for morning and evening offices and were normally responsible for Matins and the short daytime offices. It is by no means certain that all the monks were priests, although some of them certainly were. The daily liturgy must have been a unifying occupation for the diverse clergy as well as an impressive spectacle for the unbelievers. In spite of Gregory's flexibility, Canterbury became famous for its liturgical chanting in the manner of the Rome of Gregory. Similarly, the order of Mass and the sacraments was most likely Roman.

It is often asked whether Augustine built on survivals of Romano-British Christianity. An unequivocal answer is impossible. There seems to have been a shrine of an otherwise unknown Sixtus still in existence, but by the time Augustine reached England the Romans had left over 150 years before. The dominant elements of the population of eastern England were certainly Angles, Saxons, and Jutes, mainly pagan. On the other hand, the conversion of the English was not a merely insular event. It was achieved by a combination of Christian influences of which Augustine's Roman monks were one, the Irish (or Scotti) from Lindisfarne another, while the Frankish churches also contributed some diocesan priests, requested by Gregory from the Frankish rulers and bishops. These may well have been the nucleus of the earliest diocesan clergy.

Relations with the Welsh Christians, however, were bad. Augustine, as usual implementing Gregory's plan, tried to obtain their cooperation but to no avail. No doubt it was expected that the metropolitan would rule all southern Britain and that the Christianization would proceed along the same lines as elsewhere in the Roman Empire on the basis of urban dioceses being the unit in matters of both Church and State. But the Celtic Christian unit of rural monasteries, not towns, did not easily adopt either the Roman government or the Roman calculation of Easter. Bede's account of the meeting of Augustine and the Welsh bishops is legendary in detail, and his unpleasing interpretation of divine punishment overtaking their people in the later Battle of Chester is an indication of how his principal aim in his *History* was to tell of the Christianization of the Anglo-Saxon (not the Welsh) people. The non-cooperation that had ensued was doubtless due to faults on both sides; it was one factor in Augustine's decision to concentrate on the east rather than the west of England.

The favour of England's most powerful ruler of that time enabled him to found a cathedral in London (then part of the East Saxons' territory), on the site of what is now St Paul's cathedral. This venture met with political setbacks owing to the local kings' desire for independence from Ethelbert, and it was abandoned for a time. In character Augustine, like other Roman missionaries, was serious; he preferred a limited-area consolidation to more charismatic enterprises. He laid the foundations; others would complete the edifice. His achievements have sometimes been exaggerated or misunderstood. Not Augustine but Gregory was regarded by three writers of the eighth century as the "apostle of England." It is not certain that he was a Benedictine or that he brought the Rule of St Benedict into England; the latter distinction probably belongs to Benedict Biscop and Wilfrid. He was, however, reputed to have brought Gregory's *Pastoral Care*, which is likely enough, while a fragmentary "Gospel Book" called the *Gospels of St Augustine*, written in Italian uncial script, is very probably his. After about ten years of pioneering work he died, having established three dioceses and one monastery in south-east England and consecrated Laurence as his successor. The close links between the papacy and Canterbury (a miniature Rome) lasted for well over a century, being strengthened by the papal appointment of the Greek Theodore (19 Sept.) as archbishop of Canterbury (669-90).

Augustine was buried in his monastery of SS Peter and Paul, Canterbury; the location of his tomb is known, among those of other worthies of Kent's time of conversion. His relics were translated with great solemnity in 1091 to the place of greatest honour in the east end of the new church. A new account of his life and miracles was written by Goscelin, the Flemish biographer of English saints. In the Middle Ages the antiquity of St Augustine's abbey was accorded papal recognition, and its abbot ranked immediately after the abbot of Monte Cassino. Nowadays Augustine is seen as of ecumenical importance, as reflecting a time when Rome and Canterbury spoke with one voice. The feast was originally on 26 May, certainly his death-day, but is now on 27 May, while his translation feast was on 13 September.

Gregory's Letters are in D. Norberg, *Gregorii Papae registrum epistolarum*, 2 vols. (*Corpus Christianorum* 140-140A, 1982); and also in D. Norberg, *S. Gregorii Magni Registrum epistularum*, 2 vols. (*Corpus Christianorum*, 140-1140A, 1982). Bede's *Ecclesiastical History*, written in 731, is the second source and can be read in English in the edition by B. Colgrave and R.A.B. Mynors (1969) or in Penguin Classics (ed. L. Sherley-Price and D. H. Farmer); article by the latter in *Benedict's Disciples* (2d ed., 1995), pp. 41-50. The best recent study is by N. Brooks, *The Early History of the Church of Canterbury* (1984); see also P. Hunter Blair, *The World of Bede* (1970), pp. 41-79, and H. Mayr-Harting, *The Coming of Christianity to Anglo-Saxon England* (1972); J. Campbell, *The Anglo-Saxons* (1982); M. Deansley, *Augustine of Canterbury* (1964).

St Julius the Veteran, *Martyr* (d. 304)

The authentic Acts of Julian reveal the outlook of a devout soldier similar in many ways to those of our own day. He had served in seven military campaigns during twenty-seven years' unblemished service. When the prefect Maximus interrogated him, he said that he must be faithful to higher orders, and that during all his military service, including the time when he had re-enlisted as a veteran, he had reverently worshipped the God who made heaven and earth, whom also he served right up to that day. Maximus praised him as wise and serious and offered him a bonus if only he would sacrifice to the gods. If Julius would give the impression of acting voluntarily, Maximus would take on himself any blame. Julius, however, steadily refused. He was then asked why he feared a dead man more than the living emperor. He answered: "It was he who died for our sins to give us eternal life. This same man, Christ, is God and abides for ever and ever. Whoever believes in him will have eternal life; whoever denies him will have eternal punishment." Maximus then advised him compassionately to continue his life by offering sacrifice. Julius answered: "To live with you would be death for me. . . . I have chosen death that I may live with the saints for ever."

He was due to be executed at Durostorum (Silistria, Bulgaria). On his way there he was greeted by another Christian soldier in prison called Isichius. "Take the crown," he said, "which the Lord has promised to give to those who believe in him, and remember me, for I too will follow you. Give my warmest greetings to the servant of God, our brother Valentino, who has already gone before us to the Lord by his loyal confession of faith." When Julius took the blindfold, he said: "Lord Jesus Christ, I suffer this for your name. I beg you to receive my spirit together with your holy martyrs." The executioner then ended Julius' life by the sword. He was formerly commemorated today with some companions mentioned only in Greek synaxaries (summaries), but is now alone in the new Roman Martyrology.

See his Acts in *A.C.M.*, pp. 261-5, on which this entry is closely based. The Bollandists underline their authenticity in *Propylaeum*, pp. 211-2, and in *Anal. Boll.* 31 (1912), pp. 259-390.

St Eutropius, *Bishop* (476)

Born at Marseilles, Eutropius led a wordly life until his marriage. When his wife died, he became a cleric and later a priest through the help of the local bishop Eustachius. His conversion proved permanent and fruitful. On the death of its bishop, Justus, Eutropius was chosen as his successor in the ancient diocese of Orange (Vaucluse, about fifteen miles north of Avignon). This had just suffered much destruction by invading Visigoths. Its general condition of material and moral collapse led Eutropius to consider flight. A holy counsellor persuaded him to change his mind, and the new bishop proved exemplary in difficult circumstances. A contemporary letter by St Sidonius Apollinaris (21 Aug.), bishop of Clermont, who had experienced similar difficulties in his own diocese, shows much respect for Eutropius' learning and piety. Sidonius, an eloquent but verbose writer, has been regarded as the last representative of classical culture. A sepulchral inscription of Eutropius described him as faultless.

AA.SS., May, 6, pp.699-700; *O.D.C.C.*, p. 1273 (for Sidonius); *Bibl.SS.*, 5, 345.

St Melangell (date unknown)

The small church of Pennant Melangell near Llangynog (north Powys), with its twelfth-century shrine recently and lovingly restored, is and has long been a pilgrimage centre to Melangell, a Welsh princess who became a solitary and later, it is said, abbess. There is no written record of her before the sixteenth century. This story of Monacella (the Latin form of her name) claims that she was the daughter of an Irish king, who had vowed herself to God. When she was pressed to marry, she fled into Powys for fifteen years. A prince, Brochwell Ysgythrog, was hunting a hare, which took refuge in Melangell's skirt; his hounds withdrew, howling. The prince, hearing her explanation, made her a present of the land around as a perpetual refuge and place of sanctuary.

The late date of this story and the folkloric frequency of hares in Celtic legend, not to mention the absence of any firm record of facts and dates, makes this story suspect. But the existence of a long-standing shrine on a very remote site does provide some sort of archeological evidence for her existence, if not for the details of the story. The shrine makes one realize the problems William of Malmesbury had in the twelfth century when he tried to record details of largely forgotten Old English saints. In some cases at least, he had little evidence apart from a shrine. Melangell's shrine at the present time is visited by members of the Eastern Orthodox Church as well as of the Church of Wales (who are its devoted custodians) and Catholics of the neighbourhood.

See *Archaeologia Cambrensis* 1838 for further details.

BB Edmund Duke and Companions, *Martyrs* (1563-90)

Born in Kent and educated as a Protestant, Edmund became a Catholic and studied for the priesthood first at Douai and then at Rome, where he was ordained priest in 1589. With three other priests (BB Richard Hill, John Hogg, and Richard Holiday) he travelled home from Reims. They landed near Tynemouth, where there had been a centre for priests and students; but this had been discovered by pursuivants, and the four were betrayed when they sought shelter in a village. It must not be forgotten that this happened in the year after the Spanish Armada failed. Edmund and his companions suffered the usual penalty for the new "treason" charge of being priests ordained abroad (see under 4 May) by being hanged, drawn, and quartered. The burial register of St Oswald's at Durham records the interment of the four priests. They were beatified by Pope John Paul II in 1987.

See B. C. Foley, *The Eighty-Five Blessed Martyrs* (1987).

R.M.

St Clement, Studite monk (ninth century)

St Liberius or Oliver, hermit of Ancona (ninth-tenth century)

St Bruno, bishop of Franconia (1045)

St Gausbert, priest-hermit in Arvernia (1079)

SS Barbara Kim, Barbara and Teresa Yi, Martha and Lucy Kim, martyrs in Korea (1839)—see "Martyrs of Korea," 26 Feb.

SS Athanasius Bazzekuketta and Gonzaga Gonza, martyrs in Uganda (1886)—see "Martyrs of Uganda," 3 June

---

28

St Justus of Urgel (*c.* 550)

Justus was the first known bishop of Urgel (near Tarragona in eastern Spain); he took part in councils at Toledo and Lérida in 527 and 546. Little is known of his achievements apart from a short mystical commentary on the Canticle of Canticles, dedicated to his metropolitan and remarkable for its learning and piety. Three of his brothers were also bishops, of Valencia, Egara, and Heusca. Justus is described in St Isidore's work *On Famous Men*.

See *AA.SS.*, May, 6, p. 118; H. Quentin in *Revue Benedictine 23* (1906), pp. 257-60 and 487-60; *Bibl.SS.*, 7, 37.

St Germanus of Paris (*c.* 500-76)

Germanus is less well known than his namesake of Auxerre, while for Parisians their patron Genevieve (3 Jan.) is a more familiar figure. Germanus, however, had a contemporary biographer in Venantius Fortunatus (14 Dec.) and there is evidence for an early cult in both the translation of his relics and his early appearance in martyrologies.

Germanus was born at Autun (Burgundy). He was educated at Avallon with his cousin Stratidius, whose mother attempted to poison Germanus to obtain his legacy. But the poison was drunk instead by her son, who did not die but suffered ill effects for most of his life. Germanus then lived for fifteen years in semi-monastic life before being ordained priest by Agrippinus, bishop of Autun. His successor, Nectaire, appointed him abbot of the monastic church of St Symphorien, Autun, which followed the Rule of Lérins. The lands belonging to the community, sometimes distant, were efficiently administered by Germanus. After the conquest of Burgundy by the Franks, Autun and Chalon-sur-Saône were ruled by Theodebert, grandson of Clovis. He died soon after Germanus prophesied his death, and Childebert, king of Paris, succeeded him and soon invited Germanus there for a council.

Six metropolitans and twenty-one bishops from the two kingdoms had assembled, and the principal business was the deposition of the bishop of Paris, Saffaracus. He had admitted a crime (unspecified) and retired to a monastery. It seems likely that his fault was neither doctrinal nor moral but that he had opposed the king. For whatever reason, he retired, and Germanus was appointed in his place. Childebert supported him generously, both for relieving the poor and for building two important churches, the cathedral of St Stephen and the basilica of St Vincent and the

Holy Cross, where both king and bishop were buried. In the Council of 552 Germanus held an important place, as he did in the Council of Tours in 567. By now Charibert had succeeded Childebert, but he pillaged churches and was notoriously dissolute. When he married two sisters at once, Germanus excommunicated him. In 573 King Sigebert waged war on Childebert for killing his sister-in-law; but Germanus, wanting a peaceful solution, warned him not to proceed further by force. Sigebert refused and was assassinated soon afterward.

Germanus, like Gregory of Tours (17 Nov.) and others, helped to propagate the cults of saints. When abbot of St Symphorien, he used to spend long hours praying by the shrine. He launched the cult of Bishop Marcel in 566 and translated the body of Ursin of Bourges. During his lifetime Germanus had the reputation of a miracle-worker. Stories of his cures throw some light on the diseases and disabilities then most frequent. The blind were specially numerous, so was paralysis of the hands. Complications like gangrene often accompanied the maladies. Epileptics also appeared frequently, not to mention those possessed. Often he used remedies dictated by common sense, such as oil. Sometimes he healed at a distance through blessed bread or salt or hot and cold water. Prisoners and slaves of all races were the special object of his charity.

Germanus died in Paris on 28 May 576, with a great reputation for holiness, and was buried in the basilica he had founded, afterward called Saint-Germain-des-Prés in his honour. In 756 his body was translated into the choir, behind the altar of Holy Cross. The relics were removed for safety during the Viking invasions; in 1408 Abbot William provided a splendid reliquary, which was placed above the high altar in 1704. This was destroyed in the French Revolution. By about 600 his name had been added to martyrologies. About a thousand years later his abbey became famous as one of the most notable centres of Benedictine scholarship under Maurist direction.

See *H.S.S.C.*, 3, pp. 149-53, on which this entry is principally based; Life by Venantius Fortunatus in *M.G.H.*, *Scriptores Merov.*, 7 (1920), pp. 337-428.

St William of Gellone (812)

William's life was spent in a time of important political change. He was born in the reign of Pepin the Short (715-68), son of Charles Martel (see Boniface, 5 June) and father of Charlemagne (742-814). William was the son of Thierry, count of Toulouse, and had the education suitable to his rank. He went to serve at court, by which time Pepin had died and Charlemagne had become king of the Franks (768). William filled various offices at the court and was sent by him to fight against the Saracens who were threatening the Franks, mainly through Spain. William was a most successful soldier, defeated these Moors, and was regarded as an ideal Christian knight in various (later) *chansons de geste*. As a suitable reward for his military success, he was created duke of Aquitaine, which also gave him an obvious power base if hostilities were resumed. He was not completely content, however, with a fine worldly career. He wished to build a monastery and fill it with monks from

Aniane (near Narbonne), then known as the most notable centre of Benedictine monasticism in western Europe (see St Benedict of Aniane, 750-821; 12 Feb.). He found a suitable site at Gellone, about an hour's journey away, and achieved his aim of founding not one but two monasteries: one for monks, the other for nuns, where his sisters joined the community.

Still, for some years he lived at court, enjoying great favour and prestige, but eventually, with Charlemagne's consent, he left the court to become a monk in the abbey he had built. As a symbol of his determination he hung up his weapons in the church of St Julian at Brioude (Haute-Loire) on his way to Gellone from Charlemagne's court (sometimes itinerant, but usually at Aachen). Once arrived at Gellone, he received the monastic habit from St Benedict of Aniane, who now became his spiritual guide. After some years he died in the monastery on 28 May 812; it was later called after him St William in the Wilderness. He was canonized by Alexander II in 1066.

AA.SS., May, 6, pp. 154-73; G. Morin in *Revue Charlemagne 2* (1913), pp. 116-26; *Bibl. SS.*, 7, 467-70

St Gizur of Iceland (1117)

Skalholt was the first see in Iceland. Isleif, Gizur's father, was its first bishop. Gizur succeeded him, built the cathedral church, and worked strenuously for the Christian faith. Iceland had been converted to Christianity in the year 1000 after an acrimonious meeting of the Thing (assembly). Christians, who had been converted through the influence of English, Norwegian, and German settlers, were in the minority; but the assembly decided to leave the decision whether to convert or not to the wise man chosen by the assembly. To the surprise, probably, of the pagan majority, he decided that they should all follow one law and one religion. Vestiges of heathenism were tolerated for a time, like the exposure of unwanted infants and secret sacrifices; but after a few years these too were officially abolished.

From such a beginning it was not surprising that even literary Iceland did not at once conform in all things to the latest Christian thinking and practice elsewhere. At first there were few priests, usually foreigners. They introduced Roman script to Iceland. The chieftain, Gizur the White (grandfather of today's saint), was one of the first to accept baptism. His son Isleif was the most famous of the first generation of native clergy, married, like a number of other "unreformed" priests at this time. Isleif became bishop (1056-80) and was succeeded in office by his son, our Gizur, who introduced tithes, provided for the poor, carried out a census for taxation, and divided Iceland into two dioceses, Skalholt in the south-west and Holar in the north. Toward the end of his life part of Iceland's law was committed to writing for the first time. How far he was connected with Iceland's impressive development of poetry, history, and sagas or with Icelandic explorations to Greenland and North America, we do not know. It is, however, interesting to note the comment of the famous Harold Hardrada about bishop Gizur: he was fit to be a king, a leader of Vikings, or a bishop. The cult of Gizur was authorized for Reykjavik but seems never to have been confirmed. Among Scandinavian saints he is an interesting figure who belonged to the first native clergy, well before the time when other Scandinavian saints like Augustine (Eystein) of Trondheim (26 Jan.) did all they could to normalize Scandinavian Christian observance, not least by strong insistence on clerical celibacy.

See G. Jones, *A History of the Vikings* (1984); *Bibl. SS.*, 7, 55. M. Cormack, *The Saints in Iceland* (1994).

Bd Lanfranc of Canterbury, *Bishop* (1005-89)

It is a curious fact that the cult of Lanfranc, archbishop of Canterbury 1070-89, seems to have had no support from Canterbury, but it did and does flourish at Pavia, where he was born, and at Bayeux and Bec-Hellouin (Normandy). He was Italian, not Norman, but most of his later life was spent in Normandy or England.

He deserves to be remembered as scholar, monk, and archbishop. In England the last of these elements has been well covered by Sir Frank Stenton and others: he was a man of order who left a notable mark on the Church in England, whether by rebuilding the cathedral at Canterbury or reorganizing its monastery and its scriptorium, or by assuring the status of manorial priests and transferring bishoprics to fortifiable towns. He worked harmoniously with William I and even with William II for the good of both Church and State.

His earlier life has been less well chronicled. After being educated at Pavia and elsewhere, he left Italy and built up a reputation as a teacher and scholar in Burgundy and Normandy. In 1042 he became a monk at Bec, recently founded by a Norman knight, Herluin, and in 1045 he became prior. He raised its level of achievement as a centre of learning and with his gift for administration helped it in other ways too. His main works in the Bec period were commentaries on St Paul's Epistles, excerpts from which reached a wider readership through Anselm of Laon. In 1063 he became abbot of St Stephen's, Caen. He had previously attacked William's marriage to Matilda because it was in the prohibited degrees, but eventually he was entrusted with the negotiations with the pope for its being regularized. Shortly before he was appointed to Canterbury by Alexander II in consultation with William I, he wrote his most famous treatise *On the Body and Blood of the Lord*, a Eucharistic treatise against Berengarius. Lanfranc's main point was that the sacred species in the Eucharist contained the invisible body of Christ, identical with the body born of Mary, but hidden under the species of bread and wine. He was thus a precursor of the doctrine of transubstantiation. After this, he wrote his *Monastic Constitutions*.

As archbishop of Canterbury he remained very much a monk. The English writer Eadmer gave an example of his sensitive consideration both for an English monk and his mother when an alms had been lost. But he could also be stern, as in his later treatment of the monks of St Augustine's abbey who had rebelled against their new abbot and were eventually dispersed to other houses. He also had a temporary suspicion of Anglo-Saxon saints with little hard evidence for their sanctity; but when he consulted the future St Anselm (21 Apr.) about the claim of St Alphege (19 Apr.) to be a martyr, Anselm strongly supported this claim. The cult of St Dunstan (19 May) was under a cloud for a time, and Lanfranc ordered the relics of obscure Evesham saints to be subjected to an ordeal by fire, from which they emerged successfully and then proved their value as fundraisers for the new buildings. It may be that his attitude toward the English saints as well as his policy of appointing Norman bishops and abbots contributed to the lack of development of his cult at Canterbury. Most historians nowadays, however, thoroughly approve of his orderly policies for the Church in England, while the monastic Order experienced an enormous increase of personnel during his episcopate; and (against his first impressions) he added to the number of monastic cathedrals in England with Rochester, Norwich, Durham, and Coventry. His letters survive, ranging from an eloquent jeremiad to the pope on his appointment to Canterbury to perceptive treatment of problem cases of bishops and monks. All in all, Lanfranc contributed powerfully to the good of the Church in his own lifetime, and he has been appreciated as a teacher and writer as well as an administrator of a very high calibre, thanks especially to his outstanding knowledge of canon and civil law. He died on 28 May 1089.

M.T. Gibson, *Lanfranc of Bec* (1978); H. Clover and M. Gibson, *The Letters of Lanfranc, Archbishop of Canterbury* (1979); F. M. Stenton, *Anglo-Saxon England* (1965), pp. 650-70; R. W. Southern, *St Anselm* (1990); Eadmer's *History of Recent Events in England* (trans. G. Bosanquet, 1964); D. Knowles, *The Monastic Constitutions of Lanfranc* (1951); *Bibl. SS.*, 7, 1101-6.

St Ignatius of Rostov, *Abbot* (1288)

Ignatius became a monk and later abbot (archimandrite) of the monastery at Rostov (north of Moscow) and was chosen as bishop in 1262. His see was occupied for a time by the Tartars, and the nobles of his town were divided. In 1274 a synod was held at Vladimir, which complained that "people still follow the customs of the thrice-accursed heathen; they celebrate sacred feast-days with devilish observances, whistling, yelling and howling; low drunken fellows get together and beat one another with sticks until some are killed, and these they strip of their clothes." If this report is accurate, it seems clear that all was not well with the thirteenth-century Russian church. Ignatius also had to contend with false accusations, which resulted in his removal from office, followed by reinstatement. He was remembered as a great peacemaker in his country during his life and for his miracles after his death.

See *Bibl. SS.*, 7, 705-6.

Bd Margaret Pole (1473-1541)

Daughter of the Duke of Clarence and niece of Edward IV and Richard III, she was given in marriage by Henry VII to Sir Reginald Pole of Buckinghamshire, who had served the king well in the Scottish campaign and elsewhere. When Henry VIII became king in 1509, Margaret was a widow with five children. Henry at this time described her as the saintliest woman in England, gave her back her brother's estates (forfeited by attainder), and created her countess of Salisbury in her own right. When Princess Mary was born, Margaret was appointed her governess. Later, when her disapproval of Henry's marriage to Anne Boleyn was known, she had to retire from court and lost the king's favour. Her son Reginald (subsequently cardinal in Mary's reign) wrote against the royal supremacy. This so annoyed Henry that he told the French ambassador that he meant to get rid of the whole family. After Neville's rising in the north, emissaries tried hard to implicate her in the conspiracy, but they failed after interrogating her from morning till night. Her intellectual ability as well as her tall figure and dignified bearing won their respect and admiration. Nevertheless, she was imprisoned in the Tower, where she suffered extremes of cold. Because it was believed that no jury would convict her, she was never brought to trial. A servile Parliament, however, passed an act of attainder against her. On 28 May 1541 she was led out into the square to be beheaded, at the age of seventy. The understudy executioner added to her suffering by his lack of skill. Her portrait can be seen in the National Portrait Gallery, London.

See B. Camm, *Lives of the English Martyrs*, 1, pp. 502-40.

Bd Mary Bartholomaea Bagnesi (1514-77)

Born of a noble and wealthy Florentine family, she was placed with a foster mother who severely neglected her, and she suffered from this for the rest of her life. Two of her sisters had become nuns and she wished to do the same, but when her mother died when Mary was seventeen, she had to take charge of the household. She did not seem to realize that she was expected to marry, and when her father told her he had chosen her bridegroom, she had a complete nervous breakdown through shock and became bedridden. Her apostolate among her visitors was extraordinary. Enemies were reconciled, the sorrowing consoled, sinners converted, and the sick healed. At the age of thirty-two she became a Dominican tertiary, which led to a temporary improvement in her health. After a short while she was bedridden again and received extreme unction eight times. Her life of almost continual suffering was relieved by ecstasies, of which she was very reluctant to speak. After being an invalid for forty-five years, she died on this day in 1577 and was buried in the Carmelite church of St Mary of the Angels. Her cult was approved in 1804.

Life by her chaplain in *AA.SS.*, May, 3, 321-48; *Bibl.SS.*, 2, 707-8.

BB Thomas Ford and Companions, *Martyrs* (1582)

These martyrs all suffered for exercising their priestly ministry and denying that Queen Elizabeth was supreme head (or "governor") of the Church, but ostensibly they were condemned for taking part in a fictitious conspiracy. Thomas Ford, a

Devon man, took his M.A. at Oxford and became a fellow of Trinity College. A Catholic at heart, he went to the English College, Douai, and was ordained priest. From 1576 till 1581 he worked as a priest in England but was captured with St Edmund Campion (1 Dec.) at Lyford Grange, Berkshire. He was committed to the Tower and was condemned to death on the evidence of informers who had never seen him before. When he was taken to execution, he declared: "I am a Catholic and do die in that religion." On the scaffold he acknowledged the queen as his sovereign and said he had never offended her in his life.

John Shert was also an Oxford man but a native of Cheshire and a student of Brasenose College. After he left Oxford he worked as a schoolmaster in London. Like Ford, he crossed the Channel to study at Douai and was ordained in Rome. From 1579 to 14 July 1581 he worked in England as a priest. In spite of a complete lack of evidence, he was condemned to be hanged. He was obliged to watch the disembowelling of Thomas Ford and cried out: "O blessed soul, happy art thou; pray for me!" At the last moment he could have saved himself by affirming that Elizabeth was head of the Church in England, but he answered: "She is not nor cannot be, nor any other, but only the supreme pastor."

Robert Johnson came from Shropshire. He became a manservant in a private family but then went to Douai also, where he was ordained in 1576 and was sent to the English mission. In 1580 he was committed to the Tower and cruelly racked three times. In November 1581 he was sentenced to death on the same charge as the other two and suffered with them. As the rope was placed round his head, he prayed aloud in Latin. Told to pray in English, he answered: "I pray that prayer which Christ taught in a tongue I well understand." He was still praying in Latin when the execution cart was drawn away from under him. Formerly, as in earlier editions of this work, four more priests were venerated with these three; but they suffered some days later, and the new Roman Martyrology confines today's entry to the three described above.

See B. Camm, *Lives of the English Martyrs*, 2, pp. 443-563.

R.M.

St Heliconides, martyr of Corinth (third century)
St Caraunus of Chartres, martyr (fifth century)
St Podius, bishop of Florence (eleventh century)
St Ubaldesca of Pisa (1206)
Bd Herculanus, O.F.M. (1451)
St Paul Hanh, martyr in Annam (1859)

29

St Maximinus of Trier, *Bishop* (*c.* 347)

A native of Poitiers, Maximinus left for Trier for his education, attracted by the reputation of its bishop, Agritius. Maximinus eventually succeeded Agritius as bishop in 333; he became famous for his opposition to Arianism and for the practical help he gave to its victims. The most celebrated of these was St Athanasius (2 May), who was the bishop's guest for two years (336-8), but St Paul of Constantinople (7 June), banished by the emperor Constantius, also enjoyed the hospitality and protection of Maximinus. He warned the emperor Constans (a frequent visitor to Trier) against Arianism, which he opposed both in councils and in private. This earned for him the praise of St Jerome (30 Sept.) as one of the most courageous bishops of his time. Unfortunately, none of Maximinus' writings has survived.

Life by Servatus Lupus (ed. B. Krusch) in *M.G.H., Scriptores Merov.*, 3, pp. 71-82; see also J. Hau, *Sankt Maximinus* (1935).

SS Sisinnius and Companions, *Martyrs* (397)

The fact of the martyrdom of these three Cappadocians seems certain. Reference to them is found in the letters of Vigilius, bishop of Trent, and in writings of St Augustine and St Maximus of Turin. Sisinnius was a deacon, Martyrius a reader, like his brother Alexander. St Ambrose (7 Dec.) recommended them warmly to Vigilius, who was short of clergy. He commissioned the three to spread the gospel in the Tyrolian Alps (especially Anaunia or Val di Non). In spite of opposition they won a number to the Christian faith, and Sisinnius built a church at Methon (Medol). The pagans, enraged at the spread of Christianity, tried to force the newly-converted to participate in a polytheistic festival. This the Christians refused to do; the three martyrs were attacked in their church and beaten severely. Sisinnius died shortly after. The other two were burned, alive or dead, in the same fire. Their ashes were taken to Trent by the faithful, and a church was built on the site of their martyrdom.

References in *Propylaeum*, p. 281; see *AA.SS.*, May., 6, pp. 388-400. *Bibl.SS.*, 11, 1251-4. See also E.M. Sironi, *Dall'Oriente in Occidente: i santi Sisinio, Martirio e Alessandro martiri in Anaunia* (1989).

St Bona of Pisa (1156-1207)

Little is known of this saint. She was a visionary, an indefatigable pilgrim (like the medieval St Godric (21 May) in early life or like St Benedict Joseph Labre (d.

1783; 16 Apr.) and was based at Pisa, where she died. She had several times made pilgrimages to the Holy Land, Rome, and Compostela. Her cult was a local one, confined to the diocese of Pisa.

See *Bibl. SS.*, 3, 234-7.

BB William Arnaud and Companions, *Martyrs* (1242)

The existence of this cult, confirmed in 1866 by the Holy See after many cures at their burial place, is a reminder that in the troubled times of the Albigensian heresy in south-western France there were Christian martyrs who suffered for the Faith and for obedience to the Holy See. The twelve who suffered comprised three Dominicans, two Franciscans, two Benedictines, four other clerics, and one layman.

The late twelfth and early thirteenth centuries were times when the idea of crusading had been extended to expeditions against heretics. This had happened in southern France, where its real momentum was provided by the French desire to extend their effective rule into the Toulouse-Carcassonne areas. This was achieved by war in 1229, when Count Raymond VII of Toulouse asked for peace. The action against the Cathars was continued by resettlement, dispossession, and the Inquisition from 1233. This slow erosion of Catharism, whose strict form implied belief in two Gods, one the creator of the spiritual world and the other the creator of the material world in which the soul was imprisoned, was considered necessary. It was often compared to preventing the spread of disease. The Inquisition was largely effective in this aim. It must be stressed, however, that the Church did not execute heretics, but when they refused all persuasion to recant (the Cathars rejected belief in the Church and its authority), they were handed over to the secular arm, that is, the civil power, for punishment.

The papal (as distinct from the diocesan) Inquisition was entrusted to the Dominicans by Pope Gregory IX in 1233, the same year that the university of Toulouse was formally founded on the Paris model. Both events took place twelve years after the death of St Dominic (8 Aug.). One may well believe that he would have approved of the second rather than the first, while the balanced views of St Thomas Aquinas (28 Jan.) provided the best answers to the Cathars' hatred of food, drink, sex, and other human activities. Some, at least, of today's martyrs were inquisitors, as was the more famous St Peter the Martyr (d. 1252; 29 Apr.), but we do not know how many were Dominicans—presumably at least three. Members of their Order, which originated in Toulouse, had been driven out by Cathar mobs. They conducted a preaching mission at Avignonet (to the south-west) with the help of local priests. They were offered hospitality in the castle there by the local bailiff of Raymund VII. As they were retiring to bed, they were butchered by soldiers secretly admitted into the building. The priests with their dying breath praised God in the words of the *Te Deum*. Many cures at their grave led to a cult, confirmed long after.

AA.SS., May, 6, 532-5; J. Procter, *Lives of Dominican Saints*, pp. 152-55; J. Riley-Smith, *The Atlas of the Crusades* (1991); *Bibl. SS.*, 2, 647-9.

St Andrew of Constantinople, *Martyr* (1465)

This saint, who came from Chiusa in the Italian Alps, was accused in Islamic Constantinople of having renounced the religion of Mohammed. He answered that he had always been a Christian. For this he was subjected to various tortures such as scourging, flaying, and fracture of limbs; finally, he was beheaded. His cult was based at Constantinople.

Bibl.SS., 1, 1126-7; *AA.SS.*, May, 6, pp. 536-40.

Bd Richard Thirkeld, *Martyr* (1583)

Born in the diocese of Durham, Richard was one of a group of English martyrs who were educated at Oxford. Richard had been a scholar of Queen's College there, had studied at Douai and Reims, and was ordained priest in 1579, by which time he was already an old man. He was sent on the English mission and ministered in and around York. When he visited a prisoner at night suspicion was aroused, and he was arrested nine days after the execution of Bd William Hart on the charge of being a priest. He admitted his priesthood, explained why he was in England, and was placed in the Kidcote prison, York. Two months later he was tried. Because he admitted that he had absolved and reconciled to the Catholic Church some of the queen's subjects, he was pronounced guilty of treason. In the condemned cell he spent the night instructing the criminals and preparing them for death. The next day he was condemned to death with the customary tortures. He thanked God, saying: "This is the day which the Lord has made: let us be glad and rejoice therein." His execution was carried out in secret because of the widespread sympathy and admiration for this venerable and holy priest.

M.M.P., pp. 79-83, and B. Camm, *Lives of the English Martyrs*, vol. 2, pp. 635-53.

Bd Joseph Gerard (1831-1914)

Joseph was born at Bouxières-aux-Chênes (France). Like many of his compatriots, he joined the Missionary Congregation called the Oblates of Mary Immaculate, founded by Bd Charles de Mazenod (see 21 May). This Congregation flourished in the Americas, but Joseph was sent to southern Africa, where he evangelized the Kaffirs without apparent success for seven years. He then went to northern Basutoland in 1876, founded the mission of St Monica and built a convent and a school. He had a special care for the sick and the suffering, constantly exercised during an apostolate of over twenty years. Based at a place called Rome, he laboured very long and hard, becoming the respected founder of this mission and its vigilant apostle. He was beatified in 1988, by which time the laity in this country numbered 600,000.

Bibl.SS., 6, 177-8.

Bd Ursula Ledochowska, *Foundress* (1865-1939)

Born at Loosdorf in Austria, she became an Ursuline nun at Cracow (Poland), and in 1907 she was sent to St Petersburg (Russia) to practise apostolic work of various kinds. In 1914 she had to leave Russia and worked in Scandinavia. After World War I she asked Pope Benedict XV to approve her new Congregation (Ursulines of the Sacred Heart). This she obtained with the help of her brother Vladimir, then general of the Jesuits. She set up the motherhouse of her Congregation, commonly called Grey Ursulines, at Pniewy (near Poznam). The Congregation has spread into different parts of Poland and outside Europe also. The Holy See asked her to reside at Rome. There she died on 29 May 1939 and is buried in her convent on the via del Casaletto. She was beatified at Poznam in 1983 by Pope John Paul II.

R.M.

St Restitutus, martyr at Rome (fourth century)

St Olbianus, bishop and martyr in Roman Asia (*c.* 300)

St Senator, bishop of Milan (*c.* 480)

St Gerard, monk, bishop, and hermit in Burgundy (*c.* 940)

Bd Gherardesca, anchoress of Pisa (*c.* 1269)

30

SS Basil and Emmelia (*c.* 370)

These were the saintly parents of SS Basil the Great (2 Jan.), Gregory of Nyssa (10 Jan.), Peter of Sebastea (formerly 9 Jan.), and Macrina the Younger (19 July). They had been exiled under Galerius Maximinus, but after the Peace of the Church they had returned to their native city of Caesarea (Cappadocia). This Basil's mother (grandmother of St Basil the Great), called Macrina the Elder, had also suffered persecution and exile near the Black Sea.

See *The Book of Saints* (ed. monks of Ramsgate, 1989).

St Isaac of Constantinople (*c.* 410)

This saint is principally known as the founder of the first monastery in Constantinople, where he gathered many disciples. Another title to fame is an incident earlier in his life. Isaac was then a solitary but left his hermitage in order to remonstrate with the emperor Valens. He warned Valens several times that unless he ceased his oppression and restored to the Catholics their churches which had been given to the Arians, disaster and a miserable end faced him. The emperor understandably treated these predictions with contempt. Once, when Isaac seized the bridle of his horse, he ordered him to be thrown into a swamp. Isaac escaped, repeated his prophecy, and was imprisoned. Valens was defeated and killed by the Goths at Adrianople (Edirne) in 478. His successor Theodosius released Isaac and venerated him as a holy man. Isaac tried to resume his solitary life, but disciples came and refused to leave him. This was how he came to found the monastery at Constantinople, called, after his successor Dalmatus, the Dalmatian monastery. Opinions differ about the date of Isaac's death; some prefer 383, previously rejected, to the more usual 410.

AA.SS, May, 6, pp. 598–612; *Anal. Boll.* 18 (1899), pp. 430–1; *Bibl.SS.*, 7, 920–1.

St Exuperantius, *Bishop* (418)

The diocese of Ravenna was large and important, even before the Eastern emperors developed it as a counterweight to papal influence in Italy. Its first bishop was Ursus; its second, Exuperantius. He lived in the reign of the emperor Honorius (384–423), who made Ravenna his capital in 403. Most of the real power in the West was held by Flavius Stilicho (359–408), a Vandal by blood, who had married the emperor's niece and whose own daughter had married Honorius. Stilicho's important wars saved the western empire for a time; when he came to Ravenna,

Exuperantius persuaded him not to desecrate and loot the cathedral. Stilicho was eventually murdered at Ravenna. Exuperantius built the town of Argenta, which paid a silver tribute to Ravenna. He died peacefully and was buried in the church of St Agnes, but his relics now rest in Ravenna cathedral.

History of Ravenna by Andreas Agnellus is in *M.G.H., Scriptores rerum Langobardicarum*, pp. 265 ff.

St Dympna, *Martyr* (Seventh Century)

The shrine of St Dympna at Geel (Limburg, east of Antwerp), which is of considerable antiquity and interest, is the centre of admirable work done in modern times in the care of the mentally ill. It is even claimed that it has been one of the pioneers in the movement for supervision and residence of patients "in the community"; that is, in Belgium, in the homes of farmers and other local residents.

Unfortunately the legend of Dympna is almost pure folklore. Supposedly the daughter of a Celtic king whose mother died when she was a child, Dympna bore an uncommon resemblance to her dead mother. Her father fell in love with her. To escape his incestuous attention she fled with her confessor, Gerebernus, to Antwerp and then to Geel (twenty-five miles away). Her father pursued them, tracing them through coins they had used, and discovered them living as solitaries. They refused to return with him, so his attendants killed the priest and the king killed his own daughter. Both bodies (of Dympna and Gerebernus) were buried on the spot, but they were both translated in the thirteenth century, an event marked by the cure of many epileptics and lunatics. This was the reason why Dympna became the patroness of the insane.

Her legend was described by H. Delehaye, the Bollandist, as "an adaptation of the well-known tale of the donkey's skin," but the same author also notes how patients at St Dympna's shrine make the round of the choir, walking under the arcade that supports it. He adds that if there is any resemblance between this practice and those of pagan antiquity recommending squeezing through a hole in a stone or a split tree, it is very remote. A far cry, indeed, from the supposed power in holed stones to a belief based on the virtue of relics. An infirmary was built for the insane by the end of the thirteenth century, and nowadays there is a fine sanatorium for the supervision and care of mental defectives. Dympna's feast was formerly on 15 May.

See *AA.SS.*, May, 3, pp. 477-97; H. Delehaye, *The Legends of the Saints* (1962); *O.D.S. (s.v.)*, p. 141. For a recent examination of the legend in relation to the "Donkeyskin" cycle of fairy tales, see M. Warner, *From the Beast to the Blonde: On Fairy Tales and Their Tellers* (1994), pp. 335-41.

St Walstan of Bawburgh (1016)

This local saint of Norfolk had no known liturgical cult, but an unofficial following with short Lives in Latin and English is well attested, and there was certainly a shrine which attracted pilgrims during the Middle Ages. As with the cult of St

Urith of Chittlehampton (Devon; see 8 July), the local veneration continued right up to Reformation times.

The legend of Walstan contains folkloric elements but also some perfectly credible data. In order to highlight these it seems best to omit the claims to royal birth and to the presence of bishop and monks at his funeral. In its basics, the life of Walstan resembles that of St Isidore the Farmer (15 May). Both saints worked as agricultural labourers; both had stories and cures connected with rural life; both had strong and persistent local following. Walstan was born at Bawburgh and went to work for a farmer at Taverham, only seven miles away but separated by a forest. He gave alms to those poorer than himself, sometimes food, and once his shoes, so that he himself went barefoot. His master was very impressed by him and wished to make him his heir. Walstan refused but asked for a cow instead. The cow was in calf; later, the two calves born to her carried Walstan's body to the grave after he had received the last sacraments in a field, prophesied his death, and promised to help cure both men and beasts. Near Costessey, and again at Bawburgh, it was claimed that the cart tracks had given rise to springs of pure water. The shrine in the north aisle of Bawburgh church contained a Life written on vellum and placed on a wooden triptych. In addition to the vicar, there were, in the later Middle Ages, six chantry priests, and in 1309 the shrine offerings were large enough to pay for rebuilding the chancel. The shrine chapel was demolished under Henry VIII. According to Bale (1496-1563), "all mowers and scythe followers seek him once in the year"; the day when these farmers and labourers visited his shrine was 30 May. Paintings of Walstan survive on several East Anglian rood-screens, where he is depicted crowned or with a sceptre, holding a scythe, and sometimes accompanied by two calves. There is still local interest in him in Bowthorpe as well as Bawburgh and even in Rongai (Kenya).

See M.R. James, "Lives of St Walstan," in *Norfolk Archaeol. Soc. Papers* 19 (1917), pp. 238-67; *N.L.A.*, pp. 168-9; F. Husenbeth, *Life of St Walstan* (1859); C. Twinch, *Walstan of Bawburgh* (1989).

St Hubert of Liège (727)

Details of his early life are lacking, but Hubert entered the service of St Lambert, bishop of Maastricht, at an early age. He was chosen to succeed Lambert when the bishop was murdered in 705. Before and after this time Hubert was the apostle of the Ardenne, where he penetrated into remote areas and abolished the worship of idols. He was believed also to work miracles. Hubert translated the bones of St Lambert from Maastricht to Liège, then a village, now a city. With the bones he also transferred the centre of the diocese; hence Hubert is venerated as founder of the church and the city, while Lambert is its principal patron. Hubert was taken ill at Tervueren, near Brussels, soon after dedicating a church in Brabant. He died on 30 May 727 and was buried in Liège. In 825 his body was translated to Andain, now called Saint Hubert (Ardenne). He is patron of hunters and invoked against hydrophobia. Hubert has been popular with artists. During the fourteenth century the story of his conversion while hunting on Good Friday, with the stag displaying a crucifix between its horns, was borrowed from the Acts of St Eustace (formerly 20 Sept.). Two orders of chivalry (in Lorraine and Bavaria) were founded under his patronage, which implies a diffusion of his cult beyond local confines.

See *AA.SS.*, Nov., 1, pp. 759-930; M. Coens in *Anal. Boll.* 45 (1927), pp. 84-92 and 345-62; Lives by F. Peny (1961) and A. Paffrath (1961).

St Ferdinand of Castile (1199-1252)

The son of Alfonso IX of León and Berengaria of Castile, Ferdinand was born near Salamanca. He became king of Castile in 1217 and king of León in 1230. The union of these two Christian kingdoms made possible his principal achievement, the recovery from the Moors of much of southern Spain and its assimilation into the Christian State. The extent of his conquest is about one-third of present-day Spain. He campaigned successfully over twenty-seven years, and his victories included Ubeda (1234), Córdoba (1236), and Seville and Cadiz (1249). The battle of Xeres (now Jerez) was the one in which St James the Great (25 July) was believed to have led the army in person, when only twelve Spanish soldiers were killed. Ferdinand converted an important mosque at Seville into a church. After the wars, only Granada was left to the Moors, while Ferdinand induced a number of Spaniards to settle in the conquered territory, not least because many Muslims had left it. He also rebuilt Burgos cathedral in thanksgiving and restored the stolen bells to the cathedral of St James at Compostela.

Ferdinand was not only a successful soldier. He administered impartial justice and chose wise counsellors such as Ximénes, archbishop of Toledo. He founded the universities of Salamanca and perhaps Valladolid. He was politically tolerant to Jews and Muslims but encouraged the friars to convert them.

In 1219 he had married Beatrice of Swabia, and they had seven sons and three daughters. On the death of Beatrice he married Joan of Ponthieu, and they had two sons and a daughter, Eleanor, who was to become the wife of Edward I of England. Ferdinand died on 30 May 1252 and was buried not in royal robes but in the habit of a Franciscan tertiary. A widespread popular cult followed, which led to his canonization in 1671. His emblem in art is a greyhound.

AA.SS., May, 7, 281-414; D.W. Lomax, *The Reconquest of Spain* (1978); A. Mackay, *Spain in the Middle Ages: From Frontier to Empire, 1000-1500* (1977); Lives in Spanish by J. R. Coloma (1928) and in French by J. Laurentie (1910); see also *N.C.E.*, 5, 886-7; *O.D.S.*, pp. 176-7.

St Joan of Arc (1412-31)

A French patriot who was burned at the stake and rehabilitated by the Holy See in 1456, Joan was certainly important in raising French morale in the Hundred Years' War. She deserved a better fate than that of being betrayed to the English by Burgundians, neglected by her compatriots, and executed by English influence. She is a saint who has been much written about by authors who see in her much of their own presuppositions. She was a patriot but not a martyr; someone of immense courage and determination.

She was born at Domrémy (Meuse) of a peasant family; she learned spinning and sewing but not reading and writing. She apparently had a happy childhood, modified by the danger of attack from Lorraine and by the Hundred Years War. When she was three, Henry V won the battle of Agincourt and claimed the throne of the French king, the insane Charles VI. France was weakened by the divisions between the houses of Orleans and Burgundy, whose duke was murdered by the Dauphin's servants. This led the Burgundians to an alliance with the English, who continued the claim in spite of its immense cost, first under Henry V (d. 1422) and then his infant son Henry VI (aged one) and the Protector, the duke of Bedford. Meanwhile Joan, aged fourteen, in 1426 heard voices accompanied by a blaze of light. In 1428 she was told to present herself to the military authorities with a mission to "save France."

At this time Orleans was besieged and the French cause seemed uncertain. In 1429 Joan was admitted to the Dauphin's presence at Chinon. She somehow recognized him in disguise; he was impressed and she was sent to be examined by theologians at Poitiers, who found no fault in her and advised the Dauphin to make good use of her abilities. She asked for troops to relieve Orleans, and she rode at their head dressed in white armour and accompanied by a special banner bearing the words "Jesus: Maria." Military success in relieving Orleans and at the battle of Patay was due in part to the immense improvement of French morale through her novel intervention, believed to be a manifestation of divine help. The high point of her success was the crowning at Reims of the Dauphin as king Charles VII, with Joan standing by with her standard. This had been accomplished in spite of considerable opposition, since Joan was suspect in the predominantly male world of court, army, and Church.

An attack on Paris failed, but Compiègne was relieved from the Burgundian siege. By some accident the drawbridge was raised when Joan and some followers were still outside the town. She was captured and taken to the duke of Burgundy as his prisoner. No effort seems to have been made by the French king to obtain her release. On 21 November 1430 she was sold to the English. They wished to have her sentenced as a sorceress or a heretic. She was cross-examined before a tribunal presided over by Pierre Cauchon, bishop of Beauvais, with its officials chosen by him. Her "voices," her use of male dress, her faith, her willingness to submit to the Church, were all sifted. Occasionally her lack of education led her to make damaging answers; but she conducted herself, alone, with great courage and accuracy. A "grossly unfair summing-up" was made: the judges called her revelations diabolical and the University of Paris denounced her in violent terms.

They then decided she must be handed over to the secular arm as a heretic if she would not retract. This she did in part, but the exact terms are not clear. She then resumed male dress, originally worn for her own protection in a wartime environment but now regarded as provocative. Once more she declared that God had truly sent her and that her voices were from God. The judges, under Cauchon's influence, reported her as a relapsed heretic and on 30 May 1431, not yet twenty, she was burned at the stake in Rouen. Her demeanour was exemplary: a Dominican at her request held up a cross, and she died calling on the name of Jesus. After her death her ashes were thrown into the Seine. One of the English royal secretaries said, "We are lost: we have burned a saint."

About twenty years later, Joan's mother and two brothers appealed to the Holy See for the case to be reopened. Callistus III granted this, and in 1456 the original judgment was quashed and her innocence declared. This was a surprising but just decision, implying the injustice and victimization of Joan by an important bishop. This rehabilitation was important for her beatification in 1910 by St Pius X (21 Aug.) and her canonization just after World War I by Benedict XV in 1920. In France military crises have tended to favour her cult, and she has been declared a patron of France. In England there has been considerable interest in her as a victim of injustice, as manifested in G. B. Shaw's famous play and by the placing of her statue in Winchester cathedral opposite the rich tomb of Cardinal Beaufort, who had taken some part in her trial. More recently she has been hailed not as the "first Protestant," as in Shaw's play, but as a proto-feminist "ideal androgyne." In reality she was a simple country girl, able, sensible, and committed utterly to the truth of her revelations. These are not without difficulty, if only because they were supposedly due to St Margaret of Antioch and St Catherine of Alexandria, both of whom may never have existed (except in the pages of fiction). Whatever may be thought of that, the Holy See's record in the matter is impressive, and justice, if posthumous, was ultimately done. But those responsible for her death in the fifteenth century were in different degrees guilty of miscarriage of justice, all the more regrettable because of the involvement of ecclesiastics.

P. Tisset and Y. Lanhers, *Procès de Jeanne d'Arc* (3 vols., 1960-71); J. P. Barrett, *The Trial of Joan of Arc* (1931); studies by V. Sackville-West (1936), R. Pernoud (1954, Eng. trans. 1961), M. Warner (1980).

What appears to be her suit of armour, with marks coinciding with wounds she was known to have suffered, was discovered in the attic of a French country house in 1996.

BB William Scott and Richard Newport, *Martyrs* (1612)

These martyrs under James I remind us that persecution of Catholics continued after the death of Elizabeth. They were also both imprisoned more than once before execution. William Scott came from Chigwell and while studying law at Trinity Hall, Cambridge, was converted to Catholicism through reading. He went abroad and became a Benedictine in the abbey of St Facundus. After ordination he was sent on the English mission. As he entered London, he saw St John Roberts (25 Oct.), who had received him into the Church, being led to execution. Three days later William was arrested and imprisoned for a year. He was then deported, but returned. This process was repeated. After his final arrest, while in a boat from Gravesend to London, he threw into the river a bag which contained his Breviary, his faculties, and some medals and crosses. This bag was caught in a fisherman's net and was produced at his trial. His companion in prison was Richard Newport, a Northamptonshire man who had been trained in Rome and exercised a successful apostolate in England. He too had been imprisoned and banished before. The two were brought before the lord mayor, the bishop of London, the lord chief justice, and other magistrates. They defended themselves boldly, but their condemnation was a foregone conclusion simply because they were priests ordained abroad, and this fact alone made them guilty of "high treason." They were executed at Tyburn with the usual tortures on 30 May 1612.

M.M.P., pp. 323-9; B. Camm, *Nine Martyr Monks* (1931), pp. 180-237.

BB Luke Kirby and Companions, *Martyrs* (1582)

These martyrs were formerly venerated on 28 May with Thomas Ford and companions, called collectively the London Martyrs of 1582. The four priests commemorated today were in fact executed two days after the others, on 30 May. Luke Kirby was a northerner (from Yorkshire or Durham) and a Master of Arts. He joined Douai College in 1576 and was ordained priest in 1577. He went to England for a few months but returned to Rome for further study. He came back to England and was soon arrested and imprisoned. He was tortured by the instrument popularly known as the "scavenger's daughter." William Filby was an Oxford man who had been a student at Lincoln College there. Religious scruples led him overseas to the English seminary at Reims. Ordained priest in 1581, he was arrested with St Edmund Campion (1 Dec.) and shackled with manacles in the Tower of London for six months. He was twenty-seven years old. Laurence Richardson (or Johnson) was a Lancashire man who left Brasenose College, Oxford, to become a Catholic. Trained and ordained at Douai and ordained priest in early 1581, he was offered mercy on the scaffold if he would confess treason and renounce the pope, to which he answered: "I thank her Majesty for her mercy; but I must not confess an untruth or renounce my faith." Thomas Cottam also came from Lancashire and was a graduate of Brasenose College, Oxford. He too went abroad on becoming a Catholic, to Douai College. He then joined the Jesuits in Rome, but bad health prevented him from finishing his novitiate. He was ordained priest at Reims and asked to be sent on the English mission. Here he was betrayed by a notorious informer named Sledd, who had pretended to be his friend. Thomas was arrested at Dover and placed in the charge of Dr Ely, a Douai professor, who had not been recognized by the pursuivants. He allowed Thomas to escape, but the latter gave himself up when the authorities pressed Dr Ely. He was imprisoned in the Marshalsea prison and afterward in the Tower, where he too suffered from the "scavenger's daughter."

It will be noticed that all four of these martyrs had had a university education before going abroad. All were tried the previous November with St Edmund Campion, nominally for complicity in the bogus plot of Reims and Rome but really for being Catholic priests who ministered to the queen's subjects. All were imprisoned in the Tower of London and all were executed together at Tyburn.

See B. Camm, *Lives of the English Martyrs*, 2, pp. 443-563.

R.M.

St Felix, martyr of Rome (third century)
St Gabinus, martyr in Sardinia (fourth century)
St Hesychius, martyr of Antioch (fourth century)
St Anastasius, bishop of Papias (*c.* 680)
St Matthias Kalemba, martyr in Uganda (1886)—see "Martyrs of Uganda," 3
  June

ST JOAN OF ARC (pp. 171-3)
Gold crown and fleur-de-lis, sword with gold hilt
and silver blade, on gold field.

31

THE VISITATION OF THE BLESSED VIRGIN MARY

This feast commemorates the visit of Mary to her cousin Elizabeth, as recorded in Luke 1:39-56. It had a Franciscan origin, when the general chapter of 1263 introduced it at the request of St Bonaventure (15 July). During the time of the Great Schism, Urban VI and Boniface IX (1389) took it into the Roman Calendar, hoping that its celebration would end the schism. This, however, did not happen at once. The Council of Basle ordered its celebration, but only under St Pius V did it attain universal status, with the date of 2 July. In 1969 the date was changed to 31 May to stress its scriptural links with the feasts of the Annunciation (25 Mar.) and the birthday of St John the Baptist (24 June).

In considering the historical event of Mary's visit to Elizabeth, we need to recall the Annunciation, which gave rise to it. Mary had just been told that she was to be the mother of the Saviour. She went to share the good news with her cousin Elizabeth, who had conceived a son six months earlier in her mature years. This was a visit of charity, accomplished by a journey from Nazareth to Judaea. As soon as Elizabeth heard her voice, the child "leapt in her womb." She called Mary "blessed among women" and blessed for believing in the angel's message. Mary responded by saying the *Magnificat*, the perfect song of praise and thanksgiving for the Incarnation, yet one with many phrases of biblical and especially psalmic inspiration. It is at once a highly personal response and one that can be said by all. This is why it is part of Vespers every day; hence it can be said that each day of the year (and not only 31 May) is one on which the Visitation is commemorated by the Church. The reading in the Breviary for today's feast is from a homily by Bede: "Not only blessed among women, but with an eminent blessing among all blessed women. Nor is the fruit of her womb blessed after the manner of the saints, but as the Apostle says: 'Of whom is Christ according to the flesh, who is over all things, God blessed for ever.'" And again: "our earth gave its fruit when the same virgin, whose body was of our earth, gave birth to a Son co-equal to his Father in his divinity, though consubstantial with his mother in the truth of his humanity."

Although this feast was not formally instituted until the thirteenth century, representations of it were painted by artists long before. These are especially frequent and are notable in psalters and other liturgical books of the twelfth century.

O.D.C.C., p. 1446; G. MacGinty, *Today We Celebrate* (1986), pp. 137-8.

St Petronilla, *Martyr* (*c.* 251)

In the cemetery of Domitilla in Rome a fresco of the fourth century survives which represents Petronilla as a martyr. The new Roman Martyrology entry says this and no more, thereby showing its disapproval of the legend which made her a daughter of St Peter. Previous editions of this work state that "it is quite certain that Petronilla was not the daughter of St Peter . . . the idea that he had one was derived from apocryphal publications of gnostic origin." The legend by which she died in her bed (after refusing marriage) is based on the worthless Acts of Nereus and Achilleus (see 12 May).

H. Delehaye in *Sanctus* (1927), pp. 118-20; *Propylaeum*, pp. 285-6.

SS Cantius, Cantianus, and Cantianella, *Martyrs* (304)

The early cult of these martyrs at Aquileia is established by an ancient casket that bears their names, by a sermon of St Maximus of Turin, and by mentions in the verse of Venantius Fortunatus, as well as in the earliest text of the so-called martyrology of Jerome. As against this solid evidence, the Acts are of uncertain value. The two brothers and their sister were members of the Roman family of the Anicii. Left orphans, they were brought up by a Christian tutor in their own house. When the persecution of Diocletian began, they liberated their slaves, sold their possessions, and went to live in Aquileia. They were soon cited to offer sacrifice to the gods. The emperor, who was consulted, wished to be rid of them for political reasons as well as religious ones. They meanwhile left Aquileia in a chariot drawn by mules, but they were overtaken by their pursuers. When called to obey the emperor, they answered that nothing would make them unfaithful to the only true God. With their tutor, they died by the executioner's sword.

See *AA.SS.*, May, 6, pp. 776-84; *Bibl. SS.*, 3, 758-60; *Propylaeum*, p. 284.

Bd James Salomoni (1231-1314)

A noble Venetian by birth, James was brought up by his mother after his father's death, and later by a grandmother after his mother had become a Cistercian nun. At the age of seventeen he joined the Dominican Order. Many years later he was made prior in turn at Forli, Faenza, San Severino, and Ravenna. Finally he settled at Forli (near Ravenna), where he lived most austerely in constant prayer and reading as well as charity to the sick poor. Not only did he read the Bible but also the Martyrology, which gave him constant food for meditation. He experienced ecstacy, healed paralytics, and had a gift of prophecy. He seems to have suffered for four years from cancer, which was cured not long before his death. He lived to be eighty-two. A year after his death a brotherhood was formed to promote his veneration. His cult was approved for Forli in 1526, for Venice in about 1568, and for the Dominicans by Gregory XV in 1622.

AA.SS., May, 6, p. 807; *Bibl. SS.*, 11, 592-3; J. Procter, *Lives of Dominican Saints*, pp. 155-9.

BB Robert Thorpe and Thomas Watkinson, *Martyrs* (1591)

Robert was a priest, Thomas a layman; they suffered together at York, one for being a seminary priest, the other for harbouring him. Robert was born in Yorkshire, studied at Douai, and was ordained priest at Reims in 1585. In 1591, on the eve of Palm Sunday, he was captured in the house of Thomas Watkinson at Menthorpe (Yorkshire) with all the equipment needed for him to say Mass. His host, Thomas, was a widower, a fatherly old man, who had earlier left property to the Church "against the time when God should restore the Catholic religion." His family and household at this time had "fallen away," but he was imprisoned with Robert, who somehow managed to say Mass the day they died. This was on 31 May 1591. They were beatified by Pope John Paul II in 1987.

See B. C. Foley, *The Eighty-five Blessed Martyrs* (1987).

Bd Felix of Nicosia (1787)

Born the son of a shoemaker in Nicosia (Sicily), he was christened Jacopo. Unusually devout, he worked in his father's workshop from an early age but suffered from the oaths and bad language he heard there. Once a workman accidentally cut the leather upper of a shoe, but James passed his finger wet with saliva across it and the shoe was undamaged and unmarked. After his parents' deaths he applied to the local Capuchins for admission, but they refused him at intervals for seven years. He was then accepted at Mistretta (some miles further north), where he was given the habit and the name of Felix. He was professed a year later and recalled to Nicosia, where he helped the brother who begged for alms. He healed illnesses, both physical and mental; he looked after prisoners; he worked, prayed, and offered penance for all. When a fatal epidemic ravaged Cerami in 1777, the local superior asked Felix to come and help. Over sixty years old, he responded eagerly, nursing the sick with deep commitment. Obedient to the last, he even asked for permission to die. He was seventy-two years old when he died on 31 May 1787. He was beatified in 1888.

Life by Gesualdo da Bronte (1888).

R.M.

St Hermias, martyr in Pontus (third century)

SS Thecla and Companions, martyrs in Persia (347)

St Theodore, monk-martyr at Alexandria (357)

St Silvius, bishop of Toulouse (*c.* 400)

St Vitalis, monk and hermit in Umbria (1370)

Bd Baptista Varano, abbess (1524)

St Noe Mawaggali, martyr in Uganda (1886)—see "Martyrs of Uganda," 3 June

---

Glossary of Hagiographic and Some Other Terms used

*=see separate entry

ACOLYTE	Fourth and highest of the four traditional *minor orders of the Western Church, involving duties in connection with the celebration of Mass now mainly carried out by altar servers.
ACTS	Or *Acta*. Account of sufferings and death of a *martyr. Some are authentic trial records, others are spurious, written in imitation of the authentic ones.
APOSTOLIC PROCESS	Examination of witnesses in the diocese of origin of petition for *beatification, by judges appointed by the Holy See.
APPROBATIO CULTUS	Approval of *cult.
ATTRIBUTE	Feature with which a *saint is usually depicted in art, as, e.g., a palm for *martyrs.
ARCHDEACON	Diocesan official priest responsible for ruling in a particular district (in Britain usually a county) in the bishop's name and appointed by him.
ASCETIC	One who leads a life of systematic self-discipline, as a means to more perfect love of God. Applied to such as the Desert Fathers, but levels of asceticism can be exaggerated in written Lives.
BARONIUS	Oratorian and church historian, cardinal from 1596 and Vatican librarian the following year. Published new and corrected editions of the Roman *Martyrology in 1586 and 1589.
BEATIFICATION	Official declaration by the papacy that a candidate for *canonization has attained the required standards, after which he/she is referred to as *beatus/beata*, *"blessed." Indicates that veneration may be paid to the person concerned, either locally or universally. A comparatively recent development in the process, which has always started from "below," at local level, and now arguably the most significant stage, with the number of beatifications in recent years far exceeding the number of *canonizations.
BLESSED	Title accorded to persons after a papal decree of *beatification has been issued in their honour, entitling them to a local *cult.

179

BOLLANDISTS   Team of Belgian Jesuits who, from the seventeenth century to the present day, have devoted themselves to the specialist study of saints and their Lives. Their principal publications are the monumental *Acta Sanctorum* and the bi-annual periodical *Analecta Bollandiana*.

BULL, PAPAL   Solemn form of communication from the pope, named after the lead seal (Latin *bulla*) formerly attached to the document.

CANON   (1) Member of a cathedral chapter; (2) (of the Mass) Name for Eucharistic Prayer, used up to the Second Vatican Council (1962-5); (3) Article of church law.

CANONIZATION   The formal process, obtaining in the Western Church from about 1200, of papal decision on entitlement to the designation *"saint." *See* General Introduction in January volume, p. xv. The process developed gradually; before that time, authorization of a saint's feast in the calendar had been the decision of a local church or council, as it still is today in the Eastern Churches. Canonization is the culmination of a complex process that has varied considerably over the years.

CENOBITIC(ISM)   Way of monastic life distinguished by living in community, as opposed to *eremiticism.

CULT   Official, liturgical expression of veneration or honour accorded to *saints, originating in assemblies of local Christian communities on the anniversary of date of a saint's death. This replaced the pagan custom of families only assembling on the anniversary of a dead relative's birth.

DEACON   Literally "servant." Second of the traditional *major orders, preceded formerly by *sub-deacon and followed by priest. (Since St Thomas Aquinas it has generally been agreed that bishops do not constitute a separate order, but the *Catechism of the Catholic Church* [1994] states that: "There are two degrees of ministerial participation in the priesthood of Christ: the episcopacy and the presbyterate. The diaconate is intended to help and serve them." [p. 348, no. 1554]). Lowest, though, of ranks in Christian ministry. Since Vatican II their traditional duties of baptizing, administering Communion (including viaticum) and preaching have been revived.

DIES NATALIS	"Birthday into heaven." The date of a *saint's death, as recorded in *Martyrologies, which became the usual date of commemoration in the Church's calendar, and—with some exceptions—is the date on which the relevant entry is placed in this work.
DOORKEEPER	Or Porter. Lowest of the *minor orders. Their functions were similar to those of the modern verger.
ELEVATION	Removal of a *saint's *relics to a *shrine or more prominent place in a church, often under the main altar. Also *"translation."
EMBLEM	Heraldic device, often incorporating attributes, assigned to a *saint.
EQUIPOLLENT	"Equivalent." Used of acceptance of *canonization by popular acclaim before formal process was developed.
ELOGIUM	Entry in the *Martyrology briefly summarizing the achievements (and death) of a *saint.
EREMITIC(ISM)	Way of life of a hermit or solitary, whether attached to a monastery or not. *Also* Eremitical.
EXORCIST	Second of the traditional *minor orders, though the power of exorcising evil spitis was never confined to one order.
FASTING	Voluntary reduction of food for ascetical and penitential purposes, recommended and practised by Christ and the apostles, also by monastic and other religious Orders.
FIRST ORDER	Term used of the Order for men of religious Orders such as Dominicans and Franciscans, which also have a *Second Order (for women) and in some cases a *Third (for lay people).
HABIT	Distinctive religious dress. Still generally worn by members of older religious Orders. "Receiving the habit" means entering the religious life.
IGUMEN	Term still used in the Eastern Church to denote leader or guru. Roughly equivalent to "abbot," but Eastern monasteries are less structured.
INFORMATIVE PROCESS	Original examination of witnesses before ecclesiastical judges in a diocese, as first step in process of *beatification.
LIFE	Used with a capital, this denotes a written account.

MARTYR	Literally "witness." Up to the fourth century, all those venerated as *saints were martyrs, *i.e.* those who had been put to death for their faith. *See* General Introduction in January volume, pp. xii–xiii.
MARTYROLOGY	Also "Menology." Official list, originally local, of *martyrs.
MISSAL, ROMAN	Liturgical book of 1570 containing text and directions for all Masses throughout the year. Thoroughly revised in 1969.
MONASTIC(ISM)	Monks' or nuns' way of life, dedicated to God through monastic vows, originating in the fourth century.
PALLIUM	Now a circular band of white wool, with pendant strips front and back, originally a vestigial cloak reaching almost to the feet, with which archbishops are invested by the pope, signifying unity with the papacy and reception from the pope of metropolitan status and consequent authorization to consecrate other bishops. Made from wool of lambs blessed in church of St Agnes: *see* her entry on 21 January.
PAPAL RESERVE	Of *canonization, operating more or less effectively from around 1200.
PASSIO	Account of martyrdom.
PATRONAGE	Protection or guidance by a particular saint of a person, group, organization, occupation, state of life and the like.
PEREGRINATIO	Pilgrimage. Used most commonly of the Irish monks and others who went into "voluntary exile," often permanently, for the love of God and to spread the gospel— *deorad De* in Irish.
READER	Or Lector. Second of the traditional *minor orders, with duties of reading Old Testament prophecies and the Epistle at Mass. Now normally replaced by a lay reader.
RELICS	Literally "remains" of *saints, regarded as objects of devotion from early Christian times. Traditionally divided into three classes: First-class—bodies or parts of bodies; Second-class—clothes that may have been worn by a saint; Third-class—anything that has touched the body of a saint.
RELIQUARY	Casket or box containing bones (and other *relics) of *saints. These are often of considerable artistic and finan-

cial value. They were sometimes fashioned in the shape of the limb (such as arm, foot, head) of the saint, part of which was contained inside them.

SAINT(S)   Person(s) recognized by the Church as having earned the reward of heaven, and honoured on earth by a *cult, local or universal. Title accorded after the fourth and final *stage in the process. *See* Canonization.

SECOND ORDER   Religious Order of women whose founder had first established an Order for men: e.g. Dominican, Franciscan.

SERVANT OF GOD   Title given to a person who has died in the repute of holiness and on whose behalf a process of inquiry has been instituted.

SHRINE   Earlier called *martyrium*. The place where a *saint's body is buried, or (later) the *relics kept. Also a memorial church or part of a church dedicated to a saint's memory.

STAGES   In process leading ultimately to *canonization. There are four, each authorizing a title: *servant of God, *venerable, *blessed, *saint.

SYNAXARY   Term used in the Eastern Church to describe the book that contains short accounts of the *saints, arranged in calendar order, for reading aloud.

THIRD ORDER   Lay people living "in the world," but closely associated with (or even members of) a formal religious Order.

TONSURE   Shaving of part or all of the head, in some places imposed on clerics. Has taken various forms in the past. "Receiving the tonsure" means entering the monastic or clerical state of life.

TRANSLATION   Removal of *saint's body or *relics to a place of greater honour.

VENERABLE   Title accorded to a *servant of God after a favourable decision on the heroic charcter of his/her virtues, before a papal decree of *beatification has been issued.

VICAR GENERAL   The principal non-episcopal priest in a diocese, who speaks and acts on behalf of the bishop.

The above does not attempt definitions of movements, religious Orders, heresies, etc., which are generally explained where relevant in the text, and of which definitions can be found in encyclopedias or dictionaries, such as the Oxford Dictionary of the Christian Church.

Alphabetical List of Entries

(*Names are listed for those saints and blessed who have entries in the main body of the text. Those listed in the* RM *paragraph at the end of each day are not given.*)

Name	Date	Page
Acacius, St	8	41
Achilleus, St (*see* Nereus and)	12	64
Aldhelm, St	25	136
Alexander of Caesarea, St	16	86
Alphius, St (and Companions)	10	51
Amator of Auxerre, St	1	2
Andrew Abellon, Bd	15	85
Andrew Bobola, St	16	90
Andrew Fournet, St	13	74
Andrew Franchi, Bd	26	148
Andrew of Constantinople, St	29	166
Angelo, St	5	31
Ansfrid of Utrecht, St	3	20
Antonia Mesina, Bd	17	93
Antoninus of Florence, St	2	13
Antony Middleton, Bd (*see* Edward Jones and)	6	35
Argentea of Córdoba, St (and Wulfram)	13	72
Asaph, St	1	4
Athanasius, St	2	8
Augustine of Canterbury, St	27	150
Austregisilus, St	20	109
Bartholomew of Montepulciano, Bd	6	34
Basil, St (and Emmelia)	30	168
Beatrice d'Este, Bd	10	55
Bede the Venerable, St	25	130
Benedict II, St	8	43
Bernardino of Siena, St	20	107
Blandina Merten, Bd	18	99
Bona of Pisa, St	29	164
Boniface IV, St	8	42
Boniface of Tarsus, St	14	76
Brendan of Clonfert, St	16	87
Brioc, St	1	2
Calocerus, St (and Parthenius)	19	102
Cantianella, St (*see* Cantius, Cantianus, and)	31	177
Cantianus, St (*see* Cantius, and Cantianella)	31	177
Cantius, St (Cantianus and Cantianella)	31	177
Carantoc, St	16	88
Carthach, St	14	77
Catald, St	10	54
Charles de Mazenod, Bd	21	114
Columba of Rieti, Bd	20	110
Comgall of Bangor, St	10	52
Conleth of Kildare, St	3	20
Conrad of Seldenbüren, Bd	2	12
Crispin of Viterbo, St	19	105
David of Scotland, St	24	127
Denis of Milan, St	25	135
Desideratus of Bourges, St	8	42
Desiderius of Vienne, St	23	122
Dominic of the Causeway, St	12	68
Domitian of Maastricht, St	7	38
Donatian, St (and Rogatian)	24	121
Dunstan of Canterbury, St	19	100
Dympna, St	30	169
Edbert of Lindisfarne, St	6	34
Edmund Duke, Bd (and Companions)	27	155
Edward Jones, Bd (and Antony Middleton)	6	35
Eleutherius, St	26	147
Epimachus, St (*see* Gordian and)	10	51
Epiphanius of Salamis, St	12	65
Erembert, St	14	78
Eric of Sweden, St	18	97
Ethelebert of East Anglia, St	20	109
Euphrosyne of Polotsk, St	23	123
Eutropius, St	27	154
Evodius of Antioch, St	6	33
Exuperantius, St	30	168
Felix of Cantalice, St	18	98
Felix of Nicosia, Bd	31	178
Ferdinand of Castile, St	30	171
Flavia Domitilla, St	7	38
Florian, St	4	25
Forty-four Martyrs of Palestine	16	89
Frances Nisch, Bd	8	45
Francis di Girolamo, St	11	61
Francis of Quebec, Bd	6	35
Gemma of Solmona, Bd	13	73
Gengulf, St	11	59
Gennadius, St	25	138
Gerard Meccati, Bd	13	72
Germanus of Constantinople, St	12	67

Germanus of Paris, St	28	157
Gerontius, St	9	48
Gibrian, St	8	41
Giles of Portugal, Bd	14	79
Giselle of Bavaria, Bd	7	39
Gizur of Iceland, St	28	159
Godric of Finchale, St	21	112
Gordian, St (and Epimachus)	10	51
Gothard of Hildesheim, St	5	30
Gregory VII, St	25	133
Gregory of Verucchio, Bd	4	26
Hallvard of Oslo, St	14	78
Hemming of Abo, St	22	118
Hilary of Arles, St	5	29
Hubert of Liège, St	30	170
Humility of Florence, St	22	117
Ignatius of Laconi, St	11	62
Ignatius of Rostov, St	28	161
Imelda Lambertini, Bd	12	69
Indract of Glastonbury, St	8	43
Isaac of Constantinople, St	30	168
Isaiah of Rostov, St	15	84
Isidore the Farmer, St	15	84
Ivo of Brittany, St	19	104
James, St (*see* Philip and James)	3	17
James Salomoni, Bd	31	177
Jane of Portugal, Bd	12	69
Joan of Arc, St	30	171
John I, St	18	95
John Forest, Bd	22	119
John Baptist Rossi, St	23	124
John Martin Moye, Bd	4	27
John of Avila, St	10	56
John of Beverley, St	7	37
John of Parma, St	22	117
John of Prado, Bd	24	128
Joseph Gerard, Bd	29	166
Joseph Mary Rubio Peralta, Bd	2	15
Joseph the Worker, St	1	1
Julia, St	22	116
Juvenal of Narni, St	3	19
Ladislas of Warsaw, Bd	4	26
Lanfranc of Canterbury, Bd	28	160
Leontius of Rostov, St	23	122
Leopold Mandic, St	14	81
Louis Moreau, Bd	24	129
Lucius, St (*see* Montanus, and Companions)	23	121
Luke Kirby, Bd (and Companions)	30	174
Madeleine Albrici, Bd	13	73
Madeleine Sophie Barat, St	25	141
Mafalda of Portugal, St	1	5
Majolus of Cluny, St	11	59
Mamertus of Vienne, St	11	58
Marculf, St	1	4
Margaret Pole, Bd	28	161
Martyrs of England and Wales, BB	4	22
Mary Mazzarello, St	14	80
Mary Paradis, Bd	3	20
Mary Ann of Quito, St	26	148
Mary Bartolomea Bagnesi, Bd	28	162
Mary-Catherine of Cairo, Bd	6	36
Mary-Catherine de Longpré, Bd	8	44
Mary Magdalen de'Pazzi, St	25	139
Mary-Teresa Gerhardinger, Bd	9	50
Matthias, St	14	76
Maura, St (*see* Timothy and Maura)	3	19
Maximinus of Trier, St	29	164
Maximus of Jerusalem, St	5	29
Mel, St (and Sulian)	13	71
Melangell, St	27	155
Michael Garicoïts, St	14	80
Michael Giedroyc, Bd	4	26
Modoaldus, St	12	66
Montanus, St (Lucius, and Companions)	23	121
Nereus, St (and Achilleus)	12	64
Nicholas Albergati, Bd	10	55
Nicholas Hermansson, Bd	2	12
Nuntius Sulprizio, Bd	5	31
Pachomius, St	9	47
Pancras, St	12	65
Parthenius, St (*see* Calocerus and)	19	102
Paschal Baylon, St	17	92
Paternus of Vannes, St	21	114
Peregrine Laziosi, St	1	5
Peter Celestine, St	19	102
Peter Lieou, Bd	17	93
Peter Sanz, Bd (and Companions)	26	149
Peter Wright, Bd	19	105
Petronilla, St	31	177
Philip St (and James)	3	17
Philip Neri, St	26	144
Possidius, St	16	86
Potamon, St	18	96
Quiteria, St	22	116
Rheticius, St	15	83

Richard Newport, Bd			Thomas Pickering, Bd	9	49
(*see* William Scott and)	30	173	Thomas Watkinson, Bd		
Richard Pampuri, Bd	1	6	(*see* Robert Thorpe and)	31	178
Richard Thirkeld, Bd	29	166	Timothy, St (and Maura)	3	19
Rictrudis, St	12	67	Torquatus, St		
Rita of Cascia, St	22	118	(and Companions)	15	83
Robert Thorpe, Bd			Ursula Ledochowska, Bd	29	167
(and Thomas Watkinson)	31	178	Victor the Moor, St	8	41
Rogatian, St (*see* Donatian and)	24	121	Vincent of Lérins, St	24	125
Rose Venerini, Bd	7	39	Visitation of the Blessed		
Rupert of Bingen, St	15	83	Virgin Mary, the	31	176
Serenicus, St	7	39	Vitesindus of Córdoba, St	15	83
Servatius, St	13	71	Waldebert, St	2	11
Sigismund of Burgundy, St	1	3	Walter of L'Esterp, St	11	60
Simeon Stylites the			Walstan of Bawburgh, St	30	169
Younger, St	24	126	Wiborada, St	2	11
Simon Stock, St	16	89	William Arnaud, Bd		
Sisinnius, St (and Companions)	29	164	(and Companions)	29	165
Solangia, St	10	54	William Scott, Bd		
Sulian, St (see Mel and)	13	71	(and Richard Nerwport)	30	173
Theolbald of Vienne, St	21	114	William of Gelone, St	28	158
Theodotus, St			William of Rochester, St	23	123
(and Companions)	18	96	William of Toulouse, Bd	18	98
Thomas Ford, Bd			Wiro of Utrecht, St	8	44
(and Companions)	28	162	Zenobius of Florence, St	25	135